Voices from the Second World War: A Collection of Primary Documents

Bassim Hamadeh, CEO and Publisher
David Miano, Senior Specialist Acquisitions Editor
Michelle Piehl, Project Editor
Abbey Hastings, Associate Production Editor
Miguel Macias, Senior Graphic Designer
Stephanie Kohl, Licensing Associate
Natalie Piccotti, Senior Marketing Manager
Kassie Graves, Vice President of Editorial
Jamie Giganti, Director of Academic Publishing

Printed in the United States of America.

ISBN: 978-1-5165-0042-0 (pbk) / 978-1-5165-0043-7 (br)

FIRST EDITION

VOICES
FROM THE
SECOND
WORLD WAR

A Collection of Primary Documents

Stephen K. Stein & **Paul W. Doerr**
University of Memphis   *Acadia University*

cognella® | ACADEMIC PUBLISHING

TABLE OF CONTENTS

CHAPTER 3   BLITZKRIEG: THE GERMAN CONQUEST OF POLAND, NORWAY, THE LOW COUNTRIES, AND FRANCE, AND THE BATTLE OF BRITAIN — 97

PREFACE

Voices from the Second World War provides students with an accessible primary source overview of the largest and most far-reaching conflict in human history. This book covers a vast range of topics, but thematically balances the testimony from the battlefield with the conduct of war at the level of grand strategy and the ways in which civilians coped on the home front. Within these themes we focus on key decisions and turning points in the war. The book provides students and readers with an affordable yet comprehensive collection of primary documents that brings the experience of the war to life.

The book begins with an in-depth examination of the causes of the war, starting with the immediate aftermath of the First World War and the Paris Peace Conference of 1919. The first two chapters cover the crises of the 1920s and 1930s culminating in the outbreak of war in September 1939. We then move through Germany's early run of victories, the Holocaust, the bombing campaigns of both Axis and Allied powers, the wartime experiences of civilians, wartime diplomacy, the military turning points of the war, and the conduct of the war in all theaters, including North Africa, the USSR, the Atlantic, Europe, Asia, and the Pacific. A final chapter covers the aftermath of the war.

This book emphasizes multicultural and multinational approaches in exploring the war. The documents selected for this volume reflect that commitment. The documents come from an astonishing array of sources, and some have never been published before. Our sources include government documents both secret and public, private reminiscences and memoirs, and a selection of secondary assessments by professional historians. The result is that students will be exposed to as wide a range of voices from the Second World War as is possible in a single volume. As well, each chapter contains an introduction that will provide readers with the historical context for the documents, as well as questions to keep in mind when reading the chapter.

The editors would like to acknowledge and thank the people at Cognella for bringing this publication to completion. David Miano, Leah Sheets, and Berenice Quirino have been most patient in steering us through the challenging process of document selection and presentation.

INTRODUCTION

VOICES FROM THE SECOND WORLD WAR

Traditionally dated from 1939–1945, the Second World War remains the most costly conflict in human history. Fighting spanned the globe and eventually involved every continent (save Antarctica) and almost every nation. Waging this globe-spanning war required an unprecedented mobilization of industry, people, and resources, such that it affected the lives of almost everyone then living, particularly the citizens of the major combatants: China, France, Germany, Italy, Japan, the Soviet Union, the United States, and Great Britain, as well as Britain's dominions and colonial territories, particularly Australia, Canada, India, New Zealand, and South Africa.

Taking a broad approach, this reader explores the origins, conduct, and outcome of what remains the largest and most destructive war in human history. Topics addressed include the foreign policies of the major powers and how their respective ideologies shaped them; diplomacy among the respective alliances; political and strategic decision making; major battles and the operational and tactical effectiveness of military forces; the air war, bombing of cities, and use of atomic bombs; wartime mobilization and life on the home fronts; the horrors of German and Japanese occupation, the Holocaust, and other wartime atrocities; and the experience of war by combatants of diverse nations. Coverage extends from the November 1918 Armistice and Versailles Treaty that ended the First World War to the immediate aftermath of the Second World War and beginnings of the Cold War, though the emphasis is on the period from the German invasion of Poland in September 1939 to the conclusion of the Pacific War following the Soviet invasion of Manchuria, and the dropping of atomic bombs on Hiroshima and Nagasaki.

This book's documents and other readings explore the viewpoints of important political and military leaders, common soldiers, sailors, airmen, and civilians on the home front. It includes important and widely publicized wartime speeches and documents, such as speeches by U.S. president Franklin D. Roosevelt and British prime minister Winston Churchill, as well as extracts from letters, diaries, and memoirs of common participants in the war. Thought of as "the Good War" in the United States and labeled the "Great Patriotic War" in the USSR, the moral clarity of national leaders was often less apparent to those who fought the war and civilians affected by it, and these differences are highlighted in many of this book's readings.

The origins of the Second World War are rooted in unresolved issues from the First World War, the economic problems of the interwar era, and the expansionist aims of Germany, Italy, and Japan, whose leaders sought to redress their nation's grievances through military force and conquest. Chapter 1 chronicles the aftermath of the First World War and efforts to produce a stable, peaceful international order, whereas Chapter 2 describes European international relations in the 1930s as British and French leaders struggled to address Nazi Germany's increasingly strident demands for military rearmament and territorial expansion.

Benefitting from its easy conquests of Austria and Czechoslovakia and prewar development of effective techniques of air and armored warfare—and the coordination of the two—Germany's armed forces overwhelmed opponents and conquered Poland, the Low Countries, and France in a succession of rapid campaigns that the press labeled "blitzkrieg." Chapter 3 explores these from the perspective of the Germans and their enemies, as well as the Battle of Britain, the war's first great air campaign, which ended German prospects for a quick and easy war.

The increasingly strained relationship between Japan and the United States, which culminated in the Japanese government's decision for war and surprise attack on the U.S. fleet at Pearl Harbor, as well as British and Dutch possessions in the Pacific, is the subject of Chapter 4. Japan invaded first Manchuria (1931) and then the rest of China (1937) and resisted international calls for its withdrawal. In 1940, Japanese leaders cemented an alliance with Germany and Italy, the Tripartite Pact, and occupied French Indo-China. The United States responded with increasing economic sanctions against Japan. These failed to restrain Japan. Instead, Japan's military leaders convinced the government that U.S. economic sanctions, particularly restrictions on exports of oil, left them no choice but to go to with Great Britain, the Netherlands, and the United States to seize the raw materials Japan needed.

Even those who know little about the Second World War know about the Holocaust, Nazi Germany's effort to exterminate Europe's Jewish population, along with other peoples the Nazi state considered undesirable. Chapter 5 chronicles Germany's increasing persecution of Jews. As Germany conquered new territory, persecutions of Jews increased. At the Wannsee Conference

(1942), Germany's leaders decided on mass extermination, the implementation and results of which are also chronicled in this chapter, as are Jew resistance efforts, and the liberation of concentration camps by Allied soldiers who were appalled by what they found.

Defeated in the Battle of Britain, German leaders focused their attention on the Soviet Union. Italy's failed invasions of Greece and Egypt, though, required them to send aid to their ally and the arrival of German forces in the Mediterranean made it an important theater of the war. Chapter 6 offers a range of accounts on the fighting in the Mediterranean from its opening stages to the prolonged fighting in Italy, which continued into 1945. Chapter 7 covers the important battles of El Alamein and Stalingrad, turning points in their respective theaters of the war, as well as the Battle of Atlantic, the great struggle at sea between German submarines (U-boats) and Allied warships and convoys, which was an essential prelude to the Anglo-American liberation of France.

All the major powers made efforts to bomb enemy forces and factories in the First World War, but with limited success. Technological improvements and the growth of air forces in the 1920s and 1930s made the air campaigns of World War II far more devastating, and Chapter 8 covers these efforts. German bombing of Great Britain—and later rocket attacks—killed more than 50,000 civilians, whereas British and American bombing of Germany killed several hundred thousand people and left many cities in ruins, among them Hamburg and Dresden where firestorms burned out large parts of the city and killed tens of thousands. American bombing of Japan, which culminated in the dropping of atomic bombs on Hiroshima and Nagasaki, proved even more devastating.

The war's major powers mobilized civilians for war on unprecedented scales. More than half the adult populations of the major powers became involved in the war efforts in some way: serving in the military, working in the munitions or shipbuilding industries, watching the coast, supporting air defense, and assisting in other capacities. Chapter 9 details the efforts of these people and the sacrifices they made, which ranged from rationing of gasoline, rubber, and many types of foods to the starvation diets of those trapped in besieged cities such as Leningrad (today's St. Petersburg). Industrial productivity rose steadily during the war, particularly in the major Allied nations, because of the introduction of new manufacturing techniques, generally efficient management of resources by business and government leaders, and the efforts of the workers themselves who worked long hours in factories and mines. Allied industrial productivity helped win the war.

Chapter 10 looks at the formation and evolution of alliances and war aims during the war. Documents from some of the more famous wartime conferences shed light on the inner workings of the Grand Alliance, the name given to the wartime alliance between the USSR, Great Britain, and the United States. Despite tensions among its members, the alliance proved surprisingly effective—particularly the close relationships formed between American and British leaders.

The Eastern front was in many respects the key front of the Second World War. The ultimate failure of the German invasion, Operation Barbarossa, despite the devastation it inflicted on the USSR was an ominous portend for the Third Reich. Chapter 11 explores the war on the Russian Front where the German Army suffered roughly 80% of its casualties.

Described by historian John Dower as a "war without mercy," the fighting in the Pacific featured fierce combat with often heavy casualties, particularly in the succession of naval battles and amphibious invasions that characterized the war in the Central and South Pacific, as Japan first conquered these islands in the months following its attack on U.S. Pearl Harbor; and the United States then fought to recapture them, hopping island-to-island as its fleet advanced toward Japan. The documents of Chapter 12 illuminate this conflict, as well as tensions among the Allies over colonialism and the postwar world, highlighted by India's independence movement.

British, Canadian, and U.S. troops landed in Normandy, France, on June 6, 1944, beginning the liberation of Western Europe from Nazi rule. The next seven months, lasting through the Battle of the Bulge (December 16, 1944—January 25, 1945), Germany's failed winter counteroffensive, were a period of intense, almost continuous combat that exhausted soldiers. Casualties were such that personnel shortages forced Britain to consolidate many regiments. American divisions were chronically short of combat infantrymen. Chapter 13 covers the advance of Allied armies from the Normandy invasion through Germany's May 1945 surrender and the end of the war in Europe.

The costs of the war and postwar situation are the subject of the book's final chapter. More than 50 million people died as a result of the Second World War. War's end found cities in ruin and tens of millions displaced from their home nations, homeless, or both. This chapter examines the postwar situation, efforts at recovery, and how the war changed the international order. The Second World War was a transformative event that reshaped the global balance of power, international relations, and domestic affairs. The war set in motion the process of decolonization, and Europe's major powers—willingly or not—ceded control of most of their overseas colonies over the next generation.

European nations similarly found themselves displaced as the world's dominant economic and military powers by the United States and the Soviet Union. Soon called superpowers, the Cold War struggle between the two for influence around the world had its origins in the aftermath of the Second World War. So, too, did a dramatic reshaping of the world economy. The Soviet Union solidified its hold on Eastern Europe and imposed communism and centrally planned economies on these nations. The United States, in turn, encouraged capitalism and free trade through a host of new international organizations and agreements such as the General Agreement on Trade and Tariffs (GATT), International Monetary Fund (IMF), and World Bank, and provided financial and other aid through the Marshall Plan, which helped Western European nations rebuild from the war, but also increased their ties to the U.S. economy. Wartime mobilization also transformed domestic society, particularly among the western democracies. Civil rights organizations pressed for reform, and governments built on the foundation provided by wartime activism to enact sweeping social welfare programs.

CHAPTER 1

THE VERSAILLES SETTLEMENT AND THE AFTERMATH OF THE FIRST WORLD WAR, 1919–1929

Introduction

Understanding the origins of the Second World War requires readers to familiarize themselves with the problematic ending of the First World War. The United States entered the war on the side of the Allies on April 6, 1917, and immediately set about the task of mobilizing an army of millions for service in Europe. While this was going on, President Woodrow Wilson delivered the Fourteen Points speech to the U.S. Congress on January 8, 1918 (Document 1). The Fourteen Points soon came to be regarded as an unofficial statement of Allied war aims in World War I. Other Allied leaders, such as British prime minister Lloyd George and French prime minister Georges Clemenceau, may have held private reservations about Wilson's ideals behind the scenes, but the war-weary public in the Allied countries embraced Wilson and his Fourteen Points. Wilson seemed to be promising a postwar world of peace, justice, democracy, and the rule of law in international relations. What do you think were the main, guiding principles of the Fourteen Points? Wilson believed strongly in the principle of national self-determination, meaning that people should have the freedom to establish their own states and boundaries. The era of the authoritarian, multinational empire, such as Austria-Hungary, or the Ottoman Turkish empire, was apparently coming to an end. How does this ideal show up in the Fourteen Points? Why does national self-determination only seem to apply to the empires of the Central Powers, and not those of the Allies? Could the Irish or the people of the Indian subcontinent expect to benefit from the Fourteen Points?

The Paris Peace Conference opened on January 18, 1919, and concluded with the signing of the Treaty of Versailles on June 28, 1919. The Treaty of Versailles, the peace treaty between the victorious Allies and defeated Germany, was the main work of the Paris Peace Conference, but the conference also mediated the boundaries of the new states that sprung up in Europe following the war. Most historians would agree that the Treaty of Versailles and the Paris Peace Conference failed on several issues. First, national self-determination proved difficult to put into practice given the complex ethnic mixing of population in Europe. Many new states, such as Poland and Czechoslovakia had large, discontent minorities within their borders. Historian Paul W. Doerr details the way in which large numbers of Germans were left outside the borders of Germany after the war (Document 2). Why did this happen? How could German nationalists exploit such grievances?

Next, some extracts are provided from the Treaty of Versailles itself (Document 3). How was the League of Nations supposed to work? How would it maintain peace? The U.S. Senate refused to ratify the Treaty of Versailles, and because the League Charter made up the first part of the treaty text, the United States never joined the League. How serious of a setback was this to the new organization? Germany was not allowed to join until 1926 and the USSR not until 1934. The League was thus dominated by Britain and France. Would it surprise you to learn that many people saw the League as more of a "victor's club" than an impartial arbiter of the peace?

Reparations are usually seen as another great failing of the Treaty of Versailles. Why did the Allies need reparations? What do you think of the wording of Article 231? Why is it known as the "war guilt clause"? Is the term "war guilt" used in the article? How would Germans react to Article 231? What do you think would be the consequences of setting up a commission to determine the final amount of reparations, thus delaying the final bill for two years?

John Maynard Keynes resigned from the British delegation to the Paris Peace Conference in order to write a book criticizing the Treaty of Versailles. His book, *The Economic Consequences of the Peace*, published in 1920, helped to popularize the view that the treaty had been too harsh, although many have also disputed his views.[1] Keynes summarized his critique in an article for

---

1 See Sally Marks, The Myths of Reparations, *Central European History*, *11*(3), 231–255, for an excellent critique.

Everybody's Magazine in 1920 (Document 4). What were the main points of Keynes's argument?

The postwar era saw France, having endured two brutal invasions in a generation, struggling to ensure its future security. What were the terms of the Franco-Polish treaty of 1921 (Document 5)? What were the strategic benefits for France in an alliance with Poland? For Poland? In 1920–1921 the French also sponsored the creation of an alliance between Czechoslovakia, Yugoslavia, and Romania known as the Little Entente. The alliance was intended to contain postwar Hungarian ambitions, but why would the French be so keen on Eastern European alliances?[2] Do you see any connection with the Franco-Polish Treaty?

Postwar governments made strenuous efforts at international disarmament, a major theme of Wilsonian ideology. The naval race between Britain and Germany in the years leading up to 1914 was widely believed to have been a major cause of the First World War. The most ambitious and successful of the postwar disarmament efforts culminated in the Washington Naval Conference of 1921–1922 and the Washington Naval Disarmament Treaty, signed February 6, 1922. According to the treaty (Document 6), how were naval armaments to be limited and controlled? Why do you think that similar efforts to control land and air armaments failed?

The sluggish state of the postwar European economy necessitated several high-level diplomatic conferences to seek a path forward. During one of these conferences, the Genoa Conference of 1922, the German and Soviet delegations disappeared to the nearby town of Rapallo, where they proceeded to sign the Treaty of Rapallo (Document 7). The importance of this document lies more in its implications than the actual content. How do you think the Polish government would react to this treaty, given that Poland had been repeatedly partitioned by its neighbors in the late 18th century? What does this treaty say about the future of Germany and the USSR, once they had recovered their strength, which was only a matter of time? The treaty also initiated a program of secret military collaboration between Germany and the USSR, in defiance of the Treaty of Versailles. The Germans tested poison gas, tanks, and aircraft at Soviet bases until Adolf Hitler came to power in 1933 and ended the program. Again, what were the strategic benefits of the Treaty of Rapallo for the signatories?

---

2 All three members of the Little Entente contained Hungarian minorities within their new borders.

The Locarno Pact of 1925 (Document 8) is seen by some historians as the true peace treaty that ended the war. The pact came after German defaults on reparations payments led the French to occupy the Ruhr valley of Germany in 1923, an act that triggered a wave of crippling inflation in Germany and Hitler's first abortive attempt to seize power in Munich. It seemed, once again, that Germany and France were on the brink of war. But the French were persuaded to leave the Ruhr and investment capital from the United States was funneled to Germany under the terms of the Dawes Plan of 1924, which also rescheduled German debts. The recovering German economy sparked a wave of optimism, as did the Locarno Pact of 1925, which attempted to stabilize borders in Western Europe. How was this done, according to the terms of the pact? Why do you think the Germans refuse to sign similar commitments with Czechoslovakia and Poland?

The Kellogg-Briand Pact of 1928 (Document 9) is often seen as the epitome of 1920s' naiveté and optimism, but it was very much in keeping with the mood of the times. What does the pact attempt to do? Was there any enforcement mechanism? What is the significance of the date?

Hitler wrote his infamous memoir *Mein Kampf* while in jail following his treasonous attempt at a coup in 1923. As you read the excerpts (Document 10) from the book, bear in mind that Hitler was a supreme opportunist who never had a strict step-by-step plan for Germany, contrary to popular myth. That being the case, what general ideas does Hitler articulate? What role does racism play in his writing?

1

Woodrow Wilson's Fourteen Points

January 8, 1918

1. Open covenants of peace, openly arrived at, after which there shall be no private understandings of any kind but diplomacy shall proceed always frankly and in the public view.

2. Absolute freedom of navigation upon the seas, outside territorial waters, alike in peace and war, except as the seas may be closed in whole or in part by international action for the enforcement of international covenants.

3. The removal, so far as possible, of all economic barriers and the establishment of an equality of trade conditions among all the nations consenting to the peace and associating themselves for its maintenance.

4. Adequate guarantees given and taken that national armaments will be reduced to the lowest point consistent with domestic safety.

5. A free, open-minded and absolutely impartial adjustment of all colonial claims, based upon a strict observance of the principle that in determining all such questions of sovereignty the interests of the populations concerned must have equal weight with the equitable claims of the government whose title is to be determined.

6. The evacuation of all Russian territory and such a settlement of all questions affecting Russia as will secure the best and freest co-operation

Woodrow Wilson, "Woodrow Wilson's Fourteen Points, January 8, 1918," The Avalon Project, pp. 1-2. 1918.

of the other nations of the world in obtaining for her an unhampered and unembarrassed opportunity for the independent determination of her own political development and national policy and assure her of a sincere welcome into the society of free nations under institutions of her own choosing; and, more than a welcome, assistance also of every kind that she may need and may herself desire. The treatment accorded Russia by her sister nations in the months to come will be the acid test of their good will, of their comprehension of her needs as distinguished from their own interests, and of their intelligent and unselfish sympathy.

7. Belgium, the whole world will agree, must be evacuated and restored, without any attempt to limit the sovereignty which she enjoys in common with all other free nations. No other single act will serve as this will serve to restore confidence among the nations in the laws which they have themselves set and determined for the government of their relations with one another. Without this healing act the whole structure and validity of international law is forever impaired.

8. All French territory should be freed and the invaded portions restored, and the wrong done to France by Prussia in 1871 in the matter of Alsace-Lorraine, which has unsettled the peace of the world for nearly fifty years, should be righted, in order that peace may once more be made secure in the interests of all.

9. A readjustment of the frontiers of Italy should be effected along clearly recognizable lines of nationality.

10. The peoples of Austria-Hungary, whose place among the nations we wish to see safeguarded and assured, should be accorded the freest opportunity to autonomous development.

11. Rumania, Serbia and Montenegro should be evacuated; occupied territories restored; Serbia accorded free and secure access to the sea; and the relations of the several Balkan states to one another determined by friendly counsel along historically established lines of allegiance and nationality; and international guarantees of the political and economic independence and territorial integrity of the several Balkan states should be entered into.

12. The Turkish portion of the present Ottoman empire should be assured a secure sovereignty, but the other nationalities which are now under Turkish rule should be assured an undoubted security of life and an absolutely unmolested opportunity of autonomous development, and the Dardanelles should be permanently opened as a free passage to the ships and commerce of all nations under international guarantees.

13. An independent Polish state should be erected which should include the territories inhabited by indisputably Polish populations, which should be assured a free and secure access to the sea, and whose political and economic independence and territorial integrity should be guaranteed by international covenant.

14. A general association of nations must be formed under specific covenants for the purpose of affording mutual guarantees of independence and territorial integrity to great and small states alike.

2

GERMANY'S BORDERS

First, Germany returned to France the annexed parts of Alsace and Lorraine, which it had taken in 1871 at the conclusion of the Franco-Prussian War. Most of the people living in these areas considered themselves French, and German rule had been a constant source of Franco-German tension and a focus for French revanchist sentiment before the First World War. Next, small areas of territory were given by Germany to Belgium (the towns of Eupen and Malmédy) and Denmark (north Schleswig). The transfers took place after local plebiscites had demonstrated the wishes of the inhabitants. Few Germans had any serious objections to the loss of those territories.

Much more difficult was the status of the Saar valley, an important coal-producing area immediately to the southeast of Luxembourg. The vast majority of the population of the Saar was German, but the area was placed under League of Nations rule in the form of a five-man commission. The coal mines were expropriated by the French. At the end of fifteen years a plebiscite would be held so that the inhabitants should determine whether they wanted to be part of Germany or France or to continue under League rule. If they voted to return to Germany, then Germany would have the right to buy back the coal mines. Initially the French wanted to annex the Saar directly, and Lloyd George may even have been sympathetic, but Wilson had no desire to create a permanent grievance in the heart of Europe. The French government wanted compensation for the damage that the Germans had inflicted on the industries of northeastern France during the war. German nationalists took offense at the apparent violation of Wilson's principle of national self-determination. The inhabitants of the Saar clearly wanted to be part of Germany and would vote overwhelmingly to do so in 1935, giving Hitler one of his earliest triumphs. The controversy over the Saar was, however, only part of a much greater and more heated debate over the status of the Rhineland.

The Rhineland is the area of Germany that lies between the river Rhine and Germany's borders with France and Belgium. This prosperous, industrialized, urbanized region was close to the heartland of German war production in the nearby Ruhr valley. Under the final terms agreed at the conference the Rhineland was to be occupied by Allied troops. A small area near Köln *(Cologne)* in the north would be evacuated after five years and another area around Koblenz after ten, but the bulk of the region would play host to an Allied army of occupation for fifteen years. In addition, the east bank of the Rhine would be demilitarized to a distance of fifty kilometers. Fortifications in the Rhineland were prohibited in perpetuity. The occupation of the Rhineland was hated passionately by all Germans, many of whom resented France's use of troops from its African colonies on racial grounds. They referred to the unoccupied areas of their country as 'free Germany'. The Rhineland settlement could have been much harsher on Germany.

Initially the French wanted to separate the Rhineland from the rest of Germany and to set up a government that would be docile and receptive to French wishes. They even went to some lengths to encourage separatist movements in the Rhineland, none of which caught on as there was absolutely no popular support for the idea. The French plan was vetoed by both Wilson and Lloyd George for some basic reasons. A separate Rhineland would violate national self-determination and serve as a source of German revanchist sentiment, in exactly the same way as Alsace-Lorraine had for the French before 1914. For his part, Lloyd George privately opposed any occupation of the Rhineland by Allied troops. He was anxious to limit British military commitments in Europe and was worried about the effect of an occupation on German nationalism. On one hand he was sympathetic to France's fears for its security, but on the other hand he did not want to strengthen France at the expense of creating a host of grievances for German nationalists to exploit.

As a compromise solution the Allies agreed on a fifteen-year occupation of the Rhineland. A French army stationed in the Rhineland could, in a crisis, easily cross the Rhine bridgeheads and march on Berlin and the Ruhr. Occupation of the Rhineland would also serve as a means of securing German compliance with all the terms of the treaty. At the end of fifteen years, the

French hoped, Germany would be purged of the influence of the Prussian military caste known as the Junkers, who were widely blamed for perceived German aggressiveness before 1914. Germany would then take its place in the comity of European nations. Others in the French government hoped that schemes for economic co-operation would promote ties between German industry and the international community and make Germany less likely to resort to war.

Another means of ensuring French security concerned a guarantee from Britain and the United States to come to the aid of France if it were attacked by Germany. Wilson and Lloyd George proposed an Anglo-American guarantee of French security at the Paris conference, but it had to be ratified by the United States Senate and that approval was never given. Clemenceau set great store by an Anglo-American guarantee, and the Anglo-American offer was one reason why Clemenceau backed down on plans for a separate Rhenish state. Despite the offer of the guarantee the French still insisted on some degree of occupation, as it would take time for their allies to mobilize and come to their assistance in the event of war.

The territorial arrangements in the east were equally controversial. The inter-mixing of ethnic populations in Eastern Europe meant that Wilson's principle of national self-determination proved notoriously difficult to apply in reality. Virtually every one of the new states that were created in 1919 contained within its borders large numbers of citizens who wanted to belong to a different state. The difficulty of drawing viable borders was most evident in the case of Poland. The re-emergence of an independent Polish state had been raised in Wilson's Fourteen Points, together with the stipulation that the new state have an outlet to the sea. A corridor to the Baltic Sea was deemed necessary for Poland's economic viability. Unfortunately, such an outlet could only be provided by granting Poland land that was heavily populated by Germans. The corridor that was finally given to Poland under the terms of the peace settlement included the former German provinces of West Prussia and Posen. Both provinces contained numerous Germans, although the Poles formed a small majority. The port city of Danzig, which was almost exclusively populated by Germans, was made a free city, governed by the League of Nations. This arrangement came about at the insistence of Lloyd George, who argued that if Danzig were included in Poland in addition to West Prussia and Posen there would be more than two million Germans in the new Polish state. The ideal of national self-determination would thus be grossly violated and the substantial, discontented German minority in Poland would undermine Polish security. Lloyd George favoured a smaller, more cohesive

Polish state. In the long run, even Lloyd George's compromise proved to be no more viable. When war finally came in 1939 the immediate pretext was Hitler's insistence on the return of Danzig and the German-speaking areas of Poland. Finally, there was also the inconvenient matter of the corridor and Danzig isolating East Prussia and separating it from the rest of Germany—yet another grievance for the German nationalists.

The region known as Upper Silesia added further complications. Upper Silesia was an ethnically mixed area (German and Polish) that was rich in resources and industry. A strong case was made for assigning Upper Silesia to Poland, primarily to ensure the economic viability of the new state. Once again, however, many Germans would be left stranded outside German borders and Lloyd George in particular argued against granting the whole region to Poland. The dispute was not settled until 1921 when, after a plebiscite, the territory was split between Germany and Poland. Nevertheless, the new border did not in any way reflect a clear ethnic division between the two peoples.

Other aspects of Germany's eastern borders also proved worrisome. The new state of Czechoslovakia was given the horseshoe shaped area known as Sudetenland. This region had belonged to the old Austro-Hungarian Empire and had never been considered part of Germany. There was no great call in Germany for its annexation in 1919, even though it was home to more than two million Germans and its appropriation would have been perfectly consistent with the ideal of national self-determination. Sudetenland was a hilly, semi-mountainous region with a considerable amount of industry. It was granted to Czechoslovakia to enhance the strategic and economic prospects of the new state. The large number of Germans in Czechoslovakia became an important weapon for Hitler in 1938, when he exploited the grievances of the Sudeten Germans to attempt the destruction of the Czech state.

A similar situation arose on Germany's southern borders. The largest German-speaking region of the old Austro-Hungarian Empire emerged as the new state of Austria. Again, the ideal of national self-determination argues a strong case for including Austria within a post-war Germany. Ironically, there were some in Germany who opposed the incorporation of six million Austrian Catholics within the mainly Protestant German state, but the most strenuous objections came from the French, who obviously did not want to see an even larger Germany emerge from the peace conference. The final treaty contained a strict prohibition on a German-Austrian *Anschluss*, or union. In 1938 Hitler achieved the *Anschluss* after arguing that he was only trying to right the wrongs of Versailles and carry out national self-determination.

The new borders of 1919 left a Germany that was thirteen per cent smaller in size and ten percent smaller in population. These losses were hardly crippling and Germany still had the potential to become by far the most powerful state in Europe, a fact that was not lost on French military planners. Nevertheless, Germans felt an acute sense of grievance, and the large numbers of their countrymen living outside German borders ensured that tension with Germany's neighbours would continue for years to come.

The treaty also imposed heavy limits on German military strength. Here, the starting point for Wilson was the idea that all nations should reduce their national armaments to the lowest level consistent with national security. Each state should have only a pared-down frontier guard. The Treaty of Versailles limited Germany to an army of 100,000 troops, with no conscription, no air force, no submarines (a major concern to the British), no heavy artillery, no tanks and a reduced navy. It also demanded the abolition of the German General Staff and War Academy. As far as Wilson was concerned, German disarmament constituted the first step on the road to universal arms reductions, Germany being the first state to make such a move. Lloyd George sympathized with Wilson's aims, but France had a completely different agenda. The French, for reasons of their own security, had every intention of restricting the German army while maintaining French strength at a relatively high level. In the years after 1919 the German government pursued an active, secret programme of evading the arms restrictions imposed by the treaty, part of which involved the use of bases in the USSR to test tanks and aircraft.[1] But in 1919 German nationalists were able to point to the differences in armament levels between France and Germany and to charge the victorious powers with hypocrisy.

---

1   See the Treaty of Rapallo, below and the introduction.

3

THE TREATY OF VERSAILLES

THE COVENANT OF THE LEAGUE OF NATIONS

The High Contracting Parties, in order to promote international co-operation and to achieve international peace and security by acceptance of obligations not to resort to war, by the prescription of open, just and honorable relations between nations, by the firm establishment of the understandings of international law as the actual rule of conduct among Governments, and by the maintenance of justice and a scrupulous respect for all treaty obligations in the dealings of organized peoples with one another, agree to this Covenant of the League of Nations.

Articles 1 through 7 inclusive deal with membership and League organization.

Article 8. The Members of the League recognize that the maintenance of peace requires the reduction of national armaments to the lowest point consistent with national safety and the enforcement by common action of international obligations. The Council, taking account of the geographical situation and circumstances of each State, shall formulate plans for such reduction for the consideration and action of several Governments. Such plans shall be subject to reconsideration and revision at least every ten years. After these plans shall have been adopted by the several Governments, the limits of armaments therein fixed shall not be exceeded without the concurrence of the Council. The Members of the League agree that the manufacture by private enterprise of munitions

"Treaty of Versailles, Preamble, Articles 8-17, 231-234," The Avalon Project, pp. 1-5. 1919.

and implements of war is open to grave objections. The Council shall advise how the evil effects upon such manufacture can be prevented, due regard being had to the necessities of those Members of the League which are not able to manufacture the munitions and implements of war necessary for their safety. The members of the League undertake to interchange full and frank information as to the scale of their armaments, their military, naval, and air programmes, and the condition of such of their industries as are adaptable to war-like purposes.

Article 9. A permanent Commission shall be constituted to advise the (*League*) Council on the execution of the provisions of Articles 1 (*membership*) and 8 and on military, naval and air questions generally.

Article 10. The Members of the League undertake to respect and preserve as against external aggression the territorial integrity and existing political independence of all Members of the League. In case of any such aggression or in the case of any threat or danger of such aggression the Council shall advise upon the means by which this obligation shall be fulfilled.

Article 11. Any war or threat of war, whether immediately affecting any Members of the League or not, is hereby declared a matter of concern to the whole League, and the League shall take any action that may be deemed wise and effectual to safeguard the peace of nations. In case any such emergency should arise the Secretary General shall on the request of any Member of the League forthwith summon a meeting of the Council. It is also declared to be the friendly right of each Member of the League forthwith summon a meeting of the Council. It is also declared to be the friendly right of each Member of the League to bring to the attention of the Assembly or of the Council any circumstance whatever affecting international relations which threatens to disturb international peace or the good understanding between nations upon which peace depends.

Article 12. The Members of the League agree that if there should arise between them any dispute likely to lead to a rupture, they will submit the matter either to arbitration or to inquiry by the Council, and they agree in no case to resort to war until three months after the award by the arbitrators or the report by the Council. In any case under this

Article the award of the arbitrators shall be made within a reasonable time, and the report of the Council shall be made within six months after the submission of the dispute.

Article 13. The Members of the League agree that whenever any dispute shall arise between them which they recognize to be suitable for submission to arbitration and which cannot be satisfactorily settled by diplomacy, they will submit the whole subject-matter to arbitration or judicial settlement. Disputes as to the interpretation of a treaty, as to any question of international law, as to the existence of any fact which if established would constitute a breach of any international obligation, or as to the extent and nature of the reparation to be made for any such breach, are declared to be among those which are generally suitable for submission to arbitration or judicial settlement. For the consideration of any such dispute, the court to which the case is referred shall be the Permanent Court of International Justice, established in accordance with Article 14, or any tribunal agreed on by the parties to the dispute or stipulated in any convention existing between them. The Members of the League agree that they will carry out in full good faith any award or decision that may be rendered, and that they will not resort to war against a Member of the League which complies therewith. In the event of any failure to carry out such an award or decision, the Council shall propose what steps should be taken to give effect thereto.

Article 14. The Council shall formulate and submit to the Members of the League for adoption plans for the establishment of a Permanent Court of International Justice. The Court shall be competent to hear and determine any dispute of an international character which the parties thereto submit to it. The Court may also give an advisory opinion upon any dispute or question referred to it by the Council or by the Assembly.

Article 15. If there should arise between Members of the League any dispute likely to lead to a rupture, which is not submitted to arbitration or judicial settlement in accordance with Article 13, the members of the League agree that they will submit the matter to the Council. Any party to the dispute may effect such submission by giving notice of the existence of the dispute to the Secretary General, who will make all necessary arrangements for a full investigation and consideration thereof. For this purpose the parties to the dispute will communicate to the Secretary General, as promptly as possible, statements of their case with all the relevant facts and papers, and the Council may forthwith direct the publication thereof. The Council shall endeavor to effect a settlement of the dispute, and if such efforts are successful, a statement shall be made public giving such facts and explanations regarding the dispute and the terms of settlement thereof as the Council may deem appropriate. If the dispute is not settled, the Council either unanimously or by a majority vote shall make and publish a report containing a statement of the facts of the dispute and the recommendations which are deemed just and proper in regard thereto.

Article 16. Should any member of the League resort to war in disregard of its covenants under Articles 12, 13 or 15, it shall ipso facto be deemed to have committed an act of war against all other Members of the League, which hereby undertake immediately to subject it to the severance of all trade or financial relations, the prohibition of all intercourse between their nationals and the nationals of the convenant-breaking State, and the prevention of all financial, commercial or personal intercourse between the nationals of the convenant-breaking State and the nationals of any other State, whether a member of the League or not. It shall be the duty of the Council in such case to recommend to the several Governments concerned what effective military, naval or air force the Members of the League shall severally contribute to the armed forces to be used to protect the covenants of the League. The Members of the League agree, further, that they will mutually support one another in the financial and economic measures which are taken under this Article, in order to minimize the loss and inconvenience resulting from the above measures, and that they will mutually support one another in resisting any special measures aimed at one of their number by the covenant-breaking State, and that they will take the necessary steps to afford passage through their territory to the forces of any of the Members of the League which are co-operating to protect the Covenants of the League. Any member of the League which has violated any covenant of the League may be declared to be no longer a member of the League by a vote of the Council concurred in by the Representatives of all the other Members of the League represented thereon.

Article 17. In the event of a dispute between a member of the League and a State which is not a Member of the League, or between States not Members of the League, the State or States not members of the League shall be invited to accept the obligations of membership in the League for the purposes of such dispute, upon such conditions as the Council may deem just. If such invitation is accepted, the provisions of Articles 12 to 16 inclusive shall be applied with such modifications as may be deemed necessary by the Council. Upon such invitation being given the Council shall immediately institute an inquiry into the circumstances of the dispute and recommend such action as may seem best and most effectual in the circumstances. If a State so invited shall refuse to accept the obligations of membership in the League for the purposes of such dispute, and shall resort to war against a member of the League, the provisions of Article 16 shall be applicable as against the State taking such action. If both parties to the dispute when so invited refuse to accept the obligations of membership in the League for the purposes of such a dispute, the Council may take such measures and make such recommendations as will prevent hostilities and will result in the settlement of the dispute.

REPARATIONS CLAUSES

Article 231. The Allied and Associated Governments affirm and Germany accepts the responsibility of Germany and her allies for causing all the loss and damage to which the Allied and Associated Governments and their nationals have been subjected as a consequence of the war imposed upon them by the aggression of Germany and her allies.

Article 232. The Allied and Associated Governments recognize that the resources of Germany are not adequate, after taking into account permanent diminutions of such resources which will result from other provisions of the present Treaty, to make complete reparation for all such loss and damage. The Allied and Associate Governments, however, require, and Germany undertakes, that she will make compensation for all damage done to the civilian population of the Allied and Associated Powers and to their property during the period of the belligerency of each as an Allied or Associated Power against Germany by such aggression by land, by sea and from the air, and in general all damage as defined in Annex 1 hereto.

In accordance with Germany's pledges, already given, as to complete restoration for Belgium, Germany undertakes, in addition to the compensation for damages elsewhere in this Part provided for, as a consequence of the violation of the Treaty of 1839, to make reimbursement of all sums which Belgium has borrowed from the Allied and Associated Governments up to November 11, 1918, together with interest at the rate of five percent per annum upon such sums. This amount shall be determined by the Reparation Commission, and the German Government undertakes thereupon forthwith to make a special issue of bearer bonds to an equivalent amount payable in marks gold, on May 1, 1921, or, at the option of the German Government, on the 1st May in any year up to 1926. Subject to the foregoing, the form of such bonds shall be determined by the Reparations Commission, which has authority to take and acknowledge receipt thereof on behalf of Belgium.

Article 233. The amount of the above damage for which compensation is to be made by Germany shall be determined by an Inter-Allied Commission, to be called the Reparation Commission and constituted in the form and with the powers set forth hereunder and in Annexes II to VII inclusive hereto. The Commission shall consider the claims and give to the German Government a just opportunity to be heard. The findings of the Commission as to the amount of damage defined as above shall be concluded and notified to the German Government on or before May 1, 1921, as representing the extent of that Government's obligations. The Commission shall concurrently draw up a schedule of payments prescribing the time and manner for securing and discharging the entire obligation within a period of thirty years from May 1, 1921. If, however, within the period mentioned, Germany fails to discharge her obligations, any balance remaining unpaid may, within the discretion of the Commission, be postponed for settlement in subsequent years, or may be handled otherwise in such a manner as the Allied and Associated Governments, acting in accordance with the procedure laid down in this Part of the present Treaty, shall determine.

Article 234. The Reparation Commission shall after May 1, 1921, from time to time, consider the resources and capacity of Germany, and, after giving her representatives a just opportunity to be heard, shall have discretion to extend the date, and to modify the form of payments, such as are to be provided for in accordance with Article 233; but not to cancel any part, except with the specific authority of the several Governments represented upon the Commission.

4

John Maynard Keynes on Reparations

With these brief comments, I pass from the justice of the treaty, which can not be ignored even when it is not our central topic, to its wisdom and its expediency. Under these heads my criticism of the treaty is double. In the first place, this treaty ignores the economic solidarity of Europe, and by aiming at the destruction of the economic life of Germany it threatens the health and prosperity of the Allies themselves. In the second place, by making demands the execution of which is in the literal sense impossible, it stultifies itself and leaves Europe more unsettled than it found it. The treaty, by overstepping the limits of the possible, has in practise settled nothing. The true settlement still remains to be made out of the ashes of the present and the disillusionment of the future, when the imposture of Paris is recognized for what it is.

For reasons of historical experience, which are easily understood, and with which all men must sympathize (however profoundly we believe that France will deal to herself as well as to her enemy a fatal wound if she yields to them), there were powerful influences in Paris demanding for the future security of France that the peace should complete the destruction of the economic life of Central Europe, which the war had gone far to consummate.

The German economic system as it existed before the war depended on three main factors:

John Maynard Keynes, "The Peace of Versailles," *Everybody's Magazine*, Vol. 43, no. 3, pp. 36-42. 1920.

1. Overseas commerce, as represented by her mercantile marine, her colonies, her foreign investments, her exports, and the overseas connections of her merchants.
2. The exploitation of her coal and iron and the industries built upon them.
3. Her transport and tariff system.

Of these the first, while not the least important, was certainly the most vulnerable. The treaty aims at the systematic destruction of all three, but principally the first two.

The above provisions relate to Germany's external wealth. Those relating to coal and iron are more important in respect of their ultimate consequences to Germany's internal industrial economy than for the money value immediately involved. The German Empire has been built more truly on coal and iron than on blood and iron. The skilled exploitation of the Ruhr, Upper Silesia and the Saar alone made possible the development of the steel, chemical and electrical industries which established her as the first industrial nation of continental Europe. One-third of Germany's population lives in towns of more than twenty thousand inhabitants, an industrial concentration which is only possible on a foundation of coal and iron. In striking, therefore, at her coal supply, those who sought her economic destruction were not mistaking their target.

The coal clauses of the treaty are, however, among those which are likely, by reason of the technical impossibility of their execution, to defeat their own object. If the plebiscite results in Germany losing the coal districts of Upper Silesia, the treaty will have deprived her of territory from which not far short of one-third of her total coal supply was previously derived. Out of the coal that remains to her Germany is required, quite rightly, to make good for ten years the estimated loss which France has incurred by the destruction and damage of war in the coalfields of her northern provinces, such deliveries not to exceed twenty million tons in each of the first five years or eight million tons annually thereafter. She has also, over and above this, for ten years to deliver annually seven million tons to France, eight million tons to Belgium, and from four million five hundred thousand tons to eight million five hundred thousand tons to Italy.

I have estimated that this would leave Germany with about sixty million tons annually against domestic requirements, which, on the prewar basis of industry in her remaining territory, would amount to one hundred and ten million tons. In short, Germany could only execute the coal demands of the treaty by abandoning the bulk of her industries and returning to the status of an agricultural country. In this case many millions of her present population could obtain neither work nor food (nor, indeed, facilities of emigration). Yet it is not to be supposed that the population of any country will submit year after year to an export which dooms many of them to starvation and even to death. The thing is humanly and politically impossible. Men will not die so obediently to the dictates of a document. The coal clauses of the treaty are not being executed and never will be.

But in this event the treaty settles nothing, and the extent of the coal deliveries remains as a source of perpetual friction, uncertainty and inefficiency, which will inhibit the industrial activity of all the European countries alike which are parties to it. The coal will not be delivered; it may not even by mined. No plans which look ahead can be made by any one. The commodity will be the subject of a perpetual scramble; and even of military occupations and bloodshed. For, as the result of many various causes, the coal position of all Europe is nearly desperate, and no country will lightly surrender its treaty rights. I affirm, therefore, that the coal clauses are inexpedient and disastrous, and full of danger not only for the economic efficiency but for the political peace of the European continent.

The provisions relating to iron ore require less detailed attention, though their effects are destructive. They require less attention, because they are in large measure inevitable. Almost exactly seventy-five per cent of the iron ore raised in Germany in 1913 came from Alsace-Lorraine. But while Lorraine contained seventy-five percent of Germany's iron ore, only twenty-five per cent of her blast furnaces and of her foundries lay within Lorraine and the Saar basin together, a large proportion of the ore being carried into Germany proper. Thus here, as elsewhere, political considerations cut disastrously across economic. ...

* * *

That is to say, even if Germany pays seven hundred and fifty million dollars annually up to 1936, she will nevertheless owe us at that date more than half as much again as she does now (sixty-five billion dollars as compared with forty billion dollars). From 1936 onwards she will have to pay to us three billion two hundred and fifty million dollars annually in order to keep pace with the interest alone. At the end of any year in which she pays less than this sum she will owe more than she did at the beginning of it. And if she is to discharge the capital sum in thirty years from 1936, i.e. in forty-eight years from the armistice, she must pay an additional six hundred and fifty million dollars annually, making three billion nine hundred million dollars in all.

It is, in my judgement, as certain as anything can be, for reasons which I will summarize in a moment, that Germany can not pay anything approaching this sum. Until the treaty is altered, therefore, Germany has in effect engaged herself to hand over to the Allies the whole of her surplus production in perpetuity.

5

THE FRANCO-POLISH TREATY

FEBRUARY 19, 1921

Preamble: The Polish Government and the French Government, both desirous of safeguarding, by the maintenance of the treaties which both have signed or which may in future be recognized by both parties, the peace of Europe, the security of their territories, and their common political and economic interests, have agreed as follows:

1. In order to coordinate their endeavors towards peace the two Governments undertake to consult each other on all questions of foreign policy which concern both States, so far as those questions affect the settlement of international relations in the spirit of the treaties and in accordance with the Covenant of the League of Nations.

2. In view of the fact that economic restoration is the essential preliminary condition for the re-establishment of international order and peace in Europe, the two Governments shall come to an understanding in this regard with a view to concerted action and mutual support. They will endeavor to develop their economic relations, and for this purpose will conclude special agreements and a commercial treaty.

3. If, notwithstanding the sincerely peaceful views and intentions of the two contracting States, either or both of them should be attacked without giving provocation, the two Governments shall take concerted measures

"The Franco-Polish Treaty, February 19, 1921," The Avalon Project. 1921.

for the defence of their territory and the protection of their legitimate interests within the limits specified in the preamble.

4. The two governments undertake to consult each other before concluding new agreements which will affect their policy in Central and Eastern Europe. *(This treaty was supplemented by a military agreement regarding its execution signed on the same day.)*

6

THE WASHINGTON NAVAL DISARMAMENT TREATY

FEBRUARY 6, 1922

The United States of America, the British Empire, France, Italy and Japan: Desiring to contribute to the maintenance of the general peace, and to reduce the burdens of competition in armament; Have resolved, with a view to accomplishing these purposes, to conclude a treaty to limit their respective naval armament, and to that end have appointed as their Plenipotentiaries;

(There follows a long list of such plenipotentiaries)

Who, having communicated to each other their respective full powers, found to be in good and due form, have agreed as follows:

Article 1. The Contracting Powers agree to limit their respective naval armament as provided in the present Treaty.

(Articles 2 and 3 deal with specific ships that each signatory could retain, complete, replace or scrap).

Article 4. The total capital ship replacement tonnage of each of the Contracting Powers shall not exceed in standard displacement, for the United States 525,000 tons; for the British Empire 525,000 tons; for France 175,000 tons; for Italy 175,000 tons; for Japan 315,000 tons.

"The Washington Naval Disarmament Treaty, February 6, 1922," The Library of Congress. 1922.

Article 5. No capital ship exceeding 35,000 tons (35,560 metric tons) standard displacement shall be acquired by, or constructed by, for or within the jurisdiction of, any of the Contracting Powers.

Article 6. No capital ship of any of the Contracting Powers shall carry a gun with a caliber in excess of 16 inches (406 millimeters).

Article 7. The total tonnage for aircraft carriers of each of the Contracting Powers shall not exceed in standard displacement, for the United States 135,000 tons; for the British Empire 135,000 tons; for France 60,000 tons; for Italy 60,000 tons; for Japan 81,000 tons.

Article 8. The replacement of aircraft carriers shall be effected only as prescribed in Chapter II, Part 3, provided, however, that all aircraft carrier tonnage in existence or building on November 12, 1921, shall be considered experimental, and may be replaced, within the total tonnage limit prescribed in Article VII, without regard to its age.

Article 9. No aircraft carrier exceeding 27,000 tons standard displacement shall be acquired, or constructed by, for or within the jurisdiction of, any of the Contracting Powers. However, any of the Contracting Powers may, provided that its total tonnage allowance of aircraft carriers is not thereby exceeded build not more than two aircraft carriers, each of a tonnage of not more than 33,000 tons (33,528 metric tons) standard displacement, and in order to effect economy any of the Contracting Powers may use for this purpose any two of their ships, whether constructed or in the course of construction, which would otherwise be scrapped under the provisions of Article II. The armament of any aircraft carriers exceeding 27,000 tons (27, 432 metric tons) standard displacement shall be in accordance with the requirements of Article X, except that the total number of guns to be carried in case any of such guns be of a caliber exceeding 6 inches (152 millimeters), except anti-aircraft guns and guns not exceeding 5 inches (127 millimeters) shall not exceed eight.

(Articles 10 to 18 deal with additional warship restrictions, capping cruiser displacement at 10,000 tons, carrying maximum eight inch guns. Article 10 prohibited aircraft carriers from having guns over eight inch calibre).

Article 19. The United States, the British Empire, and Japan agree that the status quo at the time of the signing of the present Treaty, with regard to fortifications and naval bases, shall be maintained in their respective territories and possessions specified hereunder:

1. The insular possessions which the United States now holds or may hereafter acquire in the Pacific Ocean, except (a) those adjacent to the coast of the United States, Alaska and the Panama Canal Zone, not including the Aleutian Islands, and (b) the Hawaiian Islands;

2. Hong Kong and the insular possessions which the British Empire now holds or may hereafter acquire in the Pacific Ocean, east of the meridian of 110 degrees east longitude, except (a) those adjacent to the coast of Canada, (b) the Commonwealth of Australia and its Territories, and (c) New Zealand;

3. The following insular territories and possessions of Japan in the Pacific Ocean, to wit: the Kurile Islands, the Bonin Islands, Amami-Oshima, the Loochoo Islands, Formosa and the Pescadores, and any insular territories or possessions in the Pacific Ocean which Japan may hereafter acquire.

The maintenance of the status quo under the foregoing provisions implies that no new fortifications or naval bases shall be established in the territories and possession specified; that no measures shall be taken to increase the existing naval facilities for the repair and maintenance of naval forces, and that no increase shall be made in the coast defences of the territories and possessions above specified. This restriction, however, does not preclude such repair and replacement of worn-out weapons and equipment as is customary in naval establishments in time of peace.

7

THE TREATY OF RAPALLO

GERMANY AND THE USSR

APRIL 16, 1922

Preamble. The two Governments are agreed that the arrangements arrived at between the German Reich and the Russian Socialist Federal Soviet Republic, with regard to questions dating from the period of war between Germany and Russia, shall be definitely settled upon the following basis:

Article 1. (a)The German Reich and the Russian Socialist Federal Soviet Republic mutually agree to waive their claims for compensation for expenditure incurred on account of the war, and also for war damages, that is to say, any damages which may have been suffered by them and by their nationals in war zones on account of military measures, including all requisitions in enemy country. Both Parties likewise agree to forego compensation for any civilian damages, which may have been suffered by the nationals of on Party on account of so-called exceptional war measures or on account of emergency measures carried out by the other Party.

(b) Legal relations in public and private matters arising out of the state of war, including the question of the treatment of trading vessels which have fallen into the hands of either Party, shall be settled on a basis of reciprocity.

(c) Germany and Russia mutually agree to waive claims for compensation for expenditure incurred by either party on behalf of prisoners of war.

"The Treaty of Rapallo, April 16, 1922," The Avalon Project, pp. 1-2. 1922.

Furthermore the German Government agrees to forego compensation within regard to the expenditure incurred by it on behalf of members of the Red Army stationed in Germany. The Russian Government agrees to forego the restitution of the proceeds of the sale carried out in Germany of the army stores brought into Germany by the interned members of the Red Army mentioned above.

Article 2. Germany waives all claims against Russia which may have arisen through the application, up to the present, of the laws and measures of the Russian Socialist Federal Soviet Republic to German nationals or to their private rights and the rights of the German Reich and states, and also claims which may have arisen owing to any other measures taken by the Russian Socialist Federal Soviet Republic or by their agents against German nationals or their private rights, on condition that the government of the Russian Socialist Federal Soviet Republic does not satisfy claims for compensation of a similar nature made by a third Party.

Article 3. Diplomatic and consular relations between the German Reich and (the USSR) shall be resumed immediately.

Article 4. Both governments have furthermore agreed that the establishment of the legal status of those nationals of the one Party, which live within the territory of the other Party, and the general regulation of mutual, commercial and economic relations, shall be effected on the principle of the most favoured nation. This principle shall, however, not apply to the privileges and facilities which the Russian Socialist Federal Soviet Republic may grant to a Soviet Republic or to any State which in the past formed part of the former Russian Empire.

Article 5. The two Governments shall co-operate in a spirit of mutual goodwill in meeting the economic needs of both countries. In the event of a fundamental settlement of the above question on an international basis, an exchange of opinions shall previously take place between the two Governments. The German Government, having lately been informed of the proposed agreements of private firms, declares its readiness to give all possible support to these arrangements and to facilitate their being carried into effect.

Article 6. Articles 1(b) and 4 of this Agreement shall come into force on the day of ratification, and the remaining provisions shall come into force immediately.

8

THE LOCARNO PACT

OCTOBER 16, 1925

Preamble: Anxious to satisfy the desire for security and protections which animates the peoples upon whom fell the scourge of war 1914–1918; Taking note of the abrogation of the treaties for the neutralization of Belgium, and conscious of the necessity of ensuring peace in the area which has so frequently been the scene of European conflicts; Animated also with the sincere desire of giving to all the signatory Powers concerned supplementary guarantees within the framework of the Covenant of the League of Nations and the treaties in force between them; (*The signatories*) Have determined to conclude a treaty with these objects, and have appointed as their plenipotentiaries:

Names omitted.

Who, having communicated their full powers, found in good and due form, have agreed as follows:

Article 1. The High Contracting Parties *(Germany, Belgium, France, Britain and Italy)* collectively and severally guarantee, in the manner provided in the following Articles, the maintenance of the territorial status quo resulting from the frontiers between Germany and Belgium and between Germany and France, and the inviolability of the said frontiers as fixed by or in pursuance of the Treaty of Peace signed at Versailles on June 28, 1919, and also the observance of the stipulations

"The Locarno Pact, October 16, 1925," The Avalon Project, pp. 1-3. 1925.

of Articles 42 and 43 *(dealing with demilitarization of the Rhineland)* of the said treaty concerning the demilitarized zone.

Article 2. Germany and Belgium, and also Germany and France, mutually undertake that they will in no case attack or invade each other or resort to war against each other. This stipulation shall not, however, apply in the case of: (1) The exercise of the right of legitimate defence, that is to say, resistance to a violation of the undertaking contained in the previous paragraph or to a flagrant breach of Articles 42 or 43 of the said Treaty of Versailles. If such breach constitutes an unprovoked act of aggression and by reason of the assembly of armed forces in the demilitarized zone immediate action is necessary; (2) Action in pursuance of Article 16 of the Covenant of the League of Nations; (3) Action as the result of a decision taken by the Assembly of by the Council of the League of Nations in pursuance of Article 15, paragraph 7 of the Covenant of the League of Nations, provided that in this last event the action is directed against a State which was the first to attack.

Article 3. In view of the undertakings entered into in Article 2 of the present treaty, Germany and Belgium, and Germany and France, undertake to settle by peaceful means and in the manner laid down herein all questions of every kind which may arise between them and which it may not be possible to settle by the normal methods of diplomacy: Any question with regard to which the Parties are in conflict as to its respective rights shall be submitted to judicial decision, and the parties undertake to comply with such decision. All other questions shall be submitted to a conciliation commission. If the proposals of this commission are not accepted by the two Parties, question shall be brought before the Council of the League of Nations, which will deal with it in accordance with Article 15 of the Covenant of the League.

Article 4. (1) If one of the High Contracting Parties alleges that a violation of Article 2 of the present Treaty or a breach of Articles 42 or 43 of the treaty of Versailles has been or is being committed, it shall bring the question at once before the Council of the League of Nations.

(2) As soon as the Council of the League of Nations is satisfied that violation or breach has been committed, it will notify its finding without delay to the Powers signatory of the present Treaty, who severally

agree that in such case they will each of them come immediately to the assistance of the Power against whom the act complained of is directed.

(3) In case of a flagrant violation of Article 2 of the present Treaty or a flagrant breach of Articles 42 or 43 of the Treaty of Versailles by one of the High Contracting Parties, each of the other Contracting Parties hereby undertakes to come to the help of the Party against whom such a violation or breach has been directed as soon as the said Power has been able to satisfy itself that this violation constitutes an unprovoked act of aggression and that by reason either of the crossing of the frontier or of the outbreak of hostilities or of the assembly of armed forces in the demilitarized zone immediate action is necessary. Nevertheless, the Council of the League of Nations, which will be seized of the question in accordance with the first paragraph of this Article, will issue its findings, and the High Contracting Parties undertake to act in accordance with the recommendations of the Council, provided that they are concurred in by all the Members other than the representatives of the Parties which have engaged in hostilities.

Article 5. The provisions of Article 3 of the present Treaty are placed under the guarantee of the High Contracting Parties as provided by the following stipulations: If one of the Powers referred to in Article 3 refuses to submit a dispute to peaceful settlement or to comply with an arbitral or judicial decision and commits a violation of Article 2 of the present Treaty or a breach of Articles 42 or 43 of the Treaty of Versailles, the provisions of Article 4 of the present Treaty shall apply. Where one of the Powers referred to in Article 3, without committing a violation of Article 2 of the present Treaty or a breach of Articles 42 or 43 of the Treaty of Versailles, refuses to submit a dispute to peaceful settlement or to comply with an arbitral or judicial decision, the other Party shall bring the matter before the Council of the League of Nations, and the Council shall propose what steps shall be taken; the High Contracting Parties shall comply with these provisions.

9

KELLOGG-BRIAND PACT

1928

Preamble: (*The signatories*) deeply sensible of their solemn duty to promote the welfare of mankind;

Persuaded that the time has come when a frank renunciation of war as an instrument of national policy should be made to the end that the peaceful and friendly relations now existing between their peoples may be perpetuated;

Convinced that all changes in their relations with one another should be sought only by pacific means and be the result of a peaceful and orderly process, and that any signatory Power which shall hereafter seek to promote its national interests by resort to war should be denied the benefits furnished by this Treaty;

Hopeful that, encouraged by their example, all the other nations of the world will join in this humane endeavor and by adhering to the present Treaty as soon as it comes into force bring their peoples within the scope of its beneficent provisions, thus uniting the civilized nations of the world in a common renunciation of war as an instrument of their national policy;

Have decided to conclude a Treaty. ...

Article 1. The High Contracting Parties solemnly declare in the names of their respective peoples that they condemn recourse to war for the

"Kellogg-Briand Pact," The Avalon Project, pp. 1-4. 1928.

solution of international controversies, and renounce it, as an instrument of national policy in their relations with one another.

Article 2. The High Contracting Parties agree that the settlement or solution of all disputes or conflicts of whatever nature or of whatever origin they may be, which may arise among them, shall never be sought except by pacific means.

Article 3. The present Treaty shall be ratified by the High Contracting Parties named in the Preamble in accordance with their respective constitutional requirements, and shall take effect as between them as soon as all their several instruments of ratification shall have been deposited in Washington.

The Treaty shall, when it has come into effect as prescribed in the preceding paragraph, remain open as long as may be necessary for adherence by all the other Powers of the world. Every instrument evidencing the adherence of a Power shall be deposited at Washington and the Treaty shall immediately upon such deposit become effective as; between the Power thus adhering and the other Powers parties hereto.

10

Mein Kampf

1924

Today I consider it my good fortune that Fate designated Braunau on the Inn as the place of my birth. For this small town is situated on the border between those two German States, the reunion of which seems, at least to us of the younger generation, a task to be furthered with every means our lives long.

German-Austria must return to the great German motherland, and not because of economic considerations of any sort. No, no: even if from the economic point of view this union were unimportant, indeed if it were harmful, it ought nevertheless to be brought about. Common blood belongs in a common Reich. As long as the German nation is unable even to band together its own children in one common State, it has no moral right to think of colonization as one of its political aims. Only when the boundaries of the Reich include even the last German, only when it is no longer possible to assure him of daily bread inside them, does there arise, out of the distress of the nation, the moral right to acquire foreign soil and territory. The sword is then the plow, and from the tears of war there grows the daily bread for generations to come. Therefore, this little town on the border appears to me the symbol of a great task. But in another respect also it looms up as a warning to our present time. More than a hundred years ago, this insignificant little place had the privilege to gaining an immortal place in German history at least by being the scene of a tragic misfortune that moved the entire nation. There, during the time of the deepest humiliation of our fatherland, Johannes Palm, citizen of Nurnberg, a middle class bookdealer, die-hard 'nationalist,' an enemy of the French, was killed for the sake of the Germany he ardently loved even in the hour of its distress. He had obstinately refused to denounce his fellow offenders, or rather the chief offenders. Thus he acted like Leo Schlageter. But like him, he too was betrayed to France by a representative of his government. It was a director of the Augsburg police who earned that shoddy glory, thus setting an example for the new German authorities of Herr Severing's Reich.

In this little town on the river Inn, gilded by the light of German martyrdom, there lived, at the end of the eighties of the last century, my parents, Bavarian by blood, Austrian by nationality: my father a faithful civil servant, the mother devoting herself to the cares of the household and looking after her children with eternally the same loving kindness. I remember only little of this time, for a few years later my father had again to leave the little border town he had learned to like, and go down the Inn to take a new position at Passau, that is in Germany proper.

* * *

There are two reasons which induce me to subject the relations of Germany to Russia to a special examination: (1) in this case we are concerned with perhaps the most decisive matter of German foreign affairs as a whole; and (2) this question is also the touchstone of the political capacity of the young National Socialist movement to think clearly and to act correctly.

If we understand by foreign policy the regulation of the relations of one people to the rest of the world, then the manner of regulation is conditioned by quite definite facts. As National Socialists we can further lay down the following principle as to the essence of the foreign policy of a folkish State:

The foreign policy of the folkish State is charged with guaranteeing the existence on this planet of the race embraced by the State, by establishing between the number and growth of the population, on the one hand, and the size and value of the soil and territory, on the other, a viable, natural relationship.

Moreover, only that relationship can ever be regarded as healthy which assures the nourishment of a people from its own soil and territory. Every other situation, though it may last centuries and even millennia, is nevertheless unhealthy, and will sooner or later lead to the injuring if not the destruction of the people concerned.

Only a sufficiently extensive area on this globe guarantees a nation freedom of existence.

Moreover, the necessary extent of the domain to be occupied cannot be judged exclusively by contemporary requirements, nor even by the quantity of the produce of the soil compared to the population. For, as I have already have argued in the first volume, under 'German Alliance Policy Before the War,' the area of a State has also another, military-political significance than as a direct source of nourishment of a people. When a people has secured its nourishment for itself by virtue of the extent of its soil and territory, it is nevertheless necessary to think also of securing the territory in hand. This depends on the State's general power-political force and strength which is to no small extent conditioned by geo-military considerations.

Hence the German people can defend its future only as a world power. For almost two thousand years the defense of our nation's interests, as we shall term our more or less happy foreign policy, was world history. We ourselves witnessed this, because the great struggle of the nations in the years 1914–18 was only the German people's struggle for its existence on this planet, although we describe the type of event itself as a World War.

* * *

State frontiers are man-made and can be altered by man.

The reality of a nation having managed a disproportionate acquisition of territory is no superior obligation for its eternal recognition. It proves at most the might of the conqueror and the weakness of the victim. And, moreover, this might alone makes right. If the German people today, penned into an impossible area, face a wretched future, this is as little Fate's command as its rejection would constitute a snub to Fate. Just as little as some superior power has promised another nation more soil and territory than the German, or would be insulted by the fact of this unjust division of territory. Just as our forefathers did not get the land on which we are living today as a gift from Heaven, but had to conquer it by risking their lives, so no folkish grace but only the might of a triumphant sword will in the future assign us territory, and with it life for our nation.

Much as we today recognize the necessity for a reckoning with France, it will remain largely ineffective if our foreign-policy aim is restricted thereto. It has and will retain significance if it provides the rear cover for an enlargement of our national domain of life in Europe. For we will find this question's solution not in colonial acquisitions, but exclusively in the winning of land for settlement which increases the area of the motherland itself, and thereby not only keeps the new settler in the most intimate community with the land of origin, but insures to the total area those advantages deriving from its united magnitude.

We National Socialists, however, must go further: the right to soil and territory can become a duty if decline seems to be in store for a great nation unless it extends its territory. Even more especially if what is involved is not some little negro people or other, but the German mother of all life, which has given its cultural picture to the contemporary world. Germany will be either a world power or will not be at all. To be a world power, however, requires that size which nowadays gives its necessary importance to such a power, which gives life to its citizens.

With this, we National Socialists consciously draw a line through the foreign-policy trend of our pre-War period. We take up at the halting place of six hundred years ago. We terminate the endless German drive to the south and west of Europe, and direct our gaze towards the lands in the east. We finally terminate the colonial and trade policy of the pre-War period, and proceed to the territorial policy of the future.

But if we talk about new soil and territory in Europe today, we can think primarily only of Russia and its vassal border states.

Fate itself seems to seek to give us a tip at this point. In the surrender of Russia to bolshevism, the Russian people was robbed of that intelligentsia which theretofore produced and guaranteed its State stability. For the organization of a Russian State structure was not the result of Russian Slavdom's State-political capacity, but rather a wonderful example of the State-building activity of the German element in an inferior race. Thus have innumerable mighty empires of the earth been created. Inferior nations with German organizers and lords as leaders have more than once expanded into powerful State structures, and endured as long as the racial nucleus of the constructive State-race maintained itself. For centuries Russia drew nourishment from this Germanic nucleus of its superior strata of leaders. Today it is uprooted and obliterated almost without a trace. The Jew has replaced it. Impossible as it is for the Russians alone to shake off the yoke of the Jews through their own strength, it is equally impossible in the long run for the Jews to maintain the mighty empire. Jewry itself is not an organizing element, but a ferment of decomposition. The Persian Empire, once so powerful, is now ripe for collapse; and the end of Jewish dominion in Russia will also be the end of the Russian State itself. We have been chosen by Fate to be the witnesses of a catastrophe which will be the most powerful substantiation of the folkish theory of race.

Our task, the mission of the National Socialist movement, however, is to bring our own nation to such political insight as will make it see its future goal fulfilled, not by an intoxicating impression of a new Alexandrian campaign, but rather by the industrious labor of the German plow which needs only to be given land by the sword.

CHAPTER 2

THE ROAD TO WAR IN EUROPE
AND THE MUNICH CRISIS,
1929–1939

Introduction

Adolf Hitler was appointed chancellor of Germany on January 31, 1933. A few days later he addressed a meeting of senior German generals. In the notes taken at that meeting by one of those present (Document 1), what is Hitler saying? Do you see similarities with the *Mein Kampf* extract in Chapter 1, or does Hitler appear to be backing off somewhat? What does Hitler mean when he refers to France's "eastern satellites"?

In the text of the German-Polish Treaty of January 26, 1934 (Document 2), do you see any connection with Hitler's remarks in the first document? Why would Poland sign such a treaty? Why would Germany? What is the benefit to each signatory? How do you think the French felt about the German-Polish Treaty?

Fascist dictator Benito Mussolini seized power in Italy in 1922, but he had been relatively quiescent in his foreign policy during the 1920s, even guaranteeing the Locarno Pact of 1925. But the worldwide depression hit the Italian economy hard, and Mussolini began making incendiary speeches promising to recreate the old Roman empire and restore Italian greatness. Mussolini focused on the independent African state of Ethiopia, which could be attacked from bases in Italian-held Eritrea and Italian Somaliland. Ethiopia, however, was a member of the League of Nations and could be expected to appeal to the League for help if attacked. The governments of Britain and France both gave lip service to League ideals and a pro-League lobby group in Britain, the League of Nations Union, enjoyed immense popular support. However, Britain and France also hoped to woo Italy to their side and recreate at least part of the coalition that had fought Germany in the First World War. Can you understand the dilemma the London and Paris faced when an Italian attack on Ethiopia seemed imminent in 1935? What was senior British Foreign Office official Robert Vansittart's solution to the crisis (Document 3)? Mussolini attacked Ethiopia on October 3, 1935. The League branded Italy as the aggressor and imposed some economic sanctions but exempted oil, a crucial Italian import. Why did the British and French not take a stronger stance against Italy? In December 1935, the Hoare-Laval plan, a secret British-French plan to give Italy control over the bulk of Ethiopia while preserving the fiction of Ethiopian independence, had to be abandoned when details were leaked to the press. Popular outrage forced the resignation of British foreign minister Samuel Hoare and French foreign minister Pierre Laval. Mussolini completed the conquest of Ethiopia in 1936. It would be hard to imagine a worse outcome for the British and French. The League was shown to be ineffective, Ethiopia was conquered, and Italy as an alliance partner was lost to Britain and France.

In the Anglo-German Naval Agreement of 1935 (Document 4), what do you think the British were trying to do? The French were not informed about the negotiations for this agreement and were surprised when it was made public. How do you think the French might have interpreted British policy?

Britain and France had always hoped that an independent Austria could be used as a wedge issue to drive Germany and Italy apart. What was Germany's interest in Austria? (See Chapter 1, Document 2.) Note that Italy was the only country that could militarily assist Austria if it were threatened by Germany. France and Britain were both distant powers. Mussolini moved Italian troops to the Austrian border when an attempted *putsch* by Austrian Nazis briefly threatened Austrian independence in 1934. Austria's status as a buffer state between Italy and Germany was especially crucial due to Mussolini's concern over the north Italian territory known as South Tyrol. Formerly part of the Austro-Hungarian empire, Italy had been granted South Tyrol in 1919 for strategic reasons. But the territory came with a population of about 250,000 German-speaking citizens. If Hitler was to absorb Austria, what would stop him from demanding South Tyrol? Mussolini had therefore opposed German *anschluss* (union) with Austria, much to Hitler's fury. Following the Ethiopian crisis, however, Mussolini drifted into Hitler's camp slowly but surely. On January 7, 1936, the German ambassador to Italy, Ulrich von Hassell, recorded an astonishing conversation with Mussolini in which the Italian dictator outlines a new policy regarding Austria (Document 5). What does Mussolini tell Hassell? What does this mean for Austrian independence?

By early 1936 it was clear that Hitler was intent on remilitarizing the Rhineland. At the time of the signing of the Locarno treaties in 1925, the German government had promised to leave the Rhineland permanently demilitarized once Allied troops had left. This was intended to be a testament of goodwill on the part of Germany toward France. But all that was thrown overboard on March 7, 1936, when German troops entered the Rhineland. The next reading (Document 6) summarizes a conference held by the French chiefs of staff (heads of the army, navy, and air forces) as German troops fanned out across the Rhineland. What are their conclusions? Why did the French not go to war over the Rhineland? Remember that the Rhineland was indisputably a German-speaking territory. What role did the Franco-Soviet pact play in all this? How did the French military leaders regard the pact? What was the role of Belgium in French strategy?

Civil war erupted in Spain in July 1936. A coalition of fascist and right-wing authoritarian parties, eventually led by General Francisco Franco, attempted to overthrow the democratically elected government of Spain. The French and British governments responded with a policy of nonintervention, meaning that all the powers of Europe would pledge not to send weapons or to intervene on either side in the war. The British also needed to be on good terms with whomever won the war. A hostile Spanish government could pose a mortal threat to the British base at Gibraltar and the British lifeline through the Mediterranean to the Suez Canal and India. In the summary of the discussion on the Spanish Civil War (Document 7) between the British ambassador to France, Sir George Clerk, and the French foreign minister, Yvon Delbos, how does Gibraltar factor into their reasoning? What do the two diplomats think of the Spanish government? The German and Italian governments completely ignored the nonintervention agreement. Italy sent at least 40,000 troops to fight in Spain on Franco's side. The Germans sent an "experimental" aircraft unit known as the Condor Legion, which became notorious for the bombing of the Basque town of Guernica in 1937, an atrocity that inspired the famous painting by Pablo Picasso.

Antiwar sentiment ran strong in Britain in the mid-1930s. The enormous losses of the First World War left a bitter taste. Many feared that the next war would feature the use of mass aerial bombings and poison gas against civilians. Because the potential of radar and new fighter aircraft had not yet become clear, it was widely assumed that the "bomber would always get through" and Britain's cities would be obliterated on the outbreak of war with mass casualties. The remark about the omnipotence of the bomber was made by two-time British prime minister Stanley Baldwin in 1932, when he was temporarily out of power. By 1935 Baldwin was back again as prime minister. In the extracts from Baldwin's "appalling frankness" speech to the House of Commons in November 1936 (Document 8), what is he saying? Do you find his speech convincing? How did antiwar feeling become a justification for appeasement? How can governments best educate their citizens about potential threats to the peace? When British rearmament ramped up a few years later, the government experienced shortages of skilled labor and production bottlenecks that took more time to overcome.

The Communist International, known as the Comintern for short, had been founded by Russian Communist leader Vladimir Lenin in 1919 to serve as the general staff for the world worker's revolution. By the mid-1930s it was mainly a tool of Soviet foreign policy, with Moscow instructing foreign Communist parties in such a way as to safeguard the security of the USSR, the home of the worker's revolution. In 1934, for example, Communist parties were told to enter Popular Fronts, meaning alliances of any political party that would oppose fascism. The Anti-Comintern Pact of 1936 (Document 9) was signed by Germany and Japan (with Italy joining later) ostensibly to combat the Comintern. What were the terms of the Anti-Comintern Pact? Only a few weeks earlier, Mussolini had proclaimed the existence of the Rome-Berlin "Axis" (from which we derive the term Axis powers). According to Mussolini, the Rome-Berlin Axis would be the new axis around which the world would revolve. Do you think Britain and France should have been alarmed by these developments? Why or why not?

Neville Chamberlain was appointed prime minister of Britain on May 28, 1937, succeeding Baldwin. Chamberlain is most closely associated with the policy of appeasement, the policy that guided Britain in its dealing with Nazi Germany until at least March 1939. Appeasement has a bad reputation today and is associated with craven surrender in the face of obvious evil. But why did the British (and French, to a lesser extent) choose to follow such an obviously mistaken policy? Remember that hindsight allows us many benefits. A big part of the answer can be found in the memorandum (Document 10) compiled by the British chiefs of staff and presented to Chamberlain only a few months after he came to power. What does this report say? Remember to read it carefully. If you were prime minister, how would you have conducted your foreign policy in light of the realities portrayed by the heads of your armed forces?

The year 1938 proved to be pivotal. Hitler ordered German troops to march into Austria on March 13. Italy had abandoned Austria to Germany, so Hitler achieved *anschluss* without trouble. Hitler then turned his attention to Czechoslovakia. Here the issue was the status of the German-speaking Sudetenland. Pressure on Czechoslovakia built up steadily through summer 1938. The French soon made it clear that they would not fight for Czechoslovakia whereas the British sent an envoy, Lord Runciman, whose main job was to pressure the Czechs into settling with Germany. Nevertheless, by late summer 1938, war seemed imminent. In the letters that Chamberlain sent to his sister Ida in 1938 (Documents 11 and 12), what principles does he articulate in terms of foreign policy? Do you see any relation to the British chiefs of staff report? What does Chamberlain think of some of the alternatives put forth by his critics?

The "plan" that Chamberlain mentions in the last paragraph of his September 11 letter to Ida (Document 12) involved a personal visit to Hitler to save the peace. This was to be the third such visit that Chamberlain made to Hitler in 1938. This final meeting took place in desperate circumstances with war seemingly imminent. The Munich Conference of September 29–30, 1938 (Documents 13 and 14), was attended by Chamberlain, Hitler, Mussolini, and French premier Édouard Daladier. The Czech delegation was kept waiting at a nearby hotel and simply handed the resulting text. The Munich agreement provided for the handing over of the Sudetenland to Germany. What do you think of the agreement? How does the agreement provide for the future security of the Czech state? Pay close attention to the document immediately following the Munich agreement. What is the connection with the Anglo-German Naval Agreement of 1935?

During the House of Commons debate on the Munich agreement, Winston Churchill emerged as a leading critic of appeasement. What points does Chamberlain make in defense of Munich (Document 15)? How does Churchill counter Chamberlain's arguments (Document 16)? Without the benefit of hindsight, and bearing in mind some of the preceding documents, who would you have supported in the 1938 debate?

Hitler regarded Munich as a bitter defeat, a fact that surprises many. Hitler had wanted war over Czechoslovakia, and he was determined not to be outwitted again. The winter of 1938–1939 was tense and punctuated with repeated "war scares." Finally, on March 15, 1939, German troops marched into the remainder of Czechoslovakia. Bohemia and Moravia were absorbed into Germany while Slovakia was set up as an ostensibly independent state. Hitler's moves into the Rhineland, Austria, and the Sudetenland could all be rationalized as acts of national self-determination. But the final takeover of the

Czech state was indisputably open aggression. Most historians would agree that appeasement was now abandoned in favor of a policy of containment. The British guarantee to Poland, dated March 31, 1939 (Document 17), symbolized that new policy. Poland was Hitler's obvious next target. The alleged grievances of German-speaking citizens living in Danzig and the Polish Corridor could certainly be exploited by Hitler. What do the British and French promise Poland in this statement? Given preceding events, is this a surprise?

The only state that could provide effective assistance to Poland in the case of war with Germany was the USSR. Unfortunately, historical animosity between Russians and Poles ran deep. The Polish government feared that if they allowed Russian troops onto Polish territory to fight the Germans, they might not leave after the war ended. As it turned out, this was an entirely realistic fear. The British and French both realized that they needed Soviet assistance, and thus embarked on tortuous negotiations in summer 1939 for an alliance. Examine the first set of proposals that the Soviets made to the British and French in April 1939 (Document 18). What do the Soviets want?

In the summary of a briefing Hitler gave to the German generals in late May 1939 (Document 19), how does Hitler foresee events developing? How does he plan to move against Poland? Do you see any connections with the *Mein Kampf* excerpt from Chapter 1? Is Danzig Hitler's main concern?

The talks between Moscow, Paris, and London dragged on all summer. Unfortunately, it was not possible to overcome the deep mutual suspicions on both sides. The British and French were concerned about Soviet ambitions in the Baltic states while the Soviets were frustrated by their inability to pin down the British and French to a firm commitment. What do you think of Lord Halifax's summary of the negotiations in July 1939 (Document 20)? In August, the British and French sent a military delegation to Moscow to speed things up, but even that did not help. In fact, the low-ranking status of the negotiators, the slowness with which they were sent (via steamship and not air travel) and the fact that the British neglected to bring along their diplomatic credentials (a standard diplomatic procedure) may have done more harm than good. Examine the text of the Nazi-Soviet pact of August 23, 1939 (Document 21), and the accompanying, notorious secret protocol (Document 22). Why did Stalin decide to sign a pact with Hitler, and not the Western powers? What could Hitler offer?

In the summary of an interview given by the chief Soviet military negotiator, Marshal Voroshilov, to his French and British counterparts shortly after the announcement of the Nazi-Soviet Pact (Document 23), who does Voroshilov blame for the failure of the British-French-Soviet talks? Do you think he is being fair? What do the British and French conclude? Did the British-French talks with the Soviets ever stand a chance of success?

The Nazi-Soviet Pact allowed Hitler to attack Poland without running the risk of war with the USSR in the east and the British and French in the west. Hitler had argued that fighting a two-front had been a crucial German mistake in the First World War. On September 1, 1939, German forces attacked Poland. Two days later the British and French kept their promise to Poland and declared war on Nazi Germany. The Second World War in Europe had begun.

1

HITLER ADDRESSES THE GERMAN GENERALS[1]

FEBRUARY 3, 1933

Rebuilding of the armed forces is the most important prerequisite for attaining the goal: Reconquest of political power. Universal military service has to come back. First the leadership of the state must see to it, however, that those liable for service are not poisoned, even before they enter, by pacifism, Marxism, Bolshevism or that they do not succumb to that poison after having served.

How is political power to be used after it has been won? Not yet possible to tell. Perhaps conquest of new export possibilities, perhaps—and indeed preferably—conquest of new living space in the east and ruthless Germanization of the latter. It is certain that the present economic conditions can be changed only through political power and struggle. All that can be done now—land—settlement—stop gaps.

Armed forces remain the most important and most socialistic institution of the state. They are to remain non-political and above parties. The domestic struggle is not their business, but that of Nazi organizations. Different from Italy, no amalgamation of army and SA is intended. The most dangerous period is that of the rebuilding of the armed forces. Then we shall see, whether Fr(ance) has *statesmen*; if so, she will not leave us time but will fall upon us (presumably with eastern satellites).

---

1   Hitler's remarks were recorded by Lieutenant General Liebmann.

Adolf Hitler, "Hitler Addresses the German Generals, February 3, 1933," *Documents on German Foreign Policy, 1918-1945*, Series C, Volume One, pp. 37. 1957.

2

THE GERMAN-POLISH TREATY

JANUARY 26, 1934

The German Government and the Polish Government consider that the time has come to introduce a new phase in the political relations between Germany and Poland by a direct understanding between State and State. They have, therefore, decided to lay down the principles for the future development of these relations in the present declaration.

The two Governments base their action on the fact that the maintenance and guarantee of a lasting peace between their countries is an essential pre-condition for the general peace of Europe.

They have therefore decided to base their mutual relations on the principles laid down in the Pact of Paris of the 17th August, 1928, and propose to define more exactly the application of these principles in so far as the relations between Germany and Poland are concerned.

Each of the two Governments, therefore, lays it down that the international obligations undertaken by it towards a third party do not hinder the peaceful development of their mutual relations, do not conflict with the present declaration, and are not affected by this declaration. They establish, moreover, that this declaration does not extend to those questions which under international law are to be regarded exclusively as the internal concern of one of the two States.

Both Governments announce their intention to settle directly all questions of whatever sort which concern their mutual relations.

"The German-Polish Treaty, January 26, 1934," The Avalon Project. 1934.

Should any disputes arise between them and agreement thereon not be reached by direct negotiation, they will in each particular case, on the basis of mutual agreement, seek a solution by other peaceful means, without prejudice to the possibility of applying, if necessary, those methods of procedure in which provision is made for such cases in other agreements in force between them. In no circumstances, however, will they proceed to the application of force for the purpose of reaching a decision in such disputes.

The guarantee of peace created by these principles will facilitate the great task of both Governments finding a solution for problems of political, economic and social kinds, based on a just and fair adjustment of the interests of both parties.

Both Governments are convinced that the relations between their countries will in this manner develop fruitfully, and will lead to the establishment of a neighbourly relationship which will contribute to the well-being not only of both their countries, but of the other peoples of Europe as well. ...

The declaration is valid for a period of ten years ...

3

BRITAIN AND THE ETHIOPIAN CRISIS

BRITISH FOREIGN OFFICE PERMANENT UNDER-SECRETARY OF STATE ROBERT VANSITTART'S MEMORANDUM ON ABYSSINIA (ETHIOPIA)

JUNE 8, 1935

The position is as plain as a pikestaff. Italy will have to be bought off—let us use and face ugly words—in some form or other, or Abyssinia will eventually perish. That might in itself matter less, if it did not mean that the League would also perish (and that Italy would simultaneously perform *another* volte-face into the arms of Germany, a combination of haute politique and haute cocotterie that we can ill afford just now.) …

If we are all clear and in unison about that, it follows clearly that either there has got to be a disastrous explosion—that will wreck the League and very possibly His Majesty's Government too, if the League is destroyed on the eve of an election—or else that *we* have to pay the price … with British Somaliland, though payment would clearly have to be deferred, even if promised.

Personally I opt unhesitatingly for the latter. I have long thought the distribution of this limited globe quite unjustifiable. Like fools we have made it far worse at Versailles. What *has* happened in regard to Japan; what is happening in regard to Italy, and what is about to happen in regard to Germany, we should surely confirm this view to anyone with political antennae. We are grossly over-landed (and British Somaliland is a real debit.) Indeed, looking a little further ahead—say a couple of generations at most—who can for a

Robert Vansittart, "Britain and the Ethiopian Crisis, June 8, 1935," Documents on British Foreign Policy, 2nd Series, vol. 14, no. 301, pp. 308-309. 1976.

moment imagine that Canada and Australia will really be allowed to continue their present policies of shut door and eyes?

I should like to see the question of Somaliland considered at least, while we can still get something for less than nothing. If this cock won't fight, let some one else produce another that will. But whence? Failing these, we may prepare for a horrid autumn—and beyond.

4

ANGLO-GERMAN NAVAL AGREEMENT[1]

JUNE 18, 1935

During the last few days the representatives of the German government and His Majesty's Government in the United Kingdom have been engaged in conversations, the primary purpose of which has been to prepare the way for the holding of a general conference on the subject of the limitation of naval armaments. I have now much pleasure in notifying Your Excellency of the formal acceptance by His Majesty's Government in the United Kingdom of the proposal of the German Government discussed at those conversations that the future strength of the German navy in relation to the aggregate naval strength of the Members of the British Commonwealth of Nations should be in the proportion of 35:100. His Majesty's Government in the United Kingdom regard this proposal as a contribution of the greatest importance to the cause of future naval limitation. They further believe that the agreement which they have now reached with the German Government and which they regard as a permanent and definite agreement as from today between the two Governments, will facilitate the conclusion of a general agreement on the subject of naval limitation between all the naval Powers of the world. ...

---

1   The agreement took the form of diplomatic notes exchanged between British Secretary of State for Foreign Affairs, Samuel Hoare and the German ambassador to Britain, Joachim von Ribbentrop (known to the British press as "Herr von Brickendrop" after his penchant for diplomatic gaffes). The document produced here consists of extracts from Hoare's note to Ribbentrop.

"Anglo-German Naval Agreement, June 18, 1935," Navweaps. 1935.

2 (a). The ratio 35:100 is to be a permanent relationship, ie, the total tonnage of the German fleet shall never exceed a percentage of 35 of the aggregate tonnage of the naval forces, as defined by treaty, of the members of the British Commonwealth of Nations ...

(c) Germany will adhere to the ratio 35:100 in all circumstances, eg, the ratio will not be affected by the construction of other Powers. ...

(f) In the matter of submarines, however, Germany, while not exceeding the ration of 35:100 in respect of total tonnage, shall have the right to possess a submarine tonnage equal to the total submarine tonnage possessed by the members of the British Commonwealth of Nations. The German Government, however, undertake that, except in the circumstances indicated in the immediately following sentence, Germany's submarine tonnage shall not exceed 45% of the total of that possessed by the Members of the British Commonwealth of Nations. The German Government reserve the right, in the event of a situation arising which in their opinion makes it necessary for Germany to avail herself of her right to a percentage of submarine tonnage exceeding the 45% abovementioned, to give notice to this effect to His Majesty's Government in the United Kingdom and agree that the matter shall be the subject of friendly discussion before the German Government exercise that right. ...

5

MUSSOLINI ABANDONS AUSTRIA TO GERMANY[1]

JANUARY 7, 1936

Mussolini received me this afternoon after I had let him know that I would be in Berlin in the middle of next week. He said it would be useful for him to discuss the whole political situation with me, in order that I might report on it orally to the Führer. ...

As far as Germany was concerned, he fully appreciated her neutrality, which he described as benevolent. This being so, he thought it would now be possible to dispose of the only dispute, namely, the Austrian problem. Since we had always declared that we did not wish to infringe Austria's independence, the simplest method would be for Berlin and Vienna themselves to settle their relations on the basis of Austrian independence, e.g., in the form of a treaty of friendship with a non-aggression pact, which would in practice bring Austria into Germany's wake, so that she could pursue no other foreign policy than one parallel with Germany. If Austria, as a formally quite independent State, were thus in practice to become a German satellite, he would have no objection. He saw in this great advantages for Germany as well as for Italy, in that Germany, as already stated, would acquire a reliable satellite, while at the same time German-Italian mistrust would be eliminated ... Should this not come about, then it was feared that Austria, who was beginning to doubt Italy's ability to help her at the decisive moment, would be driven to side with

---

1 Excerpts from a telegram composed by Ulrich von Hassell, German ambassador to Italy.

"Mussolini Abandons Austria, January 7, 1936," *Documents on German Foreign Policy, Series C*, vol. 4, no. 485, pp. 974-977. Her Majesty's Stationery Office, 1962.

Czechoslovakia and thus with France. I replied that these remarks were of very great interest to me; had I rightly understood him to mean that Italy would not oppose, either directly or indirectly, a settlement of German-Austrian relations on the basis of formal independence and close German-Austrian cooperation in foreign policy? Mussolini expressly confirmed this. ...

Throughout the conversation Mussolini gave the impression of being rather tired, but very definite and resolute. His remarks about Austria were obviously the central point of his observations. ...

Hassell

6

FRANCE AND THE RHINELAND CRISIS

FRENCH MILITARY LEADERS DISCUSS WHAT TO DO IF GERMANY

REMILITARIZES THE RHINELAND

MARCH 8, 1936

Present: General Gamelin, Admiral Durand-Viel, General Pujo (respectively chiefs of army, navy and air staffs, five other serving officers).

General Gamelin: The government has asked me, 'Are you prepared to hold them?' I replied that, if a conflict between Germany and France were limited to the land front on the Franco-German border, forces on each side would be so large that saturation point would be quickly reached. The fronts would become stabilized. Only the air forces would be able to carry out offensive action on enemy territory.

If the theatre of operations extends into Belgium, what will England do?

Admiral Durand-Viel: According to the discussions which took place last night at the Foreign Ministry ... the French government, after bringing the question before the Council of the League in accordance with Article 4 of the Locarno Treaty, will ask that the League should send a Commission of Enquiry to the Rhineland. Germany would be declared an aggressor. So that it can examine what our attitude will be then, the government has asked the military, 'Are you prepared to drive the Germans out of the zone?'

General Gamelin: By the fact of our entry into the zone, war would be unleashed. Such action would thus require general mobilization. Before the Franco-Soviet pact was ratified General Gamelin gave his written opinion on the probable consequences of this ratification (German occupation of the demilitarized zone.[1] He had a conversation on this subject with M. Léger (secretary-general of the foreign ministry) and M. Sarraut, and told them, 'If we oppose this occupation by force, it means war.' M. Léger replied that everything had been done to eliminate from this treaty all that might be dangerous, that the debate on ratification had been delayed as long as possible, but that it was no longer possible to delay it further.

General Gamelin thinks that we can only enter the Rhineland zone ... at the same time as the guarantor powers of Locarno (England, Italy) .... British and Italian contingents must be with us and the Belgians. ...

Admiral Durand-Viel: At the moment England could give us nothing but moral support. Before anything more the Ethiopian affair would need to be liquidated. It is impossible to see how to envisage common action with two powers (England, Italy) which are themselves in a state of reciprocal hostility. When this hostility is ended, at least a fortnight will be needed before English naval forces are ready to act in the North Sea and the Channel. At present the British Isles are deprived of any naval protection.[2]

General Pujo: At present there are 150 fighter aircraft in England, and 150 modern bombers. The 150 fighters would probably be assigned to the defence of London. But England might still send us a few of them, and some of the 150 bombers.

The Belgians have 18 squadrons: 6 of fighter, 6 of bombers, 6 for reconnaissance. The Italians have completely reorganized their home air force. They have at present 900 aircraft in Italy, mostly of recent

---

1   The Franco-Soviet Pact was a defensive mutual assistance treaty signed May 2, 1935. It was part of a French diplomatic initiative to rally an anti-German coalition in Eastern Europe, and present Germany with the possibility of a two-front war, as in 1914. The French Parliament took almost nine months to ratify the treaty, due to obstruction from French anti-Communist opinion (including the French military). Hitler used the ratification of the treaty as a pretext to move into the Rhineland.

2   The assertion that the British Isles were devoid of naval protection was debatable, at best.

construction. They might send us 100 bombers. Employment of the air force of the USSR would involve sending munitions and spares into Czechoslovakia. It is said that airfields with underground shelters have been prepared for Russian aircraft in Czechoslovakia.

General Gamelin wonders whether the Germans would not compromise if faced by a very firm attitude. He has asked that a General should go to Geneva, where important technical problems are to be discussed. In particular it would be most important that English and Italian troops should immediately be sent to France, and that our own troops be able to enter Belgium. ...

7

THE SPANISH CIVIL WAR AND NON-INTERVENTION

BRITISH NON-INTERVENTION POLICY IN THE SPANISH CIVIL WAR

AUGUST 7, 1936

1. Yesterday Sir George Clerk (British ambassador) spoke frankly to M. Yvon Delbos (French foreign minister) about his government's anxieties in the Spanish affair. An agreement on non-intervention was a matter of extreme urgency—and pending an agreement it was essential above all that no arms deliveries should take place otherwise everything would be compromised.

2. The British ambassador was particularly afraid that if the conflict persists General Franco, who needed support at any price, might be tempted to use the Balearics to buy Italian help, or the Canaries for German help. He thought that as a consequence the situation of Gibraltar would be weakened.

3. The Belgian ambassador is anxious to see an agreement between the five Locarno powers. Sir George Clerk, as an Englishman, said that he is of the same opinion but added that allowance must be made for French anxieties.

4. Both ambassadors did not conceal that their sympathy in the Spanish affair is for the rebels, whom they considered to be the only force capable of defeating anarchy and Soviet influence.

"The Spanish Civil War and Non-Intervention, August 7, 1936," *Documents Diplomatique Francais, 1932-1939*. Copyright © 1963 by International Editors of Diplomatic Documents. Reprinted with permission.

8

BRITISH PRIME MINISTER STANLEY BALDWIN'S SPEECH TO THE HOUSE OF COMMONS

NOVEMBER 12, 1936

The difference of opinion between the right hon. Gentleman and myself is in the years from 1933 onwards. In 1931–32, although it is not admitted by the Opposition, there was a period of financial crisis. But there was another reason. The right hon. Gentleman has spoken more than once about the anxieties which were caused after the events in Germany in 1933, and the neglect of the Government to do anything or make any preparations in 1933–34. He was more modest to-day; he spoke of a couple of million pounds. I would remind the House that not once but on many occasions in speeches and in various places, when I have been speaking and advocating as far as I am able the democratic principle, I have stated that a democracy is always two years behind the dictator. I believe that to be true. It has been true in this case. I put before the whole House my own views with an appalling frankness. From 1933, I and my friends were all very worried about what was happening in Europe. You will remember at that time the Disarmament Conference was sitting in Geneva. You will remember at that time there was probably a stronger pacifist feeling running through this country than at any time since the War. I am speaking of 1933 and 1934. You will remember the election at Fulham in the autumn of 1933, when a seat which the National Government held was lost by about 7,000 votes on no issue but the pacifist. You will remember

Stanley Baldwin, "British Prime Minister Stanley Baldwin's speech to the House of Commons, November 12, 1936," *Hansard's Parliamentary Debates*, vol. 317. 1936.

perhaps that the National Government candidate who made a most guarded reference to the question of defense was mobbed for it.

That was the feeling in 1933. My position as the leader of a great party was not altogether a comfortable one. I asked myself what chance was there—when that feeling that was given expression to in Fulham was common throughout the country—what chance was there within the next year or two of that feeling being so changed that the country would give a mandate for rearmament? Supposing I had gone to the country and said that Germany was rearming and that we must rearm, does anybody think that this pacific democracy would have rallied to that cry at that moment? I cannot think of anything that would have made the loss of the election from my point of view more certain. I think the country itself learned by certain events that took place during the winter of 1934–35 what the perils might be to it. All I did was to take a moment perhaps less unfortunate than another might have been, and we won the election with a large majority; but frankly I could conceive that we should at that time, by advocating certain courses, have been a great deal less successful. We got from the country—with a large majority—a mandate for doing a thing that no one, 12 months before, would have believed possible. It is my firm conviction that had the Government, with this great majority, used that majority to do anything that might be described as arming without a mandate—and they did not do anything, except the slightly increased air programme for which they gave their reasons—had I taken such action as my right hon. Friend desired me to take, it would have defeated entirely the end I had in view. I may be wrong, but I put that to the House as an explanation of my action in that respect.

9

THE ANTI-COMINTERN PACT

NOVEMBER 25, 1936

Agreement Guarding against the Communist International

The Imperial Government of Japan and the Government of Germany,
In cognizance of the fact that the object of the Communist International (the so-called Comintern) is the disintegration of, and the commission of violence against, existing States by the exercise of all means at its command,
Believing that the toleration of interference by the Communist International in the internal affairs of nations not only endangers their internal peace and social welfare, but threatens the general peace of the world,
Desiring to co-operate for defense against communist disintegration, have agreed as follows.

Article 1. The High Contracting Parties agree that they will mutually keep each other informed concerning the activities of the Communist International, will confer upon the necessary measure of defense, and will carry out such measures in close co-operation.

Article 2. The High Contracting Parties will jointly invite third States whose internal peace is menaced by the disintegrating work of the Communist International, to adopt defensive measures in the spirit of the present Agreement or to participate in the present Agreement. ...

"The Anti-Comintern Pact, November 25, 1936," The Avalon Project. 1936.

10

BRITISH CHIEFS OF STAFF MEMORANDUM

THE BRITISH CABINET REVIEWS BRITAIN'S STRATEGIC PROSPECTS

DECEMBER 8, 1937

The Cabinet had before them a Memorandum by the Minister for Co-ordination of Defence (C.P.-295 (37)) covering a Most Secret Report by the Chiefs of Staff Sub-Committee (C.I.D. Paper No. 1366-B) on the Comparison of the Strength of Great Britain with that of certain other Nations as at January, 1938. The *draft* Conclusions reached by the Committee of Imperial Defence (303rd Meeting, Minute 3) after consideration of the above Report were as follows:

F.R. 10(38)10
'(i) To take note of:
(a) The warnings contained in the Report of the Chiefs of Staff Sub-Committee (C.I.D. Paper No. 1366-B):

F.R.1.(38)1.
(b) The statement on foreign policy made at this meeting by the Secretary of State for Foreign Affairs, which, it was agreed, takes proper account of the facts of the situation, including those mentioned in the Report by the Chiefs of Staff:
(c) The Prime Minister's observations as summarized in the above Minutes.
(ii) That the Report by the Chiefs of Staff Sub-Committee (C.I.D. Paper No. 1366-B) together with the above conclusions (but not the full Minutes) should

"British Chiefs of Staff Memorandum, December 8, 1937," UK National Archives, CAB 23/90A. 1937.

be circulated to the Cabinet; it being left to the Prime Minister to explain the gist of the discussion to the Cabinet.'

In compliance with the second of the conclusions quoted above, the Prime Minister made a statement to the Cabinet.

He pointed out that in paragraph 14 of their memorandum, the Chiefs of Staff Sub-Committee had summarized their conclusions. In paragraph 42 they had expressed the warnings referred to in conclusion (i)(a) above. From this paragraph, he quoted the following extracts:

'From the above report it will be seen that our Naval, Military and Air Forces, in their present stage of development are still far from sufficient to meet our defensive commitments, which now extend from Western Europe through the Mediterranean to the Far East. ... Without overlooking the assistance which we should hope to obtain from France, and possibly other allies, we cannot foresee the time when our defence forces will be strong enough to safeguard our territory, trade and vital interests against Germany, Italy and Japan simultaneously. We cannot, therefore, exaggerate the importance, from the point of view of Imperial defence, of any political or international action that can be taken to reduce the numbers of our potential enemies and to gain the support of potential allies.'

The Foreign Secretary, the Prime Minister continued, had circulated a short paper to the Committee of Imperial Defence dealing with certain aspects of the Chiefs of Staff paper but not pretending to give any general account of our foreign policy. At the meeting of the Committee, however, the Foreign Secretary had made a verbal statement, the general effect of which had been summarized in conclusion (i)(b). He then summarized the main considerations that had been brought to the notice of the Committee. It was true, as the Chiefs of Staff had pointed out, that we could not hope to confront satisfactorily Germany, Italy and Japan simultaneously and, when we looked round as to what help we could get from other nations, the results were not very encouraging. France was our most important friend. Though she was strong defensively and possessed a powerful army, the French Air Force was far from satisfactory. During the Anglo-French visit, M. Chautemps had admitted to an output of aircraft that was only about one-fifth (60–300) of our own. A long time must elapse before France would be able to give us much help in the air. The Power that had the greatest strength was the United States of America, but he would be a rash man who based his calculations on help from that quarter. Our position in relation to the smaller Powers was much better than formerly, but he did not think that they would add much to our offensive or defensive strength. In time of peace their support was useful, but in war less so. The Chiefs of Staff, as he had mentioned, said they could not foresee the time when our defense forces would be strong enough to safeguard our territory, trade and vital interests against Germany, Italy and Japan simultaneously. They had urged that our foreign policy must be governed by this consideration, and they had made a rather strong appeal to this effect. Of course, it would be possible to make an effort to detach one of the three Powers from the other two and it might even succeed. This, however, could only be done at the cost of concessions which would involve humiliations and disadvantages to this country by destroying the confidence of other nations. No-one would suppose, therefore, that we should try and bribe one of the three nations to leave the other two. What the Foreign Secretary was doing was to try and prevent a situation arising in which the three Powers mentioned would ever be at war with us. He recalled that before the trouble had arisen in the Far East, we had been making great efforts to improve our relations with Japan and that considerable progress had been made. Owing to recent events, we had been compelled to break off these negotiations, but we had tried to keep open the position or resuming them later on. We had avoided threats ourselves and had restrained others from making them. The improvement in relations with Italy was not easy, but we had made some efforts to get on better terms, in spite of the difficult attitude of Mussolini and we were about to make a further effort at that end of the Berlin-Rome Axis. As he himself had pointed out before, however, Germany was the real key to the question. In view of the recent consideration given by the Cabinet to the question of improving relations with Germany, it was unnecessary to develop that theme any further. He thought, however, that he had said enough to show that the strategic considerations urged by the Chiefs of Staff were fully taken into account in our foreign policy and that was what underlay the taking note by the Committee of Imperial Defence of conclusion (i)(b) quoted above, namely—

'(b) The statement on foreign policy made at this meeting by the Secretary of State for Foreign Affairs, which, it was agreed, takes proper account of the facts of the situation, including those mentioned in the Report by the Chiefs of Staff.'

In the course of a short discussion, attention was drawn to the late Prime Minister's undertaking as to the maintenance of parity between the Air Force of the United Kingdom and that of Germany.

The Minister for Co-Ordination of Defence pointed out that Lord Baldwin's statement required interpretation. He had never taken it to mean that we must have exactly the same number of fighters and bombers as Germany in order to carry out the contemplated equality.

The Prime Minister said he did not intend to repeat Lord Baldwin's words and, if the question were raised, he would make it clear that the Government did not consider it necessary to have precise equality in every class of aircraft. It might be necessary to make a statement on this subject before very long.

After some further discussion, the Cabinet agreed: To take note of the Report contained in C.P. 296(37), together with the Prime Minister's remarks thereon and summarized above.

11

PRIME MINISTER NEVILLE CHAMBERLAIN SURVEYS BRITAIN'S STRATEGIC PROSPECTS

MARCH 20, 1938

(With) Franco winning in Spain by the aid of German guns and Italian planes, with a French government in which one cannot have the slightest confidence and which I suspect to be in closish touch with our Opposition, with the Russians stealthily and cunningly pulling all the strings behind the scenes to get us involved in war with Germany (our Secret Service doesn't spend all its time looking out of the window), and finally with a Germany flushed with triumph, and all too conscious of her power, the prospect looked black indeed. In face of such problems, to be badgered and pressed to come out and give a clear, decided, bold, and unmistakable lead, show "ordinary courage", and all the rest of the twaddle, is calculated to vex the man who has to take the responsibility for the consequences. As a matter of fact, the plan of the "Grand Alliance", as Winston calls it, had occurred to me long before he mentioned it. ... I talked about it to Halifax, and we submitted it to the chiefs of the Staff and the F.O. experts. It is a very attractive idea; indeed there is almost everything to be said for it until you come to examine its practicability. From that moment its attraction vanishes. You have only to look at the map to see that nothing that France or we could do could possibly save Czechoslovakia from being overrun by the Germans, if they wanted to do it. The Austrian frontier is practically open; the great Skoda munition works are within easy bombing distance of the German aerodromes, the railways all pass through German territory, Russia is 100 miles away. Therefore we could

Neville Chamberlain, "Prime Minister Neville Chamberlain Surveys Britain's Prospects, 1938," Neville Chamberlain Papers, Birmingham University, NC 18/1/1042. 1938.

not help Czechoslovakia—she would simply be a pretext for going to war with Germany. That we could not think of unless we had a reasonable prospect of being able to beat her to her knees in a reasonable time, and of that I see no sign. I have therefore abandoned any idea of giving guarantees to Czecho-slovakia, or the French in connection with her obligations to that country.

12

CHAMBERLAIN LETTER

SEPTEMBER 11, 1938

I fully realise that, if eventually things go wrong and the aggression takes place, there will be many, including Winston, who will say that the British government must bear the responsibility, and that if only they had had the courage to tell Hitler now that, if he used force, we should at once declare war, that would have stopped him. By that time it will be impossible to prove the contrary, but I am satisfied that we should be wrong to allow the most vital decision that any country could take, the decision as to peace or war, to pass out of our hands into those of the ruler of another country, and a lunatic at that. I have been fortified in this view by reading a very interesting book on the foreign policy of Canning. ... Over and over again Canning lays it down that you should never menace unless you are in a position to carry out your threats, and although, if we have to fight I should hope we should be able to give a good account of ourselves, we are certainly not in a position in which our military advisers would feel happy in undertaking to begin hostilities if we were not forced to do so.

There is another consideration which, of course, our critics cannot have in mind, and that is the plan, the nature of which I think you have guessed correctly. The time for this has not yet arrived, and it is always possible that Hitler might act so unexpectedly as to forestall it. That is a risk which we have to take, but in the meantime I do not want to do anything which would destroy its chance of success because, if it came off, it would go far beyond the present crisis, and might prove the opportunity for bringing about a complete change in the international situation.

Neville Chamberlain, "Chamberlain Letter, September 11, 1938," Neville Chamberlain Papers, Birmingham University, NC 18/1/1042. 1938.

13

THE MUNICH PACT

SEPTEMBER 29, 1938

Germany, the United Kingdom, France and Italy, taking into consideration the agreement, which has been already reached in principle for the cession to Germany of the Sudeten German territory, have agreed on the following terms and conditions governing the said cession and the measures consequent thereon, and by this agreement they each hold themselves responsible for the steps necessary to secure its fulfillment:

1. The evacuation will begin on 1st October.

2. The United Kingdom, France and Italy agree that the evacuation of the territory shall be completed by the 10th October, without any existing installations having been destroyed, and that the Czechoslovak Government will he held responsible for carrying out the evacuation without damage to the said installations.

3. The conditions governing the evacuation will be laid down in detail by an international commission composed of representatives of Germany, the United Kingdom, France, Italy and Germany.

4. The occupation by stages of the predominantly German territory by German troops will begin on 1st October. The four territories marked on the attached map will be occupied by German troops in the following

"The Munich Pact, September 29, 1938," The Avalon Project. 1938.

order: The territory marked No. 1 on the 1st and 2nd of October; the territory marked No. II on the 2nd and 3rd of October; the territory marked No. III on the 3rd, 4th and 5th of October; the territory marked No. IV on the 6th and 7th of October. The remaining territory of preponderantly German character will be ascertained by the aforesaid international commission forthwith and be occupied by German troops by the 10th of October.

5. The international commission referred to in paragraph 3 will determine the territories in which a plebiscite is to be held. These territories will be occupied by international bodies until the plebiscite has been completed. The same commission will fix the conditions in which the plebiscite is to be held, taking as a basis the conditions of the Saar plebiscite. The commission will also fix a date, not later than the end of November, on which the plebiscite will be held.

6. The final determination of the frontiers will be carried out by the international commission. The commission will also be entitled to recommend to the four Powers, Germany, the United Kingdom, France and Italy, in certain exceptional cases, minor modifications in the strictly ethnographical determination of the zones which are to be transferred without plebiscite.

7. There will be a right of option into and out of the transferred territories, the option to be exercised within six months from the date of this agreement. A German-Czechoslovak commission shall determine the details of the option, consider ways of facilitating the transfer of population and settle questions of principle arising out of the said transfer.

8. The Czechoslovak Government will within a period of four weeks from the date of this agreement release from their military and police forces any Sudeten Germans who may wish to be released, and the Czechoslovak Government will within the same period release Sudeten German prisoners who are serving terms of imprisonment for political offenses.

Munich, September 29, 1938.
Adolf Hitler,
Neville Chamberlain,
Edouard Daladier,
Benito Mussolini.

MUNICH PACT: ANNEX TO THE AGREEMENT

His Majesty's Government in the United Kingdom and the French Government have entered into the above agreement on the basis that they stand by the offer, contained in paragraph 6 of the Anglo-French proposals of the 19th September, relating to an international guarantee of the new boundaries of the Czechoslovak State against unprovoked aggression.

When the question of the Polish and Hungarian minorities has been settled, Germany and Italy for their part will give a guarantee to Czechoslovakia.

Munich, September 29, 1939
Adolf Hitler,
Neville Chamberlain,
Edouard Daladier,
Benito Mussolini.

"Munich Pact: Annex to the Agreement," The Avalon Project. 1939.

14

POST-MUNICH TEXT

TEXT OF STATEMENT RELEASED AFTER CONVERSATION BETWEEN

HITLER AND CHAMBERLAIN IN MUNICH

SEPTEMBER 30, 1938

We, the German Führer and Chancellor and the British Prime Minister, have had a further meeting today and are agreed in recognizing that the question of Anglo-German relations is of the first importance for the two countries and for Europe.

We regard the agreement signed last night and the Anglo-German Naval Agreement as symbolic of the desire of our two peoples never to go to war with one another again.

We are resolved that the method of consultation shall be the method adopted to deal with any other questions that may concern our two countries, and we are determined to continue our efforts to remove possible sources of difference and thus to contribute to the peace of Europe.

A. Hitler
Neville Chamberlain

Adolf Hitler and Neville Chamberlain, "Post-Munich Text, September 30, 1938," *Documents on British Foreign Policy, 1919-1939: Third Series, Volume II*, no. 640.

15

CHAMBERLAIN ON MUNICH

CHAMBERLAIN DEFENDS THE MUNICH PACT IN THE HOUSE OF COMMONS

OCTOBER 3, 1938

When the House met last Wednesday, we were all under the shadow of a great and imminent menace. War, in a form more stark and terrible than ever before, seemed to be staring us in the face. Before I sat down, a message had come which gave us new hope that peace might yet be saved, and today, only a few days after, we all meet in joy and thankfulness that the prayers of millions have been answered, and a cloud of anxiety has been lifted from our hearts. ...

Ever since I assumed my present office my main purpose has been to work for the pacification of Europe, for the removal of those suspicions and those animosities which have so long poisoned the air. The path which leads to appeasement is long and bristles with obstacles. The question of Czechoslovakia is the latest and perhaps the most dangerous. Now that we have got past it, I feel that it may be possible to make further progress along the road to sanity.

My right hon. Friend has alluded in somewhat bitter terms to my conversation last Friday morning with Herr Hitler. I do not know why that conversation should give rise to suspicion, still less to criticism. I entered into no pact. I made no new commitments. There is no secret understanding. Our conversation was hostile to no other nation. The object of that conversation, for which I asked, was to try to extend a little further the personal contact which I had established with Herr Hitler and which I believe to be essential

Neville Chamberlain, "Chamberlain on Munich, October 3, 1939," *Hansard's Parliamentary Debates, 5th Series, Volume 339*. 1938.

in modern diplomacy. We had a friendly and entirely non-committal conversation, carried on, on my part, largely with a view to seeing whether there could be points in common between the head of a democratic government and the ruler of a totalitarian state. We see the result in the declaration which has been published, in which my right hon. Friend finds so much ground for suspicion. What does it say?

There are three paragraphs. The first says that we agree in "recognizing that the question of Anglo-German relations is of the first importance for the two countries and for Europe." Does anyone deny that? The second is an expression of opinion only. It says that: "We regard the agreement signed last night and the Anglo-German Naval Agreement as symbolic of the desire of the two peoples never to go to war with on another again." Once more I ask, does anyone doubt that that is the desire of the two peoples? What is the last paragraph? "We are resolved that the method of consultation shall be the method adopted to deal with any other questions that may concern our two countries, and we are determined to continue our efforts to remove possible sources of difference and thus to contribute to assure the peace of Europe." Who will stand up and condemn that sentence?

I believe there are many who will feel with me that such a declaration, signed by the German chancellor and myself, is something more than a pious expression of opinion. In our relations with other countries everything depends upon there being sincerity and good will on both sides. I believe that there is sincerity and good will on both sides in the declaration. That is why to me its significance goes far beyond its actual words. If there is one lesson which we should learn from the events of these last weeks it is this, that lasting peace is not to be obtained by sitting still and waiting for it to come. It requires active, positive efforts to achieve it. No doubt I shall have plenty of critics who will say that I am guilty of facile optimism, and that I should disbelieve every word that is uttered by rulers of other great states in Europe. I am too much of a realist to believe that we are going to achieve our paradise in a day. We have only laid the foundations of peace. The superstructure is not even begun.

For a long period now we have been engaged in this country in a great program of rearmament, which is daily increasing in pace and in volume. Let no one think that because we have signed this agreement between these four powers at Munich we can afford to relax our efforts in regard to that program at this moment. Disarmament on the part of this country can never be unilateral again. We have tried that once and we very nearly brought ourselves to disaster. If disarmament is to come it must come by steps, and it must come by the agreement and the active cooperation of other countries. Until we know that we have obtained that cooperation and until we have agreed upon the actual steps to be taken, we here must remain on guard ....

While we must renew our determination to fill up the deficiencies that yet remain in our armaments and in our defensive precautions, so that we may be ready to defend ourselves and make our diplomacy effective—(interruption)—Yes, I am a realist—nevertheless, I say with an equal sense of reality that I do see fresh opportunities of approaching this subject of disarmament opening up before us, and I believe that they are at least as hopeful today as they have been at any previous time. It is to such tasks (the winning back of confidence, the gradual removal of hostility between nations until they feel that they can safely discard their weapons, one by one) that I would wish to devote what energy and time may be left to me before I hand over my office to younger men.

16

Winston Churchill on the Munich Agreement

October 5, 1938

Mr. Churchill. I will, therefore, begin by saying the most unpopular and most unwelcome thing. I will begin by saying what everybody would like to ignore or forget but which must nevertheless be stated, namely, that we have sustained a total and unmitigated defeat, and that France has suffered even more than we have.

Viscountess Astor. Nonsense!

Mr. Churchill. When the noble Lady cries "Nonsense," she could not have heard the Chancellor of the Exchequer admit in his illuminating and comprehensive speech just now that Herr Hitler had gained in this particular leap forward in substance all he set out to gain. The utmost my right hon. Friend, the prime minister, has been able to secure by all his immense exertions, by all the great efforts and mobilization which took place in this country, and by all the anguish and strain through which we have passed in this country, the utmost he has been able to gain (Hon. Members: "Is Peace"). I thought I might be allowed to make that point in its due place, and I propose to deal with it. The utmost he has been able to gain for Czechoslovakia and in the matters which were in dispute has been that the German dictator, instead of snatching his victuals from the table has been content to have them served to him course by course.

The Chancellor of the Exchequer said it was the first time Herr Hitler has been made to retract (I think that was the word) in any degree. We really must

Winston Churchill, "Winston Churchill on the Munich Agreement," *Hansard's Parliamentary Debates, 5th Series, vol. 339*. 1938.

not waste time, after all this long debate, upon the difference between the positions reached at Berchtesgaden, at Godesberg and at Munich. They can be very simply epitomized, if the House will permit me to vary the metaphor. One pound was demanded at the pistol's point. When it was given, two pounds were demanded at the pistol's point. Finally, the dictator consented to take one pound, seventeen shillings and six pence, and the rest in promises of good will for the future.

Now I come to the point, which was mentioned to me just now from some quarters of the House, about the saving of the peace. No one has been a more resolute and uncompromising struggler for peace than the prime minister. Everyone knows that. Never has there been such intense and undaunted determination to maintain and to secure peace. That is quite true. Nevertheless, I am not quite clear why there was so much danger of Great Britain or France being involved in a war with Germany at this juncture if, in fact, they were ready all along to sacrifice Czechoslovakia. ...

I have always held the view that the maintenance of peace depends upon the accumulation of deterrents against the aggressor, coupled with a sincere effort to redress grievances. Herr Hitler's victory, like so many of the famous struggles that have governed the fate of the world, was won upon the narrowest of margins. After the seizure of Austria in March, we faced this problem in our debates. I ventured to appeal to the government to go a little further than the prime minister went, and to give a pledge that in conjunction with France and other powers they will guarantee the security of Czechoslovakia, while the Sudeten Deutsch question was being examined either by a League of Nations commission or some other impartial body, and I still believe that if that course had been followed events would not have fallen into this disastrous state. ...

France and Great Britain together, especially if they had maintained a close contact with Russia, which certainly was not done, would have been able in those days in the summer, when they had the prestige, to influence many of the smaller states of Europe. ... Such a combination, prepared at the time when the German dictator was not irrevocably committed to his new adventure, would, I believe, have given strength to all those forces in Germany which resisted this departure ....

All is over. Silent, mournful, abandoned, broken, Czechoslovakia recedes into the darkness. She has suffered in every respect by her association with the Western democracies and with the League of Nations, of which she has always been an obedient servant. ... We in this country, as in other liberal and democratic countries, have a perfect right to exalt the principle of self-determination, but it comes ill out of the mouths of those in totalitarian states who deny even the smallest element of toleration to every section and creed within their bounds. But, however you put it, this particular block of land, this mass of human beings to be handed over, has never expressed the desire to go into the Nazi rule. I do not believe that even now—if their opinion could be asked, they would exercise such an option. ...

I venture to think that in the future the Czechoslovak state cannot be maintained as an independent entity. You will find that in a period of time which may be measured by years, but may be measured only by months, Czechoslovakia will be engulfed in the Nazi regime. ... It is the most grievous consequence which we have done and of what we have left undone in the last five years: five years of futile good intention, five years of eager search for the line of least resistance, five years of uninterrupted retreat of British power, five years of neglect of our air defenses. ...

When I think of the fair hopes of a long peace which still lay before Europe at the beginning of 1933 when Herr Hitler first obtained power, and of all the opportunities of arresting the growth of the Nazi power which have been thrown away, when I think of the immense combinations and resources which have been neglected or squandered, I cannot believe that a parallel exists in the whole course of history. So far as this country is concerned the responsibility must rest with those who have the undisputed control of our political affairs. They neither prevented Germany from rearming, nor did they rearm ourselves in time. They quarreled with Italy without saving Ethiopia. They exploited and discredited the vast institution of the League of Nations and they neglected to make alliances and combinations which might have repaired previous errors, and thus they left us in the hour of trial without adequate national defense or effective international security.

We are in the presence of a disaster of the first magnitude which has befallen Great Britain and France. Do not let us blind ourselves to that. It must now be accepted that all countries of Central and Eastern Europe will make the best terms they can with the triumphant Nazi power. The system of alliances in central Europe upon which France has relied for her safety has been swept away, and I can see no means by which it can be reconstituted. The road down the Danube Valley to the Black Sea, the resources of corn and oil, the road which leads as far as Turkey, has been opened. In fact, if not in form, it seems to me that all those countries of middle Europe, all those Danubian countries, will, one after another, be drawn into this vast system of power politics (not only power military politics but power economic politics) radiating from Berlin, and I believe this can be achieved quite smoothly and swiftly and will not necessarily entail the firing of a single shot. ... We are talking about countries which are a long way off and of which, as the prime minister might say, we know nothing. (Interruption) The noble Lady says that that very harmless allusion is ...

Viscountess Astor. Rude.

Mr. Churchill. She must very recently have been receiving her finishing course in manners. What will be the position, I want to know, of France and England this year and the year afterward? What will be the position of that Western Front of which we are in full authority the guarantors? ... Relieved from all anxiety in the East, and having secured resources which will greatly diminish, if not entirely remove, the deterrent of a naval blockade, the rulers of Nazi Germany will have a free choice open to them in what direction they will turn their eyes. If the Nazi dictator should choose to look westward, as he may, bitterly will France and England regret the loss of that fine army of ancient Bohemia which was estimated last week to require not fewer than thirty German divisions for its destruction. ... Many people, no doubt, honestly believe that they are only giving away the interests of Czechoslovakia, whereas I fear we shall find that we have deeply compromised, and perhaps fatally endangered, the safety and even the independence of Great Britain and France. ... You have to consider the character of the Nazi movement and the rule which it implies. The prime minister desires to see cordial relations between this country and Germany. There is no difficulty at all in having cordial relations with the German people. Our hearts go out to them. But they have no power. You must have diplomatic and correct relations, but there can never be friendship between the British democracy and the Nazi power, that power which spurns Christian ethics, which cheers its onward course by a barbarous paganism, which vaunts the spirit of aggression and conquest, which derives strength and perverted pleasure from persecution, and uses, as we have seen, with pitiless brutality, the threat of murderous force. That power cannot ever be the trusted friend of the British democracy. ...

In a very few years, perhaps in a very few months, we shall be confronted with demands which we shall no doubt be invited to comply. ...

We have passed an awful milestone in our history, when the whole equilibrium of Europe has been deranged, and that the terrible words have for the time being been pronounced against the Western democracies: "Thou art weighed in the balance and found wanting."

And do not suppose that this is the end. This is only the beginning of the reckoning. This is only the first sip, the foretaste of a bitter cup which will be proffered to us year by year unless by a supreme recovery of moral health and martial vigor, we arise again and take our stand for freedom as in the olden times.

17

THE BRITISH GUARANTEE TO POLAND

STATEMENT BY BRITISH PRIME MINISTER TO THE HOUSE OF COMMONS

MARCH 31, 1939

The Prime Minister (Mr. Chamberlain): The right hon. Gentleman the leader of the Opposition asked me this morning whether I could make a statement as to the European situation. As I said this morning, His Majesty's Government have no official confirmation of the rumours of any projected attack on Poland and they must not, therefore, be taken as accepting them as true.

I am glad to take this opportunity of stating again the general policy of His Majesty's Government. They have constantly advocated the adjustment, by way of free negotiation between the parties concerned, of any differences that may arise between them. They consider that this is the natural and proper course where differences exist. In their opinion there should be no question incapable of solution by peaceful means, and they would see no justification for the substitution of force or threats of force for the method of negotiation.

As the House is aware, certain consultations are now proceeding with other Governments. In order to make perfectly clear the position of His Majesty's Government in the meantime before those consultations are concluded, I now have to inform the House that during that period, in the event of any action which clearly threatened Polish independence, and which the Polish Government accordingly considered it vital to resist with their national forces, His Majesty's Government would feel themselves bound at once to lend the

Neville Chamberlain, "The British Guarantee to Poland, March 31, 1939," The Avalon Project. 1939.

Polish Government all support in their power. They have given the Polish Government an assurance to this effect.

I may add that the French Government have authorized me to make it plain that they stand in the same position in this matter as do His Majesty's Government.

18

SOVIET ALLIANCE PROPOSALS[1]

APRIL 18, 1939

M. Litvinov has now handed me in writing following proposal which is also being communicated to French Government through Soviet Ambassador in Paris. ...

1. England, France and USSR to conclude with one another an agreement for a period of five to ten years by which they would oblige themselves to render mutually forthwith all manner of assistance, including that of a military nature, in case of aggression in Europe against any one of the contracting Powers.

2. England, France and USSR to undertake to render all manner of assistance, including that of a military nature, to Eastern European States situated between Baltic and Black Seas and bordering on USSR, in case of aggression against these States.

3. England, France and USSR to undertake to discuss and to settle within shortest period of time extent and forms of military assistance to be rendered by each of these States in fulfillment of paragraphs 1 and 2.

---

1   This document is a telegram from William Seeds, British ambassador to the USSR, to Lord Halifax, British Foreign Secretary. Maxim Litvinov was Soviet Foreign Commissar at the time.

"Soviet Alliance Proposals, April 18, 1939," *Documents on British Foreign Policy*, ed. E. Woodward, 3rd Series, vol. 5, pp. 228-229. 1939.

4. English Government to explain that assistance recently promised to Poland concerns exclusively aggression on the part of Germany.

5. The treaty of alliance which exists between Poland and Roumania is to be declared operative in case of aggression of any nature against Poland and Roumania, or else to be revoked altogether as one directed against USSR.

6. England, France and USSR to undertake following outbreak of hostilities not to enter into negotiations of any kind whatsoever and not to conclude peace with aggressors separately from one another and without common consent of the three Powers.

7. An agreement on above lines to be signed simultaneously with terms of conventions which has just been described above under paragraph 3.

8. The necessity is recognized for England, France (? And USSR) to enter into joint negotiations with Turkey having in view conclusion of a special agreement on mutual assistance. ...

Clause 4 was, he (Litvinov) said, inserted because recent British declaration of assistance to Poland might be read as implying the possibility of aggression by Soviet Union.

Clause 5 was required in view of the fact that existing Polish-Roumanian Treaty had originally been aimed at the Soviet Union only.

Clause 7 was necessary as previous experience had shown that difficulties arose where military agreements were only negotiated subsequently to political conventions.

Clause 8 was designed to cover possibility that Turkish Government might wish to confine its liabilities to Balkan or Mediterranean areas.

19

HITLER BRIEFS GERMAN GENERALS

MAY 23, 1939

After six years the present position is as follows:

With minor exceptions German national unification has been achieved. Further success cannot be achieved without bloodshed.

Poland will always be on the side of our adversaries. Despite the friendship agreement Poland has always intended to exploit every opportunity against us.

Danzig is not the objective. It is a matter of expanding our living space in the east, of making our food supplies secure, and of solving the problem of the Baltic states. To provide sufficient food you must have sparsely settled areas. This is fertile soil, whose surpluses will be very much increased by German, thorough management.

No other such possibility can be seen in Europe ....

The Polish regime will not resist pressure from Russia. Poland sees danger in a German victory over the West and will try and deprive us of our victory.

There is therefore no question of sparing Poland, and the decision remains *to attack Poland at the first suitable opportunity.*

We cannot expect a repetition of Czechoslovakia. There will be fighting. The task is to isolate Poland. Success in holding her will be decisive. Therefore, the Führer must reserve to himself the final command to attack. There must be no simultaneous conflict with the West (France and England).

Adolf Hitler, "Hitler briefs the German Generals, May 23, 1939," *Documents on German Foreign Policy, 1918-1945, Series D, Volume 6*, no. 433. Her Majesty's Stationery Office, 1956.

If it is not certain that a German-Polish conflict will not lead to war with the West, then the struggle will be directed in the first instance against England and France.

Basic principle: conflict with Poland, beginning with attack on Poland, will be successful only if the West keeps out. If that is impossible, then it is better to attack the West and finish off Poland at the same time.

It will be the task of dexterous diplomacy to isolate Poland ....

20

Lord Halifax on the Soviet Talks

British Foreign Secretary Lord Halifax Briefs the Cabinet on the

Slow Pace of Talks with the Soviets

June 26, 1939

(T he) Russians were extremely suspicious and feared that our real object was to trap them into commitments and then leave them in the lurch. They suffered acutely from inferiority complex and considered that ever since the Great War the Western Powers had treated Russia with haughtiness and contempt. He suspected that the Soviet Government were anxious to secure the Treaty but were no hurry to reach agreement and were content to go on bargaining so as to secure the highest terms possible.

"Lord Halifax on the Soviet Talks, June 26, 1939," UK National Archives, CAB 27/625. 1939.

21

THE NAZI-SOVIET PACT

AUGUST 23, 1939

The Government of the German Reich and the Government of the Union of the Soviet Socialist Republics desirous of strengthening the cause of peace between Germany and the USSR and proceeding from the fundamental provisions of the Neutrality Agreement concluded in April 1926 between Germany and the USSR, have reached the following agreement:

Article 1. Both High Contracting Parties obligate themselves to desist from any act of violence, any aggressive action, and any attack on each other, either individually or with other powers.

Article 2. Should one of the High Contracting Parties become the object of belligerent action by a third power, the other High Contracting Party shall in no manner lend its support to this third power.

Article 3. The Governments of the two High Contracting Parties shall in the future maintain continual contact with one another for the purpose of consultation in order to exchange information on problems affecting their common interests.

"The Nazi-Soviet Pact, August 23, 1939," The Avalon Project. 1939.

Article 4. Neither of the two High Contracting Parties shall participate in any grouping of powers whatsoever that is directly or indirectly aimed at the other party.

Article 5. Should disputes or conflicts arise between the High Contracting Parties over problems of one kinds or another, both parties shall settle these disputes or conflicts exclusively through friendly exchange of opinion or, if necessary, through the establishment of arbitration commissions.

Article 6. The present treaty is concluded for a period of ten years, with the provision that, in so far as one of the High Contracting Parties does not denounce it one year prior to the expiration of this period, the validity of this treaty shall automatically be extended for another five years.

22

SECRET ADDITIONAL PROTOCOL

On the occasion of the signature of the Nonaggression pact between the German Reich and the Union of the Socialist Soviet Republics the undersigned plenipotentiaries of each of the two parties discussed in strictly confidential conversations the question of the boundary of their respective spheres of influence in Eastern Europe. These conversations led to the following conclusions:

1. In the event of a territorial and political rearrangement in the areas belonging to the Baltic States (Finland, Estonia, Latvia, Lithuania), the northern boundary of Lithuania shall represent the boundary of the spheres of influence of Germany and the USSR. In this connection the interest of Lithuania in the Vilna area is recognized by each party.

2. In the event of a territorial and political rearrangement of the areas belonging to the Polish state the spheres of influence of Germany and the USSR shall be bounded approximately by the line of the rivers Narew, Vistula, and San. The question of whether the interests of both parties make desirable the maintenance of an independent Polish state and how such a state should be bounded can only be definitely determined in the course of further political developments. In any event both Governments will resolve this question by means of a friendly agreement.

"Secret Additional Protocol," The Avalon Project. 1939.

3. With regard to Southeastern Europe attention is called by the Soviet side to its interest in Bessarabia. The German side declares its complete disinterestedness in these areas.

The protocol shall be treated by both parties as strictly secret.

23

THE SOVIET POINT OF VIEW

BREAKDOWN OF THE BRITISH-FRENCH-SOVIET NEGOTIATIONS

AUGUST 25, 1939

Record of Conversation with Marshal Voroshilov at 1300 Hours on August 25, 1939

Present:

Marshal Voroshilov; Corps Commander Khmelnitski; Colonel Osetrov.

Admiral Drax, Colonel Firebrace.

Général Doumenc; Général Palasse.

After greeting, the General and the Admiral made the following statement:—

'We are sorry we were unfortunately not able to come and see you last night at such short notice.

'We should like now to ask you if, in view of the changed political situation announced yesterday, it is likely in your opinion that the Soviet Government will desire the Military Missions to continue their conversation.'

The Marshal replied by expressing his regrets that, as he was out duck shooting, he had been unable to answer our letter earlier. He then stated that, to his regret, in view of the changed political situation there was no sense in continuing the conversations. The Admiral said that we would report this decision to our Governments and would await instructions from them. We should report to the Marshal any decision about our movements.

The Admiral then expressed the hope that in the new political circumstances the Soviet Union would continue to work for the cause of peace. The Marshal replied that this was the traditional policy of the Soviet Union and

"The Soviet Point of View," *Documents on British Foreign Policy*, ed. E. Woodward, 3rd Series, vol. 7, pp. 613-614. 1939.

there should be no reason to doubt that they would continue their work for peace as before. He continued that they found themselves in a very original position but it was through the fault of our Governments.

The Admiral now said that he would say goodbye to the Marshal. As we were taking our leave the Marshal in an outburst said:-

> 'During the whole time of our conversations the Polish press and Polish people were continuously saying that they did not want the help of the Soviets, and from Roumania there was not answer at all. Were we to have to conquer Poland in order to offer her our help, or were we to go on our knees and offer out help to Poland? The position was impossible for us.'

This outburst, for such it was, was due, in my opinion, to the Marshal wishing to offer some excuse for the way in which we had been treated. It was, however, a genuine outburst of Russian hatred for the Poles.

R. Firebrace, *Colonel*
Military Attaché, Moscow
I concur.
R. P. E. E. Drax, *Admiral*
Chief of British Military Mission

CHAPTER 3

BLITZKRIEG: THE GERMAN CONQUEST OF POLAND, NORWAY, THE LOW COUNTRIES, AND FRANCE, AND THE BATTLE OF BRITAIN

Introduction

The Polish army fought with skill and determination against the Germans in September 1939. But the Poles were simply overwhelmed by German tanks and aircraft. On September 17, the Poles were stabbed in the back when the Soviet Red Army moved in to take its share of eastern Poland as promised under the secret protocol to the Nazi-Soviet pact (see Chapter 2). Poland surrendered on September 27 and the country underwent a brutal wartime occupation at the hands of the Nazis. In an extract from a meeting of the British war cabinet on September 23, 1939, when the collapse of Poland was imminent (Document 1), the participants offer their guesses as to the future course of the war. Whose forecast was most correct? Do you see any evidence of overly optimistic thinking?

The next phase of the war, known as the "Phony War," lasted from the fall of Poland to the German attack on Denmark and Norway in April 1940. Haunted by the memory of failed frontal offensives in the First World War, the British and French decided to hunker down behind the Maginot line, a network of imposing but static concrete fortifications built at great expense by the French in the 1930s. In the extract from the memoirs of General André Beaufre of the French army (Document 2), how does Beaufre describe the Phony War? The long period of waiting over the winter of 1939–1940 proved bad for Allied morale. Why? It was clear to all that the waiting would come to end with the arrival of spring and that is exactly what happened. German forces overran Denmark on April 9. German naval units sailed up the Norwegian coast under the nose of the British Royal Navy and landed troops at Oslo while German paratroopers seized Norwegian airfields. The Germans did not gain full control of Norway until early June, and losses to the German surface navy were severe, but the conquest of Norway meant that the Germans now had bases to attack Britain by sea and air. British defeats in Norway forced Neville Chamberlain to resign as British prime minister on May 10, 1940. According to the extracts from Chamberlain's diary (Document 3), why did the Allies lose Norway? In Beaufre's assessment of the Norwegian debacle (Document 4), what factors does he cite for the Allied defeat? Winston Churchill, who succeeded Chamberlain, is widely regarded as one of the best orators of modern times. As defeat in France loomed, Churchill, after becoming prime minister, gave his first speech to the House of Commons (Document 5). How did Churchill attempt to rally morale?

On May 10, 1940, Germany's Army Group B swept into Holland, Belgium, and Luxembourg. A few days later Army Group A broke through thin Allied defenses in the Ardennes forest, previously regarded as impenetrable by tanks. Allied forces by this stage were also advancing into Belgium to meet the oncoming Army Group B. The Allies thus fell into a German trap (Document 6). German panzers commanded by Erwin Rommel and Heinz Guderian stormed northward from the Ardennes toward the English Channel with a view to splitting the Allied armies in two. How did British Field Marshal Alanbooke (Document 6) and Captain Basil Bartlett (Document 7) see events as they unfolded during the Battle of France? What does the British intelligence summary from May 27 (Document 8) tell you about the speed and nature of the German advance? How do the Allies appear to be coping? What are the main features of the German success? The British War Cabinet extracts from May 28 and June 4 (Document 9) discuss the Allied evacuation from Dunkirk (Operation Dynamo, May 26 to June 3, 1940). The British managed to evacuate about 338,000 Allied soldiers from the beaches of Dunkirk, but all heavy equipment, including tanks and artillery, had to be left behind. Does the reality of Dunkirk agree with popular depictions of the evacuation? How does the government propose to handle public opinion?

In extracts from two of his speeches at the time (Documents 10 and 11), how does Churchill attempt to rally the morale of his people? France surrendered on June 10, 1940. German forces occupied the north and west of the country, while the rest was governed by a collaborationist regime known as Vichy France led by former French First World War hero Marshal Philippe Pétain.

German general Heinz Guderian published his memoir, *Panzer Leader*, following the war. In a famous passage extracted here (Document 12), how does he think tanks should be used in war? What are his guiding principles? The German campaigns of 1940 are popularly known as blitzkrieg (lightning) war campaigns. Why were the Allies so unable to cope with the new German tactics?

In the extracts from a secret report on the Battle of Britain written by Air Marshal Dowding in 1942 (Document 13), what does Dowding discuss in the first three paragraphs? How do you think the French would have felt about the British holding back aircraft during the Battle of France? Why does Dowding think the British won the Battle of Britain? What advantages did the British have? What was "Radio Location" and why was it important? How close, according to Dowding, did the British come to defeat in 1940?

1

THE FALL OF POLAND[1]

Arising out of the statement recorded in Minute 5, some discussion took place as to the possible course of the war.

The First Lord of the Admiralty very much doubted whether a land offensive in the West would be mounted this winter. The Eastern front had more or less closed down owing to the Russian action, and he suggested that Germany's most likely move would be an attack on our air force and aircraft industry in the near future. If this did not eventuate, it would be either because Hitler's nerve had failed, or because his advisers had restrained him from embarking on a course which would lead to a desperate struggle, the consequence of which they feared.

The Prime Minister thought that there was a considerable danger of a "peace offensive" in which Germany would hope, during a period of stalemate, to play on neutral opinion and sow dissension between ourselves and the French.

It was pointed out that a period of inactivity by the German forces might cause serious dissatisfaction inside Germany, but that, on the other hand, the Germans might hope that they would achieve their object before this took place.

---

1 The First Lord of the Admiralty was Winston Churchill. Chamberlain was still Prime Minister while the Minister without Portfolio was Lord Hankey, a senior civil servant with an extensive background in defense issues.

Neville Chamberlain, Winston Churchill and Lord Hankey, "The Fall of Poland," UK National Archives, CAB 65/1 War Cabinet 24, September 23, 1939.

The Minister without Portfolio said that the possibility of an offensive in the West this Autumn should not be under-rated. The French regarded such an offensive as probable. The Germans would never get a better chance in the future than they had now, since by the Spring our defences would be stronger and we should have more troops available in France. They might attempt to repeat their Polish tactics and employ a great weight of mechanized forces and air forces in the hope of completely disorganizing the back areas.

2

GENERAL ANDRÉ BEAUFRE ON THE PHONY WAR

Meanwhile what was happening on our front? Contrary to all logic—since logic indicated that we should have attacked to take the pressure off Poland—nothing was happening, or at any rate very little. Our great Army had been mobilized and concentrated on the frontier along the Maginot Line. Now we could see the extra-ordinary influence of these fortifications: if we advanced, we lost the benefit of their protection; and to attack, one must advance.

Gamelin, true to type, decided to do nothing more than make a gesture: he ordered an 'offensive reconnaissance' in the direction of Saarbrücken (shades of 1870!). One Army Corps advanced to contact and found nothing but masses of mines. This was a new element with which in due course we were to become only too familiar, but was surprising at the time. As at the beginning of all wars, the remedies were rudimentary: infantrymen set them off by hitting them with a stick or herds of cattle were driven on to them. ... Finally the operation, directed in a very half-hearted and desultory way, bogged down in the minefields under artillery fire after advancing no more than a few miles. The Germans did not react. Gamelin decided to pull back. So much for our help to Poland.

After this apology for an attack, our front became static. Activities were limited to patrols and the occasional *coup de main* in which we usually came off worst because our men, enervated by this static life, found themselves face to face with young and fanatical Germans on their toes who were rushed up from the rear in motorized transport to counter any move. There were a few artillery duels; no aerial combat whatever. Along the length of the Rhine (the opposite bank of which we were forbidden to shell), the Germans hung out their washing, harangued our troops through loudspeakers and, with impunity, under our noses, sent a stream of trains bearing coal from the Ruhr to Italy. ... One day I was told to escort the Prince of Cambodia, who was doing a tour with the Army Corps of General Frère. The impression I brought back from Lorraine was incredible: the Army was rotting from inaction.

This was quite absurd. Why were we acting like this? Or, more properly, why were we not acting?

3

Neville Chamberlain on the Norwegian Campaign[1]

27 April

This has been one of the worst, if not the worst, week of the war.... We hadn't reckoned on the way in which the Germans had poured in reinforcements of men, guns, tanks, and aeroplanes. In particular, this brief campaign has taught our people, many of whom were much in need of teaching, the importance of the air factor.

4 May

I am thankful that at least we got our men out of Norway. ...We could not give them what they wanted most, namely fighter aircraft, because we had no aerodrome from which they could operate. I rather doubt whether our experts realized before the power of an unopposed air arm. Both the Norwegian and the Swedish governments told us that it was essential to take Trondjem. ... We knew it was a dangerous operation, but there was a chance that we might pull it off before the Germans established themselves. That chance, as it now appears, vanished when we gave up the original idea of a direct attack with warships up the fjord, *á la* Narvik. We had not expected the Germans to come up from Oslo so fast, for we thought the Norwegians would have blown up the railway bridges and at least rolled stones on to the roads. But they refused to do either ... My own mind, and this is the view of some of the best experts, inclines to the conclusion that, even if we had been able to capture Trondjem, our success would only have been temporary. ... The most common cry, and this of course is chronic in the U.S.A., is "why are we always too late? Why do we let Hitler take the initiative?" ... The answer to these questions is simple enough, but the questioners would rather not believe it. It is, "because we are not yet strong enough". ... We have plenty of man-power, but it is neither trained nor equipped. We are short of many weapons of offence and defence. Above all, we are short of air power. If we could weather this year, I believe we should be able to remove our worst deficiencies.

4

General André Beaufre on the Norwegian Campaign

The short Norwegian campaign was a sort of dummy run in which the two sides tried out their own methods of fighting. Our inferiority was terrifying. We lacked imagination, character and organization: responsibility was shared between the two Allies, each of which in turn was divided into land, air and naval commands, the whole thing lumbered with an utterly useless committee of politicians. Furthermore our fatal weaknesses were shown up in a glaring light: no modern equipment, no ack-ack, no decisive bombing policy, no drive in the troops—except the very best—and no incisive command.[1] At its first test our military system showed itself to be out-of-date. This unpleasant fact was borne home to thinking people who were resigned to it. Hitler was the man who had judged the situation to perfection: he had hesitated to begin his offensive against France, but now he had proof that he would risk nothing if he did so because he was the stronger. The Norwegian campaign gave him the proof he needed. He made his irrevocable decision: *blitzkrieg* would destroy France.

---

1   The term 'ack-ack' refers to anti-aircraft guns.

5

Churchill's Blood, Toil, Tears and Sweat Speech

New British Prime Minister Winston Churchill

Addresses the House of Commons

May 13, 1940

I beg to move,

That this House welcomes the formation of a Government representing the united and inflexible resolve of the nation to prosecute the war with Germany to a victorious conclusion.

On Friday evening last I received His Majesty's commission to form a new Administration. It is the evident wish and will of Parliament and the nation that this should be conceived on the broadest possible basis and that it should include all parties, both those who supported the late Government and also the parties of the Opposition. ...

To form an Administration of this scale and complexity is a serious undertaking in itself, but it must be remembered that we are in the preliminary stage of one of the greatest battles in history, that we are in action at many other points in Norway and Holland, that we have to be prepared in the Mediterranean, that the air battle is continuous and that many preparations ... have to be made here at home. In this crisis I hope I may be pardoned if I do not address the House at any length today. I hope that any of my friends, or former colleagues, who are affected by the political reconstruction, will make

Winston Churchill, "Churchill's Blood, Toil, Tears and Sweat Speech, May 13, 1940," The Churchill Centre. 1940.

allowance, all allowance, for any lack of ceremony with which it has been necessary to act. I would say to the House, as I said to those who have joined this government: "I have nothing to offer but blood, toil, tears and sweat."

We have before us an ordeal of the most grievous kind. We have before us many, many long months of struggle and of suffering. You ask, what is our policy? I can say: It is to wage war, by sea, land and air, with all our might and with all the strength that God can give us; to wage war against a monstrous tyranny, never surpassed in the dark, lamentable catalogue of human crime. That is our policy. You ask, what is our aim? I can answer in one word: It is victory, victory at all costs, victory in spite of all terror, victory, however long and hard the road may be; for without victory there is no survival. Let that be realized; no survival for the British Empire, no survival for all that the British Empire has stood for, no survival for the urge and impulse of the ages, that mankind will move forwards towards its goal. But I take up my task with buoyancy and hope. I feel sure that our cause will not be suffered to fail among men. At this time I feel entitled to claim the aid of all, and I say, "come then, let us go forward together with our united strength."

6

FIELD MARSHALL ALANBROOKE ON THE BATTLE OF FRANCE

May 10

The German planes returned early this morning between 3 and 4 am and an infernal bombardment of AA guns started. A little later Ritchie came to tell me that GHQ had rung up to place us at 6 hours notice. Shortly afterward he returned and said that the Germans had invaded Belgium and Holland at 4 am and that we were at last to put into effect our famous 'D' plan. This entails a rapid move forward to the River Dyle, east of Brussels. The II Corps goes onto a one divisional front with the 3rd Div forward and the 4th and 50th Divs back.

It was hard to believe on a most glorious spring day with all nature looking quite its best, that we were taking the first step towards what must become one of the greatest battles of history! All day long planes have been droning overhead and many have been brought down, one not very far from the Corps HQ. I spent the day checking over orders for the move. Everything so far has been running like clockwork and with less interference from bombing than I had anticipated. Gort came to see us in the afternoon and discussed progress made. 3rd Div started off at 2:30 pm this afternoon, and by now its advance elements should be approaching the Dyle. It will however take some 8 days or so to assemble the whole Corps forward.

Field Marshal Lord Alanbrooke, *War Diaries 1939-1945*, pp. 58-59, 65. Copyright © 2001 by University of California Press. Reprinted with permission.

May 19

Got up at 5 am after a short night and after examining reports started off to examine the new line of defence on the Scheldt. Found travelling difficult owing to masses of refugees but succeeded in covering the whole length of the line and in going up onto Mont-St-Aubert (near Tournal), to see to what extent it overlooks our new line. It is going to be a troublesome spot. I then motored on through (to) the new HQ of the 1st Div to try and find out how they were getting on. Then on to this new HQ which we reached in the middle of an air raid on the aerodrome which is unfortunately just along side of us! I had only just arrived when I was called to GHQ for a Corps Commanders conference. It was a momentous one!

The news of the French front was worse than ever, they were attempting one full counter attack to try and restore the situation. Should this fail it looked as if the Allies forces would be cut in the centre! The BEF communications to the sea would be completely exposed and so would our right flank. GHQ had a scheme for a move in such an eventuality towards Dunkirk, establishing a defended area around this place and embarking all we could of the personnel of the BEF, abandoning stores and equipment. I preferred pivoting on our left flank which is secure and in contact with the Belgians. To swing our right back onto the River Lys, up the new empty canal to Ypres and thence by Ypres Canal to the sea. By this means I feel that at any rate we can keep the BEF as a unity and not have it destroyed by bits. If we let go our hold of the Belgians now I feel certain they will stop fighting and both our flanks will be exposed, in which case there is little hope. We are to meet again this evening for another conference if GHQ have any more news.

7

CAPTAIN BASIL BARTLETT ON THE BATTLE OF FRANCE

May 16
The situation in the Intelligence Office is getting most alarming. I sat and watched it, fascinated, as the movement of the German push was chalked in. The break-through at Sedan seems to have been completely successful. And now there's another one beginning higher up. The German Armoured Divisions must be travelling at a tremendous pace. I wonder what the French are going to do. They anticipated that the attack would come exactly when and where and as it has come. So I imagine that they have guns placed one behind the other all the way from Sedan to Paris. I hope they have.

The General was not impressed by the break-through. He put on four pairs of spectacles and stared at it calmly for a minute or two. Then he rubbed it out.

'It hasn't been confirmed,' he said.

The Field Cashier arrived this afternoon, and we all diligently changed our French money into Belgian. The food in Brussels is famous. I hope we'll get a chance of trying some of it. We'd almost eaten and drunk Lille dry.

There's been a lot of aerial activity all day. The fights over Brussels have been as good as a football match. The whole Division watched them perilously through our big plate-glass windows. The best fight was one in which three Messerschmitts and a Hurricane were brought down.

A large bomb was dropped about three hundred yards away near the railway-station.

Sir Basil Bartlett, Excerpts from: *My First War: An Army Officer's Journal for May 1940*, pp. 64-65. Macmillan Publishing Company, 1940.

Late at night we were told to move back. This order came as a great surprise. We know that the B.E.F. is fighting well. In fact, only this afternoon our next-door Division made a successful counter-attack and recaptured Louvain. The conclusion is that the Sedan break-through has been sustained and that the B.E.F must fall back in line with the French.

It's very unsatisfactory to be living without news.

The British Consul has left Brussels. An English-woman came into the office this morning, distracted. She has no proper papers and was assured only two days ago by the Consul that there was no need for her to move. And now the last train has left without her. We sent her back to Lille on an empty supply-truck.

It seems appalling to be abandoning Brussels.

The Belgian troops stand about apathetically at street-corners or sit in pubs. They don't look desperately anxious to fight.

8

THE BATTLE OF FRANCE

MAY 27, 1940

South of the Lower SOMME the Germans withdrew on the evening 26th May from the River Bresle and West of Amiens back towards the Somme.

A German attack on Carvin (seven miles North East of Lens) reached the outskirts of that town. Further North in the St. Omer area the enemy reached Hazebruck and the Foret de Nieppe but did not press elsewhere.

An air report timed 1200 hrs. 27th May stated that no movement or fighting was seen in the Quay or Citadel areas of Calais. From this and other messages it is estimated that Calais is now occupied by the Germans.

One of the usual channel passages from Dover to Dunkirk is now impracticable in daylight owing to heavy fire from shore batteries sited between Les Hommes and Gravelines. Dunkirk and anchorages were heavily bombed yesterday morning. Three ships reported being shelled off Calais and one off Gravelines in the course of the morning.

West of Courtrai German advanced elements took Gheluvelt yesterday, and are approaching Zonnebeke. North East of Courtrai the German advance continued towards Thielt, but the Belgians retook Vynckt.

Further north German attacks, assisted by intense air bombing, have succeeded in crossing the Lys canal on a ten kilometer front between Eccloo and Maldegem. It is expected that the enemy is delivering simultaneous attacks today on the axes Courtrais-Ypres and Ronsele-Bruges.

"The Battle of France, May 27, 1940," UK National Archives, PREM 3/254/3 Joint Intelligence Summary May 27, 1940.

The German Air Force operations on 26th May showed a slight increase on the scale of the 25th. Attacks were widespread, although the main effort was in southern Belgium and North East France, and on harbours and sea objectives or the French side of the Straits of Dover. Several bombing attacks were made on the Paris-Nancy railways and on railways running north from Dijon.

Constant fighter patrols appear to be established over the Dunkirk-Calais-Boulogne area.

9

DUNKIRK

MAY 28, 1940

The First Sea Lord said that the Vice-Admiral, Dover, had reported at 11 A.M. that 11,400 men had arrived the previous night and 2,500 more were in passage across the Channel. There were 5 destroyers alongside at Dunkirk, each of which was taking on about 1,000 men. Considerable numbers of troops were arriving back at Dunkirk.

A later message from Captain Tennant at Dunkirk reported that there were 2,000 troops on the beaches and 7,000 among the sand dunes. All these were very badly in need of water, which the Army could not supply. Vice-Admiral, Dover, had informed him that a maximum effort would be made that night to send in flat bottomed boats to take these men off the beaches. Embarkation by this means was impossible by day owing to machine-gun fire. Destroyers, however, would be taking men off the quays throughout the day. Practically all the men arriving at Dunkirk had their equipment with them, and most of them had their rifles. Many also carried their Bren guns.

A message had been received that S.S. *Aboukir*, which had left Ostend on the night of the 27th May with about 1,000 men on board, including the British Missions to the Belgians, had been torpedoed, probably by a motor torpedo boat, in the early hours of that morning. Thirty-three survivors had been picked up.

S.S. *Queen of the Channel*, transporting troops, had been bombed and was in a sinking condition, but it was believed that the survivors had been taken off.

Source: http://filestore.nationalarchives.gov.uk/pdfs/small/cab-65-7-wm-40-144-39.pdf.

Dunkirk itself was covered with a pall of smoke, and Vice-Admiral, Dover, had been instructed to use smoke from ships to add to this if needed.

The Secretary of State for War said that the troops evacuated from France were being despatched at once from the ports of disembarkation to Salisbury Plain and Aldershot Command. They would be attached to parent units in these places, who would ration them and look after them.

The Chief of the Air Staff said that he had ordered continuous fighter patrols in strength during the daylight hours over Dunkirk and the beaches three miles on either side of the town. The other tasks allotted to Fighter Command were the protection of our own bomber sorties and patrols over the B.E.F. area.

The Minister of Information read to the War Cabinet a message he had just received from Sir Walter Monckton pressing for a frank statement of the desperate situation of the British Expeditionary Force. He feared that, unless this was given out, public confidence would be badly shaken and the civil population would not be ready to accept the assurances of the Government of the chances of our ultimate victory. The Minister suggested that he should make a short statement in the 1 o'clock news of the B.B.C.

The Prime Minister said that he would also make a statement in the House of Commons in the afternoon to the effect that the British Expeditionary Force was fighting its way back to the coast under the protection of the Royal Air Force, and that the Navy was embarking the troops. It would be idle to try to forecast the success of this operation at this stage.

June 4, 1940

The Chief of the Imperial General Staff said that the final measure of the evacuation of French troops from Dunkirk had been carried out during the preceding night, and that no further operations had taken place. The total numbers of evacuated troops entrained in Great Britain up to midnight the previous night had been as follows:-

British—
Fit.....................211,258
Casualties............13,053

Allied—
Fit.....................84,675
Casualties............1,230
Total....................310,216

It was hoped that a considerable further number of French troops would have been landed after midnight.

The total British casualties were between 33,000 and 34,000. Deducting the wounded brought to this country, about 20,700 remained unaccounted for. Most of these must have been killed or taken prisoner. It was possible, however, that a certain number of men might be trying to make their way back independently in a south-westerly direction, since the Germans did not hold a continuous line.

The First Sea Lord said that the Navy were keeping a look-out for individual British soldiers who might reach the French coast.

10

Churchill's We Shall Fight on the Beaches Speech

Churchill Addresses the Nation

June 4, 1940

I have, myself, full confidence that if all do their duty, if nothing is neglected, and if the best arrangements are made, as they are being made, we shall prove ourselves once again able to defend our Island home, to ride out the storms of war, and to outlive the menace of tyranny, if necessary for years, if necessary alone. At any rate, that is what we are going to try to do. That is the resolve of His Majesty's Government—every man of them. That is the will of Parliament and the nation. The British Empire and the French Republic, linked together in their cause and in their need, will defend to the death their native soil, aiding each other like good comrades to the utmost of their strength. Even though large tracts of Europe and many old and famous States have fallen or may fall into the grip of the Gestapo and all the odious apparatus of Nazi rule, we shall not flag or fail. We shall go on to the end, we shall fight in France, we shall fight on the seas and oceans, we shall fight with growing confidence and growing strength in the air, we shall defend our island, whatever the cost may be.

We shall fight on the beaches, we shall fight on the landing grounds, we shall fight in the fields and in the streets, we shall fight in the hills; we shall never surrender, and even if, which I do not for a moment believe, this Island or a large part of it were subjugated and starving, then our Empire beyond the seas, armed and guarded by the British Fleet, would carry on the struggle, until, in God's good time, the New World, with all its power and might, steps forth to the rescue and the liberation of the old.

Winston Churchill, "We Shall Fight on the Beaches Speech, June 4, 1940," The Churchill Centre, pp. 8-9. 1940.

11

CHURCHILL'S FINEST HOUR SPEECH

CHURCHILL ON THE FALL OF FRANCE

JUNE 18, 1940

We do not yet know what will happen in France or whether the French resistance will be prolonged, both in France and in the French Empire overseas. The French Government will be throwing away great opportunities and casting away their future if they do not continue the war in accordance with their Treaty obligations, from which we have not felt able to release them. The House will have read the historic declaration in which, at the desire of many Frenchmen, and of our own hearts, we have proclaimed our willingness to conclude at the darkest hour in French history a union of common citizenship. However matters may go in France or with the French Government or with another French Government, we in this island and in the British Empire will never lose our sense of comradeship with the French people. If we are now called upon to endure what they have suffered we shall emulate their courage, and if final victory rewards our toils they shall share the gains, aye. And freedom shall be restored to us all. We abate nothing of our just demands—Czechs, Poles, Norwegians, Dutch, Belgians, all who have joined their causes to our own shall be restored.

What General Weygand called the "Battle of France" is over. I expect that the Battle of Britain is about to begin. The whole fury and might of the enemy must very soon be turned on us. Hitler knows that he will have to break us in this island or lose the war. If we can stand up to him all Europe may be free, and the life of the world may move forward into broad, sunlit uplands; but if

Winston Churchill, "Finest Hour Speech, June 18, 1940." The Churchill Centre. 1940.

we fail then the whole world, including the United States, and all that we have known and cared for, will sink into the abyss of a new dark age made more sinister, and perhaps more prolonged, by the lights of a perverted science. Let us therefore brace ourselves to our duty and so bear ourselves that if the British Commonwealth and Empire lasts for a thousand years men will still say, "This was their finest hour."

12

GENERAL HEINZ GUDERIAN ON BLITZKRIEG

'It has been said, "only movement brings victory." We agree with this proposition and wish to employ the technical means of our time to prove its truth. Movement serves to bring the troops in contact with the enemy: for this purpose one can use the legs of men or of horses, the railways or—recently—the automobile and the aeroplane engine. Once contact with the enemy has been made, movement is generally paralysed by hostile fire. In order to permit the relaxation of this paralysis, the enemy must either be destroyed or made inoperative or driven from his positions. This can be done by employing fire-power so superior that his powers of resistance collapse. Fire-power from fixed positions has an effective range corresponding exactly to the observed range of the mass of the weapons employed. That is as far as the infantry can make use of its covering fire; when that point is reached the heavy weapons and the artillery must change their position in order to permit a further advance under cover of their fire-power. Vast numbers of weapons and an even vaster quantity of ammunition are needed to fight this sort of battle. The preparations for an attack of this sort require considerable time and are difficult to conceal. Surprise, that important element of success, is very hard to achieve. And even if the original attack does catch the enemy unawares, the moment it is launched the attacking force will have shown its hand, and the reserves of the defence will converge on the point of attack and block it; since reserve forces will now be motorized, the building up of new defensive fronts is easier than it used to be; *the chances of an offensive based on the timetable of artillery and infantry co-operation are, as a result, even slighter today than they were in the last war.*

'Everything is therefore dependent on this: to be able to move faster than has hitherto been done: to keep moving despite the enemy's defensive fire and thus to make it harder for him to build up fresh defensive positions: and finally to carry the attack deep into the enemy's defenses. The proponents of tank warfare believe that, in favourable circumstances, they possess the means for achieving this; the sceptics, on the other hand, say that since the element of surprise can no longer be produced as in 1918 "conditions for a successful tank attack can no longer be anticipated." But is it true that a tank attack can no longer take the enemy by surprise? How then does it happen that surprises have been achieved in warfare regardless of whether old or new methods were employed to bring them about? In 1916 General von Kuhl proposed to the High Command that in order to make a break-through primary importance must be attached to the element of surprise in launching the attack; and yet at that time he had no new methods or weapons at his disposal. As a result of surprise achieved, the March Offensive of 1918 was outstandingly successful, despite the fact that no new types of weapons were employed. If, in addition to the normal methods of achieving surprise, new weapons are also employed, then the effects of the surprise will be greatly increased; but the new weapons are not a prerequisite to those effects. We believe that by attacking with tanks we can achieve a higher rate of movement than has been hitherto obtainable, and—what is perhaps even more important—that we can keep moving once a break-through has been made. We believe that movement can be kept up if certain conditions, on which the success of a tank attack depend, exist: these include among others, concentration of force in suitable terrain, gaps in the enemy's defence, and an inferior enemy tank force. When we are blamed because we cannot storm fortifications with tanks armed only with machine-guns, then we can only say that we are sorry and point out that other arms of the service possess in many respects even less attacking power than we do. We do not claim to be omnipotent.

'It has been maintained that a weapon only achieves its maximum effectiveness while it is new and before it need fear defensive counter-measures. Pity the artillery! It is already hundreds of years old. Pity the air force! Age is creeping up on it in the form of anti-aircraft. We believe that the effectiveness of any weapon is a relative quality, depending on the effectiveness of the counter weapons employed against it. If tanks run into a superior enemy—whether in the form of hostile tanks or of anti-tank weapons—they will be beaten; their effectiveness will be reduced; if conditions are reversed, then they will achieve startling success. Every weapon is dependent not only on the strength of the opposition but also on its own willingness to make immediate, maximum use of the latest technical developments and thus to remain at the summit of its period. From this point of view the tank will not admit that it has been surpassed by any other weapon. It has been said: "The shells of defensive artillery travel faster than the tanks that are attacking that artillery." Nobody, up to now, has questioned this fact. Yet as long ago as 1917 and 1918 hundreds of tanks could be moved up to a concentration area immediately behind the front lines of the infantry: could penetrate in their swarms the enemy's line of defensive fire: could clear a way for dozens of infantry and even of cavalry divisions: and what is more could do all this without any preliminary artillery bombardment, that is to say in the teeth of an intact enemy artillery. It is only in unusually unfavourable conditions that the hostile artillery can have any serious effect on the movement of tanks: and once the tanks have succeeded in breaking through to the gun lines, the batteries will soon fall silent and will thus be no longer capable of even hurting the following infantry. Even the immutable artillery tactics of having guns registered on all localities of possible danger proved a failure in the last war. The defensive fire will throw up columns of earth, dust, smoke and so on and this will limit the vision of the tank crews; but such limitation is not intolerable; even in peacetime we have learned how to overcome that. In fact tanks can now advance through night and fog on compass bearings.

In an attack that is based on a successful tank action the "architect of victory" is not the infantry but the tanks themselves, for if the tank attack fails then the whole operation is a failure, whereas if the tanks succeed, then victory follows.

FIRE

'Armour and movement are only two of the combat characteristics of the tank weapon; the third and the most important is fire-power.

'Tank guns can be fired whether the tank is stationary or on the move. In both cases the gun is laid by direct observation. If the tank is stationary range can be quickly adjusted and the target destroyed with a minimum expenditure of ammunition. When the tank is in motion the recognition of targets becomes harder owing to difficulties in observation, but this is compensated for to a certain extent by the fact that the gun is situated comparatively high above ground, which is particularly useful if the terrain is overgrown; thus the high silhouette, which has been so frequently the cause of adverse comments as presenting the enemy with an easy target, is not without a certain advantage for the tank gunner. If it is necessary to shoot while in movement the chances of short-range accuracy are good; they decrease with longer range, higher speed and when travelling over uneven ground.

'In any event, in land battles the tanks possesses the unique quality of being able to bring its fire-power to bear while actually advancing against the enemy, and it can do this even though all the defence's guns and machine guns have not been silenced. We do not doubt that guns fired from stationary positions are more accurate than guns fired in motion; we are well able to judge this, since we are capable of both types of engagement. However: "Only movement brings victory." Now should a tank attack be envisaged simply as a means of steam-rolling a path through thick and deep defensive positions held by infantry and artillery fully equipped with anti-tank weapons, as was done during the battles of *matériel* of the last war? Certainly not. A man who would attempt this would be thinking purely in terms of the infantry tank, a weapon whose sole function was the closest co-operation with the infantry, a weapon adjusted to the foot-soldier's scale of time and space values. This was a concept which we hung on to for far too long. We neither can nor wish to devote weeks or even months to reconnaissance; we have no desire to rely on an enormous expenditure of ammunition; *what we do want to do is, for a short period of time, to dominate the enemy's defence in all its depth.* We are well aware that with the limited fire-power of our tanks we cannot mount a "planned artillery preparation" or achieve a "concentrated artillery bombardment"; our intention is exactly the contrary, it is to knock out our targets with single, surely aimed shells. For we have not forgotten how during the war week-long barrages by the most powerful artillery on earth failed to enable the infantry to achieve victory. *We have been taught by our enemies to believe that a successful, rapid tank attack, in sufficient width and depth to penetrate all the way through the opposing defence system, can achieve more towards ensuring victory than the system of limited advances as practiced in the World War.* Our shells, being aimed at specific targets, will not whistle over the enemy's heads as they did during those costly though pointless creeping barrages: rather if the attack is carried out with sufficient concentration, width and depth we shall destroy recognizable targets as they present themselves and thus drive a hole in the enemy's defences through which our reserves can follow more speedily than was possible in 1918. *We want these reserves to be available in the form of Panzer Divisions, since we no longer believe that other formations have the fighting ability, the speed and the manoeuvrability necessary for full exploitation of the attack and break-through.* Therefore

we do not regard the tank force as "an additional means for winning battles, which on many forseeable occasions could, in co-operation with other
weapons, help the infantry to advance." If that were all that tanks were for,
the situation would be the same now as in 1916; and if that were true then
one might as well be resigned to positional warfare from the very beginning
and give up all hope of quick decisions in the future. But neither the alleged
superiority in armaments of our enemy in any future war, nor the increased
accuracy and range of guns of all calibres, nor the technical advances made
in the employment of artillery suffice to shake our beliefs. On the contrary!
In the tank we see the finest weapon for the attack now available: we will not
change our minds until such time as the technicians can show us better. We
will in no circumstances agree to time-wasting artillery preparation and the
consequent danger of losing the element of surprise, simply because the old
maxim says that "only fire can open the way to movement." We believe, on the
contrary, that the combination of the internal combustion engine and armour
plate enable us to take our fire to the enemy without any artillery preparation, provided always that the important conditions for such an operation
are fulfilled: suitable terrain, surprise and mass commitment.

The idea of mass commitment gives our critics cold feet. They write: "There
is also the question of organization: of whether the massing of all tank strength
in one striking force is a sound basic idea, or whether the alternative theory
of allotting tanks organically to the infantry, in order to enable it to attack,
is not worthy of equally serious consideration." We assume from this remark
that the infantry without tanks is at present incapable of attacking; it follows
that the weapon which can attack, and which can enable other arms of the
Service to advance, must indubitably be the principal weapon. The question
of whether or not tanks should be allotted to infantry can be clarified by the
following imaginary story:

'Red and Blue are at war. Each side has 100 Infantry Divisions and 100 Tank
Battalions. Red has split up its tanks among its Infantry Divisions; Blue has
massed them in Panzer Divisions under direct control of supreme headquarters. On a front of, shall we say, 300 miles, 100 are tank-proof, 100 are difficult
for tanks and 100 are good tank country. So in battle the following picture
emerges: Red has deployed a sizeable proportion of its divisions, along with
their tank components, opposite the Blue positions in country where tanks
cannot operate and are therefore useless, while a further portion are in difficult
tank country where, though not entirely wasted, their chances of a successful
action are small. Whatever happens, only a fraction of Red's tank forces can
be employed in the country for which they are suited. Blue, on the other hand,

has collected all its armour in the one place where a decision can be reached and where the ground can be made use of; he therefore has the opportunity of going into battle with at least double his adversary's tank strength while assuming the defensive along the rest of the front against Red's very small-scale tank attacks. An Infantry Division with, say, 50 anti-tank weapons can stand up far more easily to an attack by 50 tanks than to an attack by 200. We conclude that the suggestion that our tanks be divided among Infantry Divisions is nothing but a return to the original English tactics of 1916–17, which were even then a failure, for the English tanks were not successful until they were used in mass at Cambrai.

13

Air Marshal Dowding's Report on the Battle of Britain[1]

39. When the Dunkerque evacuation was complete I had only 3 Daylight Fighting Squadrons which had not been engaged in Continental fighting, and 12 Squadrons were in the line for the second time after having been withdrawn to rest and re-form.

40. All this time, it must be remembered, the attack on this Country had not begun; with a few accidental exceptions no bomb had been dropped on our soil. I was responsible for the Air Defense of Great Britain, and I saw my resources slipping away like sand in an hour-glass. The pressure for more and more assistance to France was relentless and inexorable. In the latter part of May, 1940, I sought and obtained permission to appear in person before the War Cabinet and to state my case. I was accorded a courteous and sympathetic hearing, and to my inexpressible relief my arguments prevailed and it was decided to send no more Fighter Reinforcements to France except to cover the final evacuation.

---

1   Battle of Britain Despatch by Air Chief Marshal Sir Hugh C.T. Dowding. (The report was formatted in numbered paragraphs. A squadron normally consisted of 16 aircraft). The RAF lost 436 fighter aircraft during the Battle of France.

Hugh C. T. Dowding, "Air Marshal Dowding's Report on the Battle of Britain," United Kingdom National Archives, AIR 8/863, August 20, 1941.

41. I know what it must have cost the Cabinet to reach this decision, but I am profoundly convinced that this was one of the great turning points of the war.

54. This is not the place to give an account of the romantic discovery and development of Radio Location. It may be explained, however, that the backbone of the system consisted of a series of large "chain" stations at intervals averaging about 30 miles. These gave warning, by means of reflected electrical echoes, of the presence of aircraft within the radius of their effective action, which attained to nearly 200 miles in the most favourable circumstances. The average effective radius was about 80 miles, but they had the serious limitation that they failed altogether to give indications of aircraft flying below 1,000 feet.

88. I must now give a brief account of the characteristics of the aircraft commonly employed on both sides. As regards the Fighter types available in the Command, the bulk of the force consisted of Hurricanes and Spitfires; the former were beginning to be outmoded by their German counterparts. They were comparatively slow and their performance and manoeuvrability were somewhat inadequate at altitudes above 20,000 feet. The Spitfires were equal or superior to anything which the Germans possessed at the beginning of the Battle.

89. The Hurricanes and Spitfires had bullet-proof windscreens and front armour between the top of the engine and the windscreen. They also had rear armour directly behind the pilot, which was previously prepared and fitted as soon as we began to meet the German Fighters. The early adoption of armour gave us an initial advantage over the Germans, but they were quick to imitate our methods. While German aircraft remained unarmoured, I think it is now generally agreed that the single-seater multi-gun fighter with fixed guns was the most efficient type which could have been produced for the day fighting. With the advent of armour some change in armament and/or tactics became necessary, and the subject is discussed in more detail in Appendix F.

98. It is very difficult to give any kind of concise description of the types of Enemy Aircraft used during the Battle. The Germans, while adhering to broad standard types, were continually modifying and improving them by fitting more powerful engines and altering the armament. The original Messerschmitt 109, for instance, had a performance comparable with that of the Hurricane, but the latest type could compete with the

Spitfire, and had a better ceiling. Some of them had 4 machine guns and other had 2 machine guns and 2 cannons. Some of them were fitted to carry bombs and some were not.

107. This statement, even if intended only for popular consumption, tends to lead to an attitude of complacency which may be very dangerous in the future. Whatever the study of paper returns may have shown, the fact is that the situation was critical in the extreme. Pilots had to be withdrawn from the Bomber and Coastal Commands and from the Fleet Air Arm and flung into the Battle after hasty preparation. The majority of squadrons had been reduced to the status of training units, and were fit only for operations against unescorted bombers. The remainder were struggling daily against heavy odds.

108. The indomitable courage of the Fighter Pilots and the skill of their Leaders brought us through the crisis, and the morale of the Germans eventually cracked because of the stupendous losses which they sustained.[2]

122. The Battle may be said to have divided itself broadly into 4 Phases: First, the attack of convoys and Coastal objectives, such as Ports, Coastal Aerodromes and Radio Location Stations. Second, the attack of Inland Fighter Aerodromes. Third, the attack on London. And, fourth, the Fighter-Bomber stage, where the target was of importance quite subsidiary to the main object of drawing our Fighters into the air and engaging them in circumstances as disadvantageous to us as possible. These phases indicated only general tendencies; they overlapped and were not mutually exclusive.

193. The effective strength of the Command was running down, though the fact was not known to the public, nor, I hoped, to the Germans. They for their part must certainly be feeling the effect of their heavy losses, but there was very little indication of any loss of morale, so far as could be seen from a daily scrutiny of the examinations of Prisoners of War. Our own pilots were fighting with unabated gallantry and determination.[3]

---

2   In these paragraphs Dowding is criticizing an Air Ministry publication about the Battle of Britain that Dowding believed made serious mistakes. Also note that both sides exaggerated the losses of their enemy during the battle.

3   This paragraph refers to phase two of the battle.

196. As I have said, our own pilots were fighting with the utmost gallantry and determination, but the mass raids on London, which were the main feature of the third phase of the Battle, involved a tremendous strain on units which could no longer be relieved as such. Some Squadrons were flying 50 and 60 hours per diem.

205. The most critical stage of the Battle occurred in the third phase. On the 15th September the Germans delivered their maximum effort, when our Guns and Fighters together accounted for 185 aircraft.[4] Heavy pressure was kept up till the 25th September, but, by the end of the month, it became apparent that the Germans could no longer face the Bomber wastage which they had sustained, and the operations entered upon their fourth phase, in which a proportion of enemy Fighters themselves acted as Bombers.

209. In the fourth phase, the apparent ratio of losses in our favour dropped appreciably. I say "apparent" because, in fighting at extreme altitudes, fighters often could not see their victims crash, and the percentage reported as Certainly Destroyed was unfairly depressed. Our own casualties, nevertheless, were such that the C. Category squadrons, which I was hoping to build up to operational strength again, remained in their condition of semi-effectiveness.

210. Serious as were our difficulties, however, those of the enemy were worse, and by the end of October the Germans abandoned their attempts to wear down the Fighter Command, and the country was delivered from the threat of immediate invasion.

---

4   The Germans actually lost 60 aircraft that day, but their overall losses remained heavy.

CHAPTER 4

THE ROAD TO WAR IN THE PACIFIC

Introduction

Japan's war with China increasingly strained its relationship with the United States and other nations with interests in the Pacific. The documents in this chapter chart their steady decline following Japan's 1931 invasion of Manchuria. Following international condemnation, Japan withdrew from the League of Nations (Document 1). The United States responded with the Stimson Doctrine (Document 2), refusing to recognize Japan's conquests. Japan escalated its war with China in 1937, which the Japanese government justified by blaming the Chinese for starting the war (Document 3). The United States first responded weakly, with President Franklin D. Roosevelt's "Quarantine Speech" (Document 4), but the continued fighting, along with Germany's conquests of Poland, France, and other countries in 1939–1940, encouraged Roosevelt to take stronger measures to deter Japan. In 1940, Roosevelt convinced Congress to fund the construction of the largest navy in the nation's history (Document 5) and followed this with an escalating series of economic sanctions against Japan, restricting trade in a growing list of products and resources, among them scrap steel, which Japan vigorously protested (Document 6). Japan's leaders prepared for war (Document 7) and formed an alliance with Nazi Germany and fascist Italy, the Tripartite Pact. The United States sent military advisors and aid to China (Document 8), and Japan invaded French Indochina to block this aid.

Many Japanese and American leaders hoped to avoid war, but by 1941 most of them saw war as likely. Japan's military leaders, in fact, argued that the only practical response to U.S. economic sanctions was to go to war to secure the resources it needed, particularly oil, which was plentiful in the islands of Indonesia, which Britain and the Netherlands controlled (Document 9). Fearing the United States would oppose a Japanese invasion of these resource-rich islands, Japan's leaders determined to open the war with a surprise attack on the U.S. fleet at Pearl Harbor, Hawaii. Destruction of the American fleet would then allow the Japanese to move against American, British, and Dutch territories including Indonesia, Malaysia, Singapore, and Philippines (Document 10). Outraged by the attack, which he declared "a day of infamy," Roosevelt asked Congress to declare war on Japan, which it promptly did (Document 11). In an excerpt from his book *Pearl Harbor: FDR Leads the Nation to War* (2011), historian Steven M. Gillon provides an overview of the events that led to war (Document 12). In an excerpt from Diane Burke Fessler's *No Time for Fear* (1996), a U.S. Army nurse describes her experience of the Pearl Harbor attack (Document 13).

1

JAPAN'S STATEMENT ON WITHDRAWING FROM THE LEAGUE OF NATIONS

THE IMPERIAL RESCRIPT RELATING TO WITHDRAWAL FROM

THE LEAGUE OF NATIONS

PROCLAIMED ON MARCH 27, 1933

When the League of Nations came into being upon the restoration of a general peace, Our Imperial Father was pleased to order the entry of Our Empire thereinto; and We, in Our turn, have laboured assiduously to fulfill the high purpose of the late Emperor. It is thus that Our Empire has for these 13 years past extended consistently its cooperation to the League.

Now Manchoukuo having of late been founded, Our Empire deems it essential to respect the independence of the new State and to encourage its healthy development, in order that the sources of evil in the Far East may be eradicated and an enduring peace thereby established. Unhappily, there exists between Our Empire and the League of Nations a wide divergence of view in this regard and it has devolved upon Us to cause Our Government to take, upon mature deliberation, the necessary steps for the withdrawal of Our Empire from the League.

However, the advancement of international peace is what, as evermore, We desire, and Our attitude toward enterprises of peace shall sustain no change. By quitting the League and embarking on a course of its own, Our Empire does not mean that it will stand aloof in the Extreme Orient, nor that it will isolate itself thereby from the fraternity of nations. It is Our desire to promote

Japanese Government, "Japan's Statement on Withdrawing from the League of Nations," Ibiblio. 1933.

mutual confidence between Our Empire and all the other Powers and to make known the justice of its cause throughout the world.

Every country is overtaken today be emergencies of an unprecedented magnitude. Our Empire itself is confronted by a situation fraught with momentous possibilities. It is indeed an hour that calls for an intensification of effort on the part of Our entire nation. We command that all public servants, whether civil or military, shall faithfully perform each his appointed duty, and that all private citizens shall pursue their wonted tasks with diligence. Stray not, in advancing, from the path of rectitude; and in action, embrace always the golden mean. Strive to meet the present situation with a united will and with courage and resolution. So may We carry forward the glorious work bequeathed by Our Grandsire and contribute to the prosperity and well-being of Mankind.

2

STIMSON DOCTRINE

THE SECRETARY OF STATE TO THE AMBASSADOR IN CHINA (FORBES)

WASHINGTON, JANUARY 7, 1932

[IDENTICAL NOTE DELIVERED TO JAPANESE GOVERNMENT.]

Please deliver to the Foreign Office on behalf of your Government as soon as possible the following note:

With the recent military operations about Chinchow, the last remaining administrative authority of the Government of the Chinese Republic in South Manchuria, as it existed prior to September 18th, 1931, has been destroyed. The American Government continues confident that the work of the neutral commission recently authorized by the Council of the League of Nations will facilitate an ultimate solution of the difficulties sow existing between China and Japan. But in view of the present situation and of its own rights and obligations therein, the American Government deems it to be its duty to notify both the Imperial Japanese Government and the Government of the Chinese Republic that it cannot admit the legality of any situation *de facto* nor does it intend to recognize any treaty or agreement entered into between those Governments, or agents thereof, which may impair the treaty rights of the United States or its citizens in China, including those which relate to the sovereignty, the independence, or the territorial and administrative integrity of the Republic of China, or to the international policy relative to China, commonly known as the open door policy; and that it does not intend to recognize any situation, treaty or agreement which may be brought about by means contrary to the covenants and obligations of the Pact of Paris of August 27, 1928, to which Treaty both China and Japan, as well as the United States, are parties.

"Stimson Doctrine," Foreign Relations of the United States Diplomatic Papers, 1932. *The Far East: Volume III*, pp. 7-8. 1932.

3

JAPANESE STATEMENT ON INTERVENTION IN CHINA

1937

1. In the evening of July 7, 1937, a detachment of the Japanese troops stationed at Fengtai, near Peiping [Beijing], was engaged in a night maneuver in the vicinity of Lukow Kiao. At 11:40 PM Chinese troops under the command of Feng Chih-an (29th Army) made an attack upon the Japanese soldiers for no cause at all.

Thereupon the detachment stopped the maneuver and asked the command at Fengtai to send out reinforcements.

2. At such maneuvers, the Japanese troops carry a very small quantity of loaded shells for use in case of emergency. In point of fact the commanding officer of the said detachment had with him one box of loaded shells for the machine guns. In view of these facts, it is absolutely impossible for the Japanese soldiers to have challenged the Chinese.

3. The right of maneuver of the Japanese troops stationed in North China is clearly stipulated in the China-Japanese Protocol of 1902 concerning the restoration of Tientsin to China. Moreover, the Japanese authorities had informed the Chinese in advance of the holding of the maneuver in question. It is entirely groundless to say that the recent maneuver

"Japan's Statement on Intervention in China," *US State Department Papers Relating to the Foreign Relations of the United States: Japan: 1931-1941, vol. 1*, pp. 318-319. 1943.

of the Japanese troops is an unlawful act committed outside the region stipulated in the said Protocol as reported in the newspapers.

4. Since the night of July 7, the Japanese authorities have made an earnest endeavor to localize the incident and once succeeded in bring the Chinese authorities to agree to a peaceful settlement. On the night of July 10th, however, the 29th Army, in violation of the agreement, suddenly fired on the Japanese troops, causing considerable casualties. In addition, it is reported, China had been increasing the forces of the first line by ordering Suiyan troops to march south and by sending central forces and air corps to the front.

Since the night of July 10, China not only has failed to manifest any sincerity toward a peaceful settlement but has flatly rejected the local negotiation at Peiping [Beijing].

5. The presence of the disorderly Chinese troops in the Peiping [Beijing] and Tientsin area not only disturbs peace and order in North China which is of vital importance to Japan, but also endangers the lives and property of the Japanese nationals there.

    In the circumstances, the Japanese Government has decided to take all precautionary steps to meet all situations, including the dispatch of additional military forces to North China.

6. The Japanese Government, desirous as ever to preserve peace in East Asia, has not abandoned hope that through peaceful negotiations the aggravation of the situation may yet be prevented.

An amicable solution can yet be attained if China agrees to offer apologies for the recent lawless action and to give adequate guarantees against such outrages in the future.

In any case the Japanese Government is prepared to give full consideration to the rights and interests of the Powers in China

4

U.S. President Franklin D. Roosevelt Quarantine Speech

Chicago, October 5, 1937

Relations between the United States and Japan worsened following Japan's invasion of China on July 7, 1937. With tensions also increasing in Europe, U.S. President Franklin D. Roosevelt suggested that the United States, along with other nations, quarantine aggressor nations. Spoke against isolationism and those determined to keep the U.S. neutral and out of any future war. While vague about what this quarantine would entail, it prefigured the economic sanctions the United States later imposed on Japan.

... The political situation in the world, which of late has been growing progressively worse, is such to cause grave concern and anxiety to all the peoples and nations who wish to live in peace and amity with their neighbors.

Some 15 years ago the hopes of mankind for a continuing era of international peace were raised to great heights when more than 60 nations solemnly pledged themselves not to resort to force of arms ... The high aspirations expressed in the Briand-Kellog Pact and the hopes for peace thus raised have of late given way to a haunting fear of calamity. The present reign of terror and international lawlessness began a few years ago.

It began through unjustified interference in the internal affair of other nations or the invasion of alien territory in violation of treaties. It has now reached the stage where the very foundations of civilization are seriously threatened. The landmarks, the traditions which have marked the progress

Franklin Roosevelt, "Quarantine Speech," *The Public Papers and Addresses of Franklin D. Roosevelt*, ed. Samuel I. Rosenman, 1937, pp. 406-411. 1941.

of civilization toward a condition of law and order and justice are being wiped away.

Without a declaration of war and without warning or justification of any kind, civilians, including vast numbers of women and children are being ruthlessly murdered with bombs from the air. In times of so-called peace, ships are being attacked and sunk by submarines without cause or notice. Nations are fomenting and taking sides in civil warfare in nations that have never done them any harm. Nations claiming freedom for themselves deny it to others.

Innocent peoples, innocent nations are being cruelly sacrificed to a greed for power and supremacy which is devoid of all sense of justice and humane considerations.

* * *

If those things come to pass in other parts of the world, let no one imagine that America will escape, that America may expect mercy, that this Western hemisphere will not be attacked and that it will continue tranquilly and peacefully to carry on the ethics and arts of civilization.

... if we are to have a world in which we can breathe freely and live in amity without fear—then the peace-loving nations must make a concerted effort to uphold laws and principles on which alone peace can rest secure.

The peace-loving nations must make a concerted effort in opposition to those violations of treaties and those ignorings of human instincts which today are creating a state of international anarchy and instability from which there is no escape through mere isolation or neutrality.

Those who cherish their freedom and recognize and respect the equal right of their neighbors to be free and live in peace, must work together for the triumph of law and moral principles in order that peace, justice, and confidence may prevail throughout the world. There must be a return to a belied in the pledged word, in the value of a signed treaty. There must be recognition of the fact that national morality is as vital as private morality.

* * *

There is a solidarity and interdependence about the modern world, both technically and morally, which makes it impossible for any nation completely to isolate itself from economic and political upheavals in the rest of the world, especially when such upheavals appear to be spreading and not declining. There can be no stability or peace either within nations or between nations except under laws and moral standards adhered to by all. International anarchy destroys every foundation for peace. It jeopardizes either the immediate or the future security of every nation, large or small. It is, therefore, a matter of vital interest and concern to the people of the United States that the sanctity of international treaties and the maintenance of international morality be restored.

* * *

How happy we are that the circumstances of the moment permit us to put our money into bridges and boulevards, dams and reforestation, the conservation of our soil, and many other kinds of useful works rather than into huge standing armies and vast supplies of implements of war.

Nevertheless, my friends, I am compelled, as you are compelled, to look ahead. The peace, the freedom, and the security of 90 per cent of the population of the world is being jeopardized by the remaining 10 per cent who are threatening a breakdown of all international order and law. Surely the 90 per cent who want to live in peace under law and in accordance with moral standards that have received almost universal acceptance through the centuries, can and must find some way to make their will prevail.

The situation is definitely of universal concern. The questions involved relate not merely to violations of specific provisions of particular treaties; they are questions of war and of peace, of international law and especially of principles of humanity. It is true that they involve definite violations of agreement, and especially of the Covenant of the League of Nations, the Briand-Kellog Pact and the Nine Power Treaty. But they also involve problems of world economy, world security and world humanity.

* * *

It seems to be unfortunately true that the epidemic of world lawlessness is spreading.

AND MARK THIS WELL: When an epidemic of physical disease starts to spread, the community approves and joins in a quarantine of the patients in order to protect the health of the community against the spread of the disease.

It is my determination to pursue a policy of peace and to adopt every practicable measure to avoid involvement in war. It ought to be inconceivable that in this modern era, and in the face of experience, any nation could be so foolish and ruthless as to run the risk of plunging the whole world into war by invading and violating, in contravention of solemn treaties, the territory of other nations that have done them no real harm and are too weak to protect themselves adequately. Yet the peace of the world and the welfare and security of every nation are today being threatened by that very thing.

* * *

War is a contagion, whether it be declared or undeclared. It can engulf states and peoples remote from the original scene of hostilities. We are determined to keep out of war, yet we cannot insure ourselves against the disastrous effects of war and the dangers of involvement. We are adopting such measures as will minimize our risk of involvement, but we cannot have complete protection in a world of disorder in which confidence and security have broken down.

If civilization is to survive, the principles of the Prince of Peace must be restored. Shattered trust between nations must be revived.

Most important of all, the will for peace on the part of peace-loving nations must express itself to the end that nations that may be tempted to violate their agreements and the rights of others will desist from such a course. There must be positive endeavors to preserve peace.

5

U.S. President Roosevelt Message to the Congress Recommending Additional Appropriations for National Defense

July 10, 1940

To the Congress:

* * *

From time to time during the last seven years, I have not failed to advise the people and their representatives of grave dangers threatening the United States and its people, and the institutions of democracy everywhere. ...

A year and a half ago, on January 4, 1939, in my address to the Congress, I referred to the fact that I had felt it necessary on previous occasions to warn of disturbances abroad, and the need of putting our own house in order in the face of storm signals from across the seas. On that day I said that a war which threatened to envelope the world in flames had been averted, but that it had become increasingly clear that peace was not assured. I said then that all about us raged undeclared wars, military and economic. I said then that all about us were threats of new aggression, military and economic. ...

Unhappily, many Americans believed that those who thought they foresaw the danger of a great war, were mistaken. Unhappily, those of us who did foresee that danger, were right.

* * *

"FDR to Congress Recommending Additional Appropriations for National Defense, July 10, 1940," *Peace and War: United States Foreign Policy, 1931-1941*, pp. 66-69. 1943.

At the beginning of September the storm broke, and on the twenty-first of that month, in a message to the extraordinary session of the Congress, I said that this Government must lose no time or effort to keep this nation from being drawn into the war, and I asserted my belief that we would succeed in these efforts. We have succeeded. I believe we shall continue to succeed.

In September last, I increased the strength of the Army, Navy, Coast Guard and the Federal Bureau of Investigation within statutory authorizations made by the Congress. In January 1940, I submitted a budget to the Congress which included provision for that expansion of personnel, as well as estimates for the national defense, amounting to approximately two billion dollars for the fiscal year 1941.

On May 16, in a message to the Congress, I pointed out that the swift and shocking developments of that time [Germany's invasion of France, Belgium, and the Netherlands] forced every neutral nation to look to its defenses in the light of new factors loosed by the brutal force of modern offensive war. ... and called especial attention to the necessity for the protection of the whole American Hemisphere from control, invasion or domination. I asked at that time for a sum totaling $1,182,000,000 for the national defense.

On May 31, 1940, I again sent a message to the Congress, to say that the almost incredible events of the then past two weeks in the European conflict had necessitated another enlargement of our military program, and at that time I asked for $1,277,741,170 for the acceleration and development of our military and naval needs as measured in both machines and men.

Again today, in less than two months time, the changes in the world situation are so great and so profound that I must come once again to the Congress to advise concerning new threats, new needs, and the imperative necessity of meeting them. Free men and free women in the United States look to us to defend their freedom against all enemies, foreign and domestic. Those enemies of freedom who hate free institutions now deride democratic Governments as weak and inefficient.

We, the free men and women of the United States, with memories of our fathers to inspire us and the hopes of our children to sustain us are determined to be strong as well as free. The apologists for despotism and those who aid them by whispering defeatism or appeasement, assert that because we have not devoted our full energies to arms and to preparation for war that we are now incapable of defense.

I refute that imputation.

We fully understand the threat of the new enslavement in which men may not speak, may not listen, may not think. As these threats become more numerous and their dire meaning more clear, it deepens the determination of the American people to meet them with wholly adequate defense.

We have seen nation after nation, some of them weakened by treachery from within, succumb to the force of the aggressor. We see great nations still gallantly fighting against aggression, encouraged by high hope of ultimate victory.

That we are opposed to war is known not only to every American, but to every government in the world. We will not use our arms in a war of aggression; we will not send our men to take part in European wars.

But, we will repel aggression against the United States or the Western Hemisphere. The people and their representatives in the Congress know that the threats to our liberties, the threats to our security, the threats against our way of life, the threats to our institutions of religion, of democracy, and of international good faith, have increased in number and gravity from month to month, from week to week, and almost from day to day.

It is because of these rapid changes; it is because of the grave danger to democratic institutions; and above all, it is because of the united will of the entire American people that I come to ask you for a further authorization of $4,848,171,957 for the national defense.

* * *

The principal lesson of the war up to the present time is that partial defense is inadequate defense.

If the United States is to have any defense, it must have total defense.

We cannot defend ourselves a little here and a little there. We must be able to defend ourselves wholly and at any time.

Our plans for national security, therefore, should cover total defense. I believe that the people of this country are willing to make any sacrifice to attain that end.

* * *

In broad outline our immediate objectives are as follows:

1. To carry forward the Naval expansion program designed to build up the Navy to meet any possible combination of hostile naval forces.

2. To complete the total equipment for a land force of approximately 1,200,000 men, though of course this total of men would not be in the Army in time of peace.

3. To procure reserve stocks of tanks, guns, artillery, ammunition, etc., for another 800,000 men or a total of 2,000,000 men if a mobilization of such a force should become necessary.

4. To provide for manufacturing facilities, public and private, necessary to produce critical items of equipment for a land force of 2,000,000 men, and to produce the ordnance items required for the aircraft program of the Army and Navy-guns, bombs, armor, bombsights and ammunition.

5. Procurement of 15,000 additional planes for the Army and 4,000 for the Navy, complete with necessary spare engines, armaments, and the most modern equipment.

The foregoing program deals exclusively with materiel requirements. The Congress is now considering the enactment of a system of selective training for developing the necessary man power to operate this materiel and man power to fill army non-combat needs. In this way we can make certain that when this modern materiel becomes available, it will be placed in the hands of troops trained, seasoned, and ready, and that replacement materiel can be guaranteed.

* * *

We are keeping abreast of developments in strategy, tactics, and technique of warfare, and building our defenses accordingly.

The total amount which I ask of the Congress ... is $2,161,441,957, which it is estimated would be spent out of the Treasury between now and July 1, 1941, and an additional $2,686,730,000 for contract authorizations.

So great a sum means sacrifice. So large a program means hard work-the participation of the whole country in the total defense of the country. This nation through sacrifice and work and unity proposes to remain free.

6

Japan Protests Scrap Steel Embargo

Statement handed to U.S. Secretary of State by Japan's Ambassador

October 8, 1940

Since iron and steel scrap classified as No. 1 heavy melting scrap was placed under export-licensing system on July 26, 1940, permission of the United States government was obtained up to August 19 of the same year for 99 percent of applications for shipments to Japan.

In the light of this fact, the sudden enlargement of the iron and steel scrap licensing system to include all grades of these materials is hardly explicable from the standpoint of national defense, on which the regulation of September 30, 1940 is purported to be based.

The discriminatory feature of the announcement, the licenses will be issued to permit shipments to the countries of the Western Hemisphere and Great Britain only, has created a widespread impression in Japan that it was motivated by a desire to bring pressure upon her.

The fact that the majority of essential articles and materials that Japan desires to import from America is placed under licensing system is casing a feeling of tension among the people of Japan, who naturally presume that the system is intended to be a precursor of severance of economic relations between Japan and the United States.

In view of the high feeling in Japan it is apprehended that, in the event of continuation by the United States Government of the present attitude toward Japan in matters of trade restriction, especially if it leads to the imposition

"Japan Protests Scrap Steel Embargo, 8 Oct 1940," *Peace and War: United States Foreign Policy, 1931-1941*, pp. 579. 1943.

of further measures of curtailment, future relations between Japan and the United States will be unpredictable.

It is a matter of course that the Governments of both Japan and the United States should endeavor as best they can to preclude such an eventuality. To this endeavor the Japanese Government will devote itself and trusts it may have the full cooperation of the United States Government.

7

OUTLINE OF NATIONAL POLICIES IN VIEW OF THE CHANGING SITUATION

JULY 2, 1941

POLICY

1. Our Empire is determined to follow a policy that will result in the establishment of the Greater East Asia Co-prosperity Sphere and will thereby contribute to world peace, no matter what change may occur in the world situation.

2. Our Empire will continue its efforts to effect a settlement of the China Incident, and will seek to establish a solid basis for the security and preservation of the nation. This will involve taking steps to advance south, and, depending on changes in the situation, will involve a settlement of the Northern Question as well

3. Our Empire is determined to remove all obstacles in order to achieve the above-mentioned objectives.

SUMMARY

1. Pressure applied from the southern regions will be increased in order to force the capitulation of the Chiang regime. At the appropriate time, depending on future developments, the rights of a belligerent will be

"Outline of National Policies in View of the Changing Situation," *Japan's Decision for War: Records of the 1941 Policy Conferences*, ed. and trans. Nobutaka Ike, pp. 78-79. Copyright © 1967 by Stanford University Press. Reprinted with permission.

exercised against the Chungking regime, and hostile Foreign Settlements will be taken over.

2. In order to guarantee the security and preservation of the nation, our Empire will continue all necessary diplomatic negotiations with reference to the southern regions, and will also take such other measures as may be necessary.

3. In order to achieve the following objectives, preparations for war with Great Britain and the United States will be made. First of all, on the basis of "Outline of Policies Toward French Indochina and Thailand" and "Acceleration of Policies Concerning the South," various measures relating to French Indochina and Thailand will be taken, with the purpose of strengthening our advance into the southern regions. In carrying out the plans outlined above, our Empire will not be deterred by the possibility of being involved in a war with Great Britain and the United States

4. Our attitude with reference to the German-Soviet war will be based on the spirit of the Tripartite Pact. However, we will secretly strengthen our military preparedness vis-à-vis the Soviet Union, and we will deal with this matter independently. In the meantime, we will conduct diplomatic negotiations with great care. If the German-Soviet war should develop to the advantage of our Empire, we will, by resorting to armed force, settle the Northern Question and assure the security of the northern borders.

5. In carrying out the various policies mentioned above [In Section 3], and especially in deciding on the use of armed force, we will make certain that there will be no great obstacles to the maintenance of our basic posture with respect to war with Great Britain and the United States.

6. In accordance with established policy, we will strive to the utmost, by diplomatic and other means, to prevent the entry of the United States into the European war. But if the United States should enter the war, our Empire will act in accordance with the Tripartite Pact. However, we will decide independently as to the time and method of resorting to force.

7. We will immediately turn our attention to putting the nation on a war footing. In particular, defense of the homeland will be strengthened.

8. Concrete plans covering this program will be drawn up separately.

8

WHITE HOUSE PRESS RELEASE ON SENDING A MILITARY MISSION TO CHINA

AUGUST 26, 1941

This Government is preparing to send a military mission to China. The mission will be sent for the purpose of assisting in carrying out the purposes of the Lend-Lease Act. It is being organized and it will operate under the direction of the Secretary of War. Its chief will be Brigadier General John Magruder.

The function of the mission will be to study, in collaboration with Chinese and other authorities, the military situation in China, the need of the Chinese Government for materiel and materials; to formulate recommendations regarding types and quantities of items needed; to assist in procurement in this country and in delivery in China of such materiel and materials; to instruct in the use and maintenance of articles thus provided; and to give advice and suggestions of appropriate character toward making Lend-Lease assistance to China as effective as possible in the interest of the United States, of China, and of the world effort in resistance to movements of conquest by force.

The sending of this mission is in keeping with and is on parallel lines to the sending of a similar mission to the Soviet Union. The purposes of the two missions are identical.

General Magruder has had long experience in China where he twice served as Military Attaché. He, therefore, will be working on familiar ground, among people he knows well and to whom he is well known. An adequate staff of thoroughly qualified officers will accompany General Magruder.

"White House Press Release on Sending Military Mission to China," *The Public Papers and Addresses of Franklin D. Roosevelt, 1941*, ed. Samuel I. Rosenman. 1941.

9

THE ESSENTIALS FOR CARRYING OUT THE EMPIRE'S POLICIES

SEPTEMBER 6, 1941

In view of the current critical situation, in particular, the offensive attitudes that such countries as the United States, Great Britain, and the Netherlands are taking toward Japan, and in view of the situation in the Soviet Union and the condition of the Empire's national power, we will carry out our policy toward the South, which is contained in the "Outline of National Policies in View of the Changing Situation," as follows:

1. Our Empire, for the purposes of self-defense and self-preservation, will complete preparations for war, with the last ten days of October as a tentative deadline, resolved to go to war with the United States, Great Britain, and the Netherlands if necessary.

2. Our Empire will concurrently take all possible diplomatic measures vis-à-vis the United States and Great Britain, and thereby endeavor to attain our objectives. The minimum objectives or our Empire to be attained through negotiations with the United States and Great Britain and the maximum concessions therein to be made by our Empire are noted in the attached documents.

3. In the event that there is no prospect of our demands being met by the first ten days of October through the diplomatic negotiations mentioned

"The Essentials for Carrying out the Empire's Policies," *Japan's Decision for War: Records of the 1941 Policy Conferences*, ed. and trans. Nobutaka Ike, pp. 135-136. Copyright © 1967 by Stanford University Press. Reprinted with permission.

above, we will immediately decide to commence hostilities against the United States, Great Britain, and the Netherlands.

Policies other than those toward the South will be based on established national policy; and we will especially try to prevent the United States and the Soviet Union from forming a united front against Japan.

10

Draft Proposal for Hastening the End of the War against the United States, Great Britain, the Netherlands, and Chiang [Kai-shek]

November 15, 1941

Policy

1. We will endeavor to quickly destroy the American, British, and Dutch bases in the Far East, and assure our self-preservation and self-defense. We will endeavor at the same time to hasten the fall of the Chiang regime by taking positive measures, to work for the surrender of Great Britain in co-operation with Germany and Italy, and to destroy the will of the United States to continue the war.

2. We will do our utmost to prevent an increase in the number of countries at war against us; and we will endeavor to influence the countries not presently involved.

Summary

1. Our Empire will engage in a quick war, and will destroy American and British bases in Eastern Asia and in the Southwest Pacific region. At the same time that it secures a strategically powerful position, it will

control those areas producing vital materials, as well as important transportation routes, and thereby prepare for a protracted period of self-sufficiency.

At the appropriate time, we will endeavor by various means to lure the main fleet of the United States [near Japan] and destroy it.

2. First of all, Japan, Germany, and Italy will cooperate and work for the surrender of Great Britain.

* * *

3. Japan, Germany, and Italy will cooperate and endeavor to deal with Great Britain, and at the same time endeavor to destroy the will of the United States to fight.

* * *

4. In China we will stop support going to Chiang by utilizing the results of our military operations (especially against the United States, Great Britain, and the Netherlands), and will destroy Chiang's power to resist. We will also work for the collapse of the Chiang regime by vigorously undertaking various strategies—the seizure of the Foreign Settlements, utilization of the overseas Chinese in the South Pacific, stepping up military operations, etc.

5. The Empire will endeavor to the utmost to prevent the outbreak of war with the Soviet Union while we are engaged in military operations in the South.

* * *

6. We will continue our present policy toward French Indochina. We will persuade Thailand to cooperate with us by restoring to her territory she lost to the British.

7. While paying full attention to changes in the war situation, the international situation, and popular feelings in enemy countries, we will endeavor to seize the following opportunities in order to bring the war to a close: (a) conclusion of the principal military operations in the South; (b) conclusion of the principal military operations in China, especially the capitulation of the Chiang regime; (c) favorable developments in the war situation in Europe, especially the conquest of the British Isles, the end of the war between Germany and the Soviet Union, and the success of the policy vis-à-vis India.

For this purpose we will step up our diplomatic and propaganda activities directed against Latin America, Switzerland, Portugal, and the Vatican.

The three countries—Japan, Germany, and Italy—agree not to sign separate peace agreements; at the same time, they will not immediately make peace with Great Britain when she surrenders, but will endeavor to use Great Britain to persuade the United States. In the planning to promote peace with the United States, attention will be paid to supplies of tin and rubber in the South Pacific region, and to the treatment of the Philippines.

11

PRESIDENT FRANKLIN D. ROOSEVELT DAY OF INFAMY ADDRESS TO CONGRESS

DECEMBER 8, 1941

To the Congress of the United States:

Yesterday, Dec. 7, 1941—a date which will live in infamy—the United States of America was suddenly and deliberately attacked by naval and air forces of the Empire of Japan.

The United States was at peace with that nation and, at the solicitation of Japan, was still in conversation with the government and its emperor looking toward the maintenance of peace in the Pacific.

Indeed, one hour after Japanese air squadrons had commenced bombing in Oahu, the Japanese ambassador to the United States and his colleagues delivered to the Secretary of State a formal reply to a recent American message. While this reply stated that it seemed useless to continue the existing diplomatic negotiations, it contained no threat or hint of war or armed attack.

It will be recorded that the distance of Hawaii from Japan makes it obvious that the attack was deliberately planned many days or even weeks ago. During the intervening time, the Japanese government has deliberately sought to deceive the United States by false statements and expressions of hope for continued peace.

The attack yesterday on the Hawaiian Islands has caused severe damage to American naval and military forces. Very many American lives have been lost. In addition, American ships have been reported torpedoed on the high seas between San Francisco and Honolulu.

Franklin Roosevelt, "Day of Infamy" *Peace and War: United States Foreign Policy, 1931-1941*, pp. 838-839. 1943.

Yesterday, the Japanese government also launched an attack against Malaya.

Last night, Japanese forces attacked Hong Kong.

Last night, Japanese forces attacked Guam.

Last night, Japanese forces attacked the Philippine Islands.

Last night, the Japanese attacked Wake Island.

This morning, the Japanese attacked Midway Island.

Japan has, therefore, undertaken a surprise offensive extending throughout the Pacific area. The facts of yesterday speak for themselves. The people of the United States have already formed their opinions and well understand the implications to the very life and safety of our nation.

As commander in chief of the Army and Navy, I have directed that all measures be taken for our defense.

Always will we remember the character of the onslaught against us.

No matter how long it may take us to overcome this premeditated invasion, the American people in their righteous might will win through to absolute victory.

I believe I interpret the will of the Congress and of the people when I assert that we will not only defend ourselves to the uttermost, but will make very certain that this form of treachery shall never endanger us again.

Hostilities exist. There is no blinking at the fact that that our people, our territory and our interests are in grave danger.

With confidence in our armed forces—with the unbounding determination of our people—we will gain the inevitable triumph—so help us God.

I ask that the Congress declare that since the unprovoked and dastardly attack by Japan on Sunday, Dec. 7, a state of war has existed between the United States and the Japanese empire.

12

"THIS MEANS WAR"

FDR was still in bed on Sunday morning when he received notice that his military aide, Admiral John Beardall, would be bringing the locked pouch containing the fourteenth part of Japan's diplomatic message. Beardall delivered the pouch to the president at 10:00 a.m. and waited patiently while FDR read it. It contained the missing fourteenth part of the message that began arriving the previous evening. It stated that the chances of achieving peace in the Pacific "through cooperation of the American Government" had "been lost."

The pouch likely also contained a second message that instructed the Japanese ambassador to destroy the code machines at their Washington embassy and to deliver the message to the secretary of state at one o'clock. But if these instructions were included in the package that FDR read, he apparently was not alarmed. After reading the materials, the president turned to the admiral and said, "It looks as though they are breaking off negotiations." It was obvious to FDR that the Japanese were planning to strike, but when? And where? There was nothing that suggested to him that an American installation would be a target.[12]

Roosevelt confronted a dilemma: The Japanese response made clear they were breaking off diplomatic relations and were likely to strike Allied possessions in the Pacific. He assumed that the likely target would be either British Malaya or the Dutch East Indies. Without American intervention, the Japanese could control a vast area that was rich in natural resources that stretched from the Aleutian Islands to India. This aggression would strengthen the Japanese war machine and make them a more formidable enemy for the United States. It would also weaken the British, forcing them to expend precious resources to protect their colonial possessions that could be better used to fight Hitler.

Although a Japanese offensive against British possessions would present a long-term danger to the United States, FDR doubted if he could motivate the nation to go to war to save British imperial land in the Pacific. Congress had only reluctantly agreed to support FDR's efforts to defend Britain. As Sherwood noted, "Why, then, should Americans die for Thailand, or for such outposts of British imperialism as Singapore or Hong Kong or of Dutch imperialism in the East Indies, or for Communism in Vladivostok?"[13]

Even if the president were to muster all of his political skills, a congressional debate over war could drag on for weeks. FDR had been warning the American people about the danger in the Atlantic and the need to support Britain. How could he now convince them to go to war in the Pacific? Much of his rhetoric had been focused on convincing Americans to supply aid to Britain so that American soldiers would not have to fight and die in another foreign war. He was reluctant to abandon that message or to remove the focus from the war in Europe.[14]

The hawkish Stimson and Hull were pondering the same question on Sunday morning at their 10:00 a.m. meeting. "Hull is very certain that the Japs are planning some deviltry and we are all wondering where the blow will strike," Stimson noted in his diary. Like Roosevelt, they were convinced that the likely target would be British, not American. One question persisted: What should the United States do if the Japanese attacked Singapore, Malaysia, or Thailand? Stimson and Hull were convinced that the United States needed to join the British if a fight erupted. But they clearly wondered whether Roosevelt would agree.

The possibility that Japan would strike America or its possessions seemed remote to all. The day before, while holding his daily briefing with civilian aides and military chiefs, Knox had reviewed all the intelligence information. Reports claimed that a large Japanese task force was at sea, apparently headed along the south coast of Indochina. "Gentlemen," Knox asked, "are they going to hit us?'" His advisers were unanimous in their response. "No, Mr. Secretary," declared Admiral Richmond Kelly Turner, who was in charge of war planning for the navy. "They are going to attack the British. They are not ready for us yet." As a naval aide noted, "There was no dissenting voice. Turner's concise statement apparently represented the thinking of the Navy Department."[15]

And so in the hours before the Japanese attacked Pearl Harbor, FDR's main foreign policy advisers were busy developing a strategy for getting him to declare war against Japan if it attacked either a British or a Dutch possession. Knox dictated a memorandum that urged the president to recognize that "any threat to any one of the three of us is a threat to all of us." As Knox later told a congressional committee investigating the attack, his goal was to convince Roosevelt to state that the United States would respond by force if the Japanese attacked Thailand or "British, Dutch, United States, Free French, or Portuguese territory in the Pacific area."[16]

Notes

12. Testimony of Rear Admiral John R. Beardall, United States Navy, *Hearings Before the Joint Committee*, 2nd sess., pt. 11, 5283–5284; *Report of the Joint Committee on the Investigation of the Pearl Harbor Attack*, 79th Cong., 2nd sess., document 244, appendix D, "The Last Hours," 436; Weintraub, *Long Day's Journey into War*, 183; Bratton, *Hearings Before the Joint Committee*, Army Pearl Harbor Board, September 30, 1944, 1st sess., pt. 29, 2344–2345.

13. Sherwood, *Roosevelt and Hopkins*, 429.

14. Ibid., 337.

15. Weintraub, *Long Day's Journey into War*, 34–35; Frank E. Beatty, "The Background of the Secret Report," *National Review*, December 13, 1966, 1261.

16. Statement by Henry L. Stimson, Former Secretary of War, *Hearings Before the Joint Committee*, 79th Cong., 2nd sess., pt. 11, March 1946, 5440–5441.

13

Pearl Harbor, Hawaii 7 December 1941

7:55 A.M

"Like rats in a trap"

Agnes Shurr U.S. Navy   **USS Solace**

A native of North Dakota, Agnes joined the navy in the 1930s; it was the pay and the chance to see the world which attracted her She retired thirty years later.

Before the war, we nurses were often invited to dinner on other ships in Pearl Harbor, and I remember one of the captains asking me something that I have remembered often over the years. He said, "What do you folks think of the situation? Do you think there is going to be a war?" He must have thought we had information he didn't.

I was asleep that Sunday morning on the hospital ship *Solace* out in the middle of Pearl Harbor, "in the stream," as we say. "COMMAND BATTLE STATIONS!" was the first thing I heard. Our sailors were in their dress whites waiting to go ashore on liberty, but when the explosions started, they went around in the liberty boats, picking up injured and wounded out of the water. We received casualties almost immediately. Our ship was painted white, had a red cross on each side, and must have stood out among the other ships in the harbor. But it was never hit. Later that morning the ship moved to a more secluded area in the harbor.

We worked all through the day without stopping. Late at night, I was sitting at the dinner table with other nurses when the executive officer came and

Diane Burke Fessler, "Like Rats in a Trap," *No Time for Fear: Voices of American Military Nurses in World War II*, pp. 11-13. Copyright © 1996 by Michigan State University Press. Reprinted with permission.

talked to us for awhile. "Well," he said, "we don't know what's going to happen next. But we're all still here, kind of like rats in a trap! We're going to carry on the best we can." Because we were so busy, I hadn't been aware really of the seriousness of our own situation. I could see the ships in the water and the smoke rolling up and hear the sounds of ships firing at aircraft. But around the table, it began to dawn on me that we were really in a precarious and dangerous position in the harbor.

A few days later we were allowed to go ashore for the day, and the air raid siren sounded, so we had to return to the ship. Somehow that was more frightening to me because I didn't know if we would be able to get back on the ship or be stranded. The ship was my safe haven. In Honolulu one day, I was carrying a lot of art supplies and dropped them as I was crossing the street. A young American-Japanese boy stopped and picked them up for me. I remember thinking, "These are the people who just bombed us." Of course, he was probably a good American, but I couldn't help thinking that.

After all these years, I still recall one boy who was very badly burned. His mother wrote him a letter that I'm sure she meant to be encouraging, that said, "When you think your troubles are terrible, you need to put on a tight pair of shoes, and you'll forget about your other troubles." All I could think was that he couldn't even get shoes on. Of course, she didn't know how bad he was, but he did kind of smile.

Valera Vaubel Wiskerson U.S. Navy   Navy Hospital, Pearl Harbor

Val left a position with a Chicago hospital to join up in 1937. After a tour in San Diego, she arrived for duty in Hawaii in 1940

I'd just served breakfast to the patients who couldn't go to the mess hall and was going across to get some food for myself, when I heard a horrible explosion. I looked across the water at the hangar on Ford Island. It looked like it was picked up into the air and dropped down—PLUNK! There was nothing but smoke where there had been that great big airplane hangar with all the planes sitting in a row.

A plane with a huge red circle came close enough to tell it was Japanese. It dived over the hospital, and if I'd had a gun I could have killed him. I was a sharpshooter at the time, because a fellow had been taking me with him to practice shooting.

They started bringing men in with burns and fractures by whatever means they could get there in. Patients had tags on them telling how much morphine or whatever had been done for them. Doctors decided who went to which ward or what treatment they needed. I was an acting dietitian but also worked in other wards for the next several days. The diets were mostly liquids because of so many burn cases.

Patients who'd been there before the bombing left to return to duty and didn't take their records with them, so we never knew what happened to them.

An experience I can't forget to this day was a patient who was in shock. When I went to get him a blanket, none were there, so I went upstairs to get one. A doctor called me over to help lift a patient in the burn ward. We'd lift a patient up and draw the sheet from underneath, and because the burned skin came off, fresh oil was put on the sheet. I was holding under the patients' thigh and lower leg to raise him when his leg separated from the knee in my hands. I turned white as the sheet, and the doctor looked at my face. I took deep breaths to keep from fainting. After the patient was put on the sheet, I found a blanket and took it downstairs. The patient who needed the blanket had died, and a new one was in his place, so I covered him with the blanket.

I remember the burn cases where eyelids and lashes were burned, and you couldn't see the nose. Burns smell horrible. Our chief nurse kept a perfumed handkerchief in her pocket, and while she was feeding a burn patient, she would sniff it. Once a patient asked if he could sniff it too, because he couldn't stand the smell. She thinks it saved his life because he ate better then.

Volunteers came to the hospital to help, such as service wives and friends. Prostitutes from Honolulu came too, but they weren't all helpful, because some tried to get a little business, and we had to throw them out.

Soon after the "blitz" I was assigned to the shipyard dispensary. Everyone on the base had to be given tetanus and other shots, and we were just changing needles and giving shots to civilians as well as military families by the hundreds. Then I set up a dispensary at the main gate so the families wouldn't have to go into the shipyard.

CHAPTER 5

THE HOLOCAUST

Introduction

Anti-Semitic propaganda figured prominently in Adolf Hitler's election rhetoric, blaming Jews for Germany's problems, real and perceived. After the Nazi Party seized power in 1933, Germany's Nazi government implemented an escalating series of anti-Jewish laws that culminated in genocide. Nazi policy toward Jews began with laws that defined and segregated them, followed by efforts to concentrate them in camps and ghettos, and then to eliminate them entirely through a campaign of genocide. This chapter's documents showcase the development of Nazi policy toward Jews.

Passed in 1935, the Reich Citizenship Laws stripped Jews of their political rights, banned them from many professions, and restricted their associations with Germans (Document 1). In October 1939, Hitler ordered his personal physician, Karl Brandt, and Phillip Bouhler, the chief of Hitler's Chancellery, which oversaw Nazi Party maters, to euthanize euthanize disabled children (Document 2). Similar orders were issued to murder other people with disabilities. Nazi leaders organized this as the T-4 Program, which murdered about 200,000 Germans with physical or mental disabilities, including 5,000 children.

The Commissar Order (Document 3), issued for the invasion of Russia (June 1941) ordered German soldiers to immediately shoot any captured Soviet commissars, who were political officers serving in the Soviet army. As the German offensive stalled in late 1941, Nazi officials claimed Jews were responsible for

Germany's military setbacks and other problems, as in the article "The Jews Are to Blame" from the newspaper *Das Reich* (Document 4).

By 1940, many German and Austrian Jews had already been sent to concentration camps, and this process accelerated in 1941 as Nazi officials organized the mass deportation of Jews in occupied Europe to central Poland (renamed Reichskommissariat Ost by Germany), particularly the overcrowded Warsaw Ghetto (Document 5). Meeting at Wannsee, a Berlin suburb, on January 20, 1942, Nazi leaders decided to exterminate the Jews in their entirety and established six death camps in Poland to which they would be sent and murdered (Document 6). As Stanislav Rozycki, a Jewish refugee who managed to escape to Britain, recounts, conditions in the concentration camps and ghettos were such that many Jews were already dying from disease and starvation (Document 7).

Nazi leaders justified the necessity of extermination to those who carried out the murders, as Minister of the Interior Heinrich Himmler did when speaking to members of the Einsatzgruppen, special units that followed the German army into Russia that rounded up and murdered Jews by the tens of thousands, as at Babi Yar, near Kiev, where Einsatzgruppen and German soldiers murdered more than 30,000 Jews over several days. Although the Wannsee Protocol used a variety of circumlocutions and euphemisms to elide the nature of the "final solution," Himmler's three-hour speech pointedly exhorts SS officers to murder or work to death non-German peoples (Document 8).

The Korherr Report (Document 9) shows that Germany officials kept meticulous track of the number of Jews they killed. In total, they killed about six million Jews—two-thirds of Europe's Jewish population, and the killing continued into the closing months of the war. The Nazis murdered other people, as well, including labor leaders, political opponents, communists, gypsies, and homosexuals, but Jews were always their primary target, and it was to kill Jews that they established the Einsatzgruppen, death camps, and the rest of their infrastructure of genocide.

As they advanced into Poland and Germany in late 1944 and 1945, Allied soldiers were horrified by their discoveries of concentration camps and death camps, among them Harold Porter who described the liberation of Dachau (Document 10).

1

Reich Citizenship Laws

I. The Reich Citizenship Law of September 15, 1935

The Reichstag has unanimously adopted the following law, which is herewith promulgated.

§ 1. (1) A subject of the State is a person who belongs to the protective union of the German Reich, and who therefore has particular obligations towards the Reich.

(2) The status of subject is acquired in accordance with the provisions of the Reich and State Law of Citizenship.

§ 2. (1) A citizen of the Reich is only that subject who is of German or kindred blood and who, through his conduct, shows that he is both willing and able to faithfully serve the German people and Reich.

(2) The right to citizenship is acquired by the granting of Reich citizenship papers.

(3) Only the citizen of the Reich enjoys full political rights in accordance with the provision of the law.

Source: http://germanhistorydocs.ghi-dc.org/sub_document.cfm?document_id=1523

§ 3. The Reich Minister of the Interior in conjunction with the Deputy of the Fu''hrer will issue the necessary legal and administrative decrees for implementing and supplementing this law.
Nuremberg, September 15, 1935
The Führer and Reich Chancellor Adolf Hitler
The Reich Minister of the Interior Frick

II. First Regulation to the Reich Citizenship Law of November 14, 1935

On the basis of § 3, Reich Citizenship Law, of September 15, 1935 (RGBl [Reich Law Gazette] I, page 1146) the following is ordered:

§ 1. (1) Until further regulations regarding citizenship papers are issued, all subjects of German or kindred blood who possessed the right to vote in Reichstag elections at the time the Citizenship Law came into effect shall, for the time being, possess the rights of Reich citizens. The same shall be true of those to whom the Reich Minister of the Interior, in conjunction with the Deputy of the Führer, has given preliminary citizenship.
(2) The Reich Minister of the Interior, in conjunction with the Deputy of the Fu''hrer, can withdraw preliminary citizenship.

§ 2. (1) The regulations in § I are also valid for Reich subjects of mixed Jewish blood [Mischlinge].
(2) An individual of mixed Jewish blood is one who is descended from one or two grandparents who were fully Jewish by race, insofar as he or she does not count as a Jew according to § 5, Paragraph 2. One grandparent shall be considered as full-blooded if he or she belonged to the Jewish religious community.

§ 3. Only the Reich citizen, as bearer of full political rights, exercises the right to vote in political affairs or can hold public office. The Reich Minister of the Interior, or any agency empowered by him, can make exceptions during the transition period, with regard to occupying public offices. The affairs of religious organizations will not be affected.

§ 4. (1) A Jew cannot be a citizen of the Reich. He has no right to vote in political affairs, he cannot occupy a public office.
(2) Jewish civil servants will retire as of 31. December 1935. If these civil servants served at the front in the World War, either for Germany or her

allies, they will receive in full, until they reach the age limit, full pension to which they were entitled according to the last salary they received; they will, however, not advance in seniority. After reaching the age limit, their pensions will be calculated anew, according to the last salary they received, on the basis of which their pension was calculated.

(3) The affairs of religious organizations will not be affected.

(4) The employment status of teachers in Jewish public schools remains unchanged until new regulations for the Jewish school systems are issued.

§ 5. (1) A Jew is anyone who descended from at least three grandparents who were fully Jewish by race. § 2, par. 2, second sentence will apply.

(2) A Jew is also anyone who descended from two fully Jewish grandparents, if:

   (a) he belonged to the Jewish religious community at the time this law was issued or joined the community later;

   (b) he was married to a Jewish person at the time the law was issued or married one subsequently;

   (c) he is the offspring from a marriage with a Jew, in the sense of Section 1, which was contracted after the Law for the Protection of German Blood and German Honor became effective (RGBl. [Reich Law Gazette] I, page 1146 of September 15, 1935);

   (d) he is the offspring of an extramarital relationship with a Jew, according to Section 1, and will be born out of wedlock after July 31, 1936.

§ 6. (1) In case Reich laws or orders by the NSDAP and its organizations make demands for racial pureness that exceed § 5, they will not be affected.

(2) Any other demands for pureness of blood that exceed § 5 can only be made with permission from the Reich Minister of the Interior and the Deputy of the Führer. If any such demands have been made, they will be void as of January 1, 1936, if they have not been requested from the Reich Minister of the Interior in agreement with the Deputy of the Führer. These requests must be made to the Reich Minister of the Interior.

§ 7. The Führer and Reich Chancellor can grant exemptions from the regulations laid down in the law.

Berlin, November 14, 1935

The Führer and Reich Chancellor Adolf Hitler

The Reich Minister of the Interior Frick

The Deputy of the Führer

R. Hess (Reich Minister without Portfolio)

2

Hitler Orders Euthanasia Program

(Signed in October, backdated to September 1, 1939)

Hitler authorized his personal physician **Dr. Karl Brandt** (1904–1948) and the head of his Chancellery Phillip Bouhler (1899–1945) to introduce the so-called Children's Euthanasia in early 1939. This authorization was probably given only verbally. At least 5,000 children and infants with hereditary diseases or physical and mental disabilities fell victim to this state-organized killing initiative. In July of the same year, Hitler asked Brandt and Bouhler to develop a similar program for adult patients, a program that would eliminate "life not worth living." The following order, which Hitler signed in October 1939 and backdated to the beginning of the war, constitutes the official written authorization for Bouhler and Brandt to carry out the program of murder.

Berlin, 1. September 1939

Reichsleiter Bouhler and Dr. Brandt, M.D. are charged with the responsibility of enlarging the authority of certain physicians to be designated by name in such a manner that persons who, according to human judgment, are incurable can, upon a most careful diagnosis of their condition of sickness, be accorded a mercy death.

(signed) A. Hitler

Source: http://germanhistorydocs.ghi-dc.org/sub_document.cfm?document_id=1528

3

COMMISSAR ORDER

DIRECTIVES FOR THE TREATMENT OF POLITICAL COMMISSARS

JUNE 6, 1941

High Command of the Armed Forces WFSt. (Armed Forces Operational Staff) Department L (IV Q) ("Intelligence")

No 44822/41 Top Secret for general officers only

Fuehrer Headquarters, 6 June 1941

In addition to the Fuehrer's decree of 14 May regarding Military jurisdiction in the "Barbarossa" zone (Supreme Command of the Armed Forces/Armed Forces Operational Staff/Department L (IV Q) (Intelligence) No 44718/41, (Top Secret, for General Officers only), the enclosed "directives for the treatment of political commissars" are being transmitted herewith:

You are requested to limit the distribution to Commanders in Chief of Armies or of Air Commands, respectively, and to inform the Junior commanders by word of mouth.

The Chief of the Supreme Command Of the Armed Forces

By Order.

Signed: Warlimont

Source: http://germanhistorydocs.ghi-dc.org/sub_document.cfm?document_id=1548

1

Enclosure to Supreme Command of the Armed Forces/Department L IV Q (Intelligence) No. 44822/41 Top Secret

For General Officers only.

Directives for the treatment of political commissars.

When fighting Bolshevism one can not count on the enemy acting in accordance with the principles of humanity or International Law. In particular it must be expected that the treatment of our prisoners by the political commissars of all types who are the true pillars of resistance, will be cruel, inhuman and dictated by hate.

The troops must realize:

1. That in this fight it is wrong to trust such elements with clemency and consideration in accordance with International Law. They are a menace to our own safety and to the rapid pacification of the conquered territories.
2. That the originators of the asiatic-barbaric methods of fighting are the political commissars. They must be dealt with promptly and with the utmost severity.

Therefore, if taken while fighting or offering resistance they must, on principle, be shot immediately.

For the rest, the following instructions will apply:

I. Theatre of Operations.

1. Political commissars who oppose our troops will be dealt with in accordance with the "decree concerning jurisdiction in the "Barbarossa" area". This applies to commissars of any type and position, even if they are only suspected of resistance, sabotage or instigation thereto. Reference is made to "Directives on the behavior of troops in Russia."
2. Political commissars in their capacity of officials attached to the enemy troops are recognizable by their special insignia—red star with an inwoven golden hammer and sickle on the sleeves—[...]. They are to be segregated at once, i.e. while still on the battlefield, from the prisoners of war. This is necessary in order to deprive them of any possibility of influencing the captured soldiers. Those commissars will not be recognized as soldiers; the protection granted to prisoners of war in accordance with International Law will not apply to them. After having been segregated they are to be dealt with.

3. Political commissars who are not guilty of any hostile act or are not suspected of such will remain unmolested for the time being. Only in the course of a deeper penetration into the country will it be possible to decide whether they are, or should be handed over to the "Sonderkommandos". The latter should preferably scrutinize these cases themselves.

As a matter of principle, when deliberating the question of "guilty or not guilty", the personal impression received of the commissar's outlook and attitude should be considered of greater importance than the facts of the case which may not be decisive.

2

4. In cases 1) and 2) a brief report (report form) on the incident is to be submitted:

    a.   to the Division (Ic) (Field Intelligence Officer) by troops subordinated to a Division.

    b.   to the Corps Command or other respective Commands, as follows (Ic) by troops directly subordinated to a Corps Command, an Army High Command or the Command or an Army group, or Armored Group.

5. None of the above mentioned measures must delay the progress of operations. Combat troops should therefore refrain from systematic rounding-up and cleansing measures.

II. In the Rear Areas.

Commissars arrested in the rear area on account of doubtful behavior are to be handed over to the "Einsatzgruppe" or the "Einsatzkommandos" of the SS Security Service (SD) respectively.

III. Restriction with regard to Court Martials and Summary Courts.

The Court Martials and Summary Courts of regimental and other commanders must not be entrusted with the carrying out of the measures as under I and II.

4

"THE JEWS ARE TO BLAME"

DAS REICH

NOVEMBER 16, 1941

The historical guilt of world Jewry for the outbreak and extension of the war is so clearly proven that there is no point in wasting words on it. The Jews wanted war, and now they have it. But now they are feeling the effects of the prophesy which the Führer made on 30 January 1939 in the German Reichstag that, if international finance Jewry should succeed in plunging the nations once again into a world war, the result would not be the Bolshevization of the world and consequently the victory of Jewry, but the annihilation of the Jewish race in Europe.

We are now experiencing the implementation of this prophecy and in the process the Jews suffering a fate which, while harsh, is more than earned. Sympathy, let alone regret, is entirely inappropriate in this case. In provoking this war, World Jewry has completely miscalculated the forces at its disposal and its now experiencing a gradual process of annihilation which it intended us to suffer and would inflict on us without any qualms if it had the power to do so. It is now heading for destruction on the basis of its own law: "An eye for an eye, a tooth for a tooth."

In this historic confrontation, every Jew is our enemy irrespective of whether he is vegetating in a Polish ghetto or is continuing his parasitic existence in Berlin or Hamburg or is blowing a war trumpet in New York or Washington. All Jews are part of an international conspiracy against national socialist Germany on the basis of their birth and race. They desire its defeat and destruction, and are doing whatever is in their power to bring this about. The fact that in the Reich itself they have few opportunities to do so is not a result of the fact that they are loyal but is entirely due to the fact that we have taken what seemed to us the appropriate measures to prevent it.

One of these measures is the introduction of the yellow Jewish star which every Jew has to wear so that it is visible. Through this we wanted to mark them out above all so that, in the event of the slightest attempt to offend against the German national community, they could be instantly recognized as Jews. It is an extraordinarily humane regulation, so to speak, a hygienic and prophylactic measure that is intended to prevent the Jews from slipping into our ranks unrecognizable in order to provoke discord.

When a few weeks ago the Jews appeared on the Berlin street scene adorned with their Jewish star, the first impression of the citizens of the Reich capital was one of general surprise. Only very few people knew there were so many Jews in Berlin. Everyone discovered among their acquaintance if their neighborhood someone who appeared to be harmless, who may have stood our by their periodic grumbling and complaining, but nobody would have imagined he was Jewish. He had evidently disguised himself, made the right gestures, adapted himself to the milieu in which lived and awaited his moment. Which of us had the slightest idea that the enemy was standing right next to him, that he was quietly listening in to conversations on the street, in the subway, or in the queues in front of tobacconists or cleverly inciting people? There are Jews who one can hardly recognize as Jews from their outward appearance. Here too they have adapted themselves as far as they can. These are the most dangerous ones. It's typical that every measure that we take against the Jews is reported the following day in the English or American press. So the Jews still have secret contacts with the enemy and make use of them not only in their own interests but in all matters of military importance to the Reich. So the enemy is amongst us. Is it not then obvious that we should make sure that every citizen can recognize him?

* * *

Therefore, let me repeat for the nth time:

1. The Jews are aiming to destroy us. They have provoked and brought about this war. They want to use it to destroy the German Reich and our people. This plan must be thwarted.

2. There are no difference between Jews. Every Jew is a sworn enemy of the German people. If he does not show his enmity toward us that is only through cowardice or cunning, and not because he is not an enemy at heart.

3. The Jews bear the guilt for every German soldier killed in this war. They have him on their conscience, and must therefore pay for it.

4. If someone wears the Jewish star then he is marked out as an enemy of the people. Anyone who maintains social contact with him and belongs to him and must be considered and treated as a Jew. He deserves the contempt of the whole nation which he is abandoning in its darkest hour in order to be on the same side as those who hate it.

5. The Jews enjoy the protection of our enemies abroad. There is no further proof needed of their destructive role in our nation.

6. The Jews are the envoys of our enemies among us. Anyone who supports them has gone over to the enemy.

7. The Jews have no right to prance around among us on an equal footing. Wherever they seek to make their views known on the streets, in queues in front of shops, on public transport they should be told to keep quiet not only because their views are fundamentally wrong but because they are Jews and have no right to a voice in the affairs of the community.

8. If the Jews try to appeal to your sympathy you should be aware that they are relying on your forgetfulness; show them at once that you have seen through them and punish them with your contempt.

9. A decent enemy deserves our magnanimity on defeat. But the Jew is not a decent enemy; he only pretends to be one.

10. The Jews are guilty for the war. They do not suffer an injustice through out treatment of them. They have more than earned it.

It is a matter for the government to deal with them. No one has the right to act off his own bat, but everyone has the duty to respect the state's measures against the Jews, to give them their support and not to allow themselves to led astray by the Jews by any tricks or subterfuges they may use.

The security of the state requires this of us all.

5

The Deportation of Jews to the Reichskommissariat Ostland

November 18, 1941

Stuttgart Gestapo Branch Office Directive to the Police Chiefs of Würtemburg

1. Within the frame of the de-jewifying of the whole of Europe, railway transports contained 1,000 Jews each are at present leaving from Germany, the *Ostmark* [Austria] and the Protectorate of Bohemia and Moravia for the *Reichskommissariat Ostland*. Würtemburg and Hohenzollern are participating initially with a transport of 1,000 Jews which will leave Stuttgart on 1 December 1941.

2. Those Jews involved have already been selected and registered here. They were selected in accordance with Section 5 of the first supplementary decree of the Reich Citizenship Law of 14 November 1935. ... The following were exempted:

    a. Jews living in German-Jewish mixed marriages.

    b. Jews of foreign nationality.

    c. Jews over 65 years of age.

* * *

"The Deportation of Jews to the Reichskommissariat Ostland," *Nazism 1919-1945, Volume 3: Foreign Policy: War and Racial Extermination: A Documentary Reader*, ed. and trans. Jeremy Noakes and Geoffrey Pridham, pp. 521-523. Copyright © 2001 by Liverpool University Press. Reprinted with permission.

3. The train scheduled for transporting the Jews is timetabled to leave Stuttgart on 1 December 1941 between 8 and 9 o'clock.

   The Jews who are to be evacuated from Stuttgart itself as well as from the country areas will be concentrated in a transit camp in the grounds of the former Reich Garden Show in Stuttgart from 27 November onwards.

4. Each person may take with them:
   a. Money up to 50 RM [Reichmarks] in Reich credit notes. This money will be supplied from here so in practice Jews should not bring any money with them on their journey here.
   b. 1 or 2 cases (no bulky goods). This luggage may not weigh more than 50 kg.
   c. Bedding consisting of 1–2 blankets, 2 sheets and 1 mattress for two people (but without bolster).
   d. A complete set of clothing (particularly warm underwear and decent shoes).
   e. Food for 1–2 days. We have already seen to the further adequate provisioning of all participants in the transport.
   f. Crockery (a plate or pot with a spoon).

* * *

6. To prevent fraudulent transfers, the entire property of the Jews being deported will be confiscated by the police. ...

* * *

8. Your task, therefore, is to collect the Jews together at the proper time, to secure their property in cooperation with their financial authorities, to seal their dwellings and if necessary appoint caretakers, search the Jews' persons and their luggage and, deploying an appropriate number of officers, to deliver the Jews on 27 or 28 November 1941 to the camp in Stuttgart. ...

6

WANNSEE PROTOCOL

JANUARY 20, 1942

On July 31, 1941, Hermann Goring (1893–1946), ordered by Hitler, assigned Reinhard Heydrich (1904–1942), head of the Reich Security Main Office, to draw up a plan for the "final solution of the Jewish question." Heydrich's Special Operations Units [*Einsatzgruppen*] had already murdered tens of thousands of Jews in mass shootings on the Eastern Front. They sought more efficient methods for eliminating Europe's Jewish population of about 11 million. ... To accelerate the future deportation and murder of the European Jews and to coordinate the efforts of the state and party offices involved, Heydrich hosted a secret conference on January 20, 1942. It was held in Berlin at a Wannsee villa used by the Reich Security Main Office as a guest house and conference center. ... The protocol of the conference was recorded by Adolf Eichmann (1906–1962), who concealed the planned genocide behind a series of euphemisms.

The protocol was discovered in Berlin in 1947 by Robert Kempner, assistant U.S. chief counsel in the Nuremberg Trials. A year later, it was used as important piece of evidence in the trial against the leading officials of the ministries.

Stamp: Top Secret

Minutes of discussion.

Source: http://germanhistorydocs.ghi-dc.org/sub_document.cfm?document_id=1532

I. The following persons took part in the discussion about the final solution of the Jewish question which took place in Berlin, am Grossen Wannsee No. 56/58 on 20 January 1942.

Gauleiter Dr. MEYER and Reichsamtsleiter Dr. LEIBBRANDT
Reich Ministry for the Occupied Eastern territories
Secretary of State Dr. STUCKART
Secretary of State NEUMANN
Secretary of State Dr. Freisler
Secretary of State Dr. Bühler
Under Secretary of State Luther
SS-Oberfuehrer KLOPFER
Ministerialdirektor KRITZINGER
SS-Gruppenfuehrer HOFMANN
SS-Gruppenfuehrer MUELLER
SS-Obersturmbannfuehrer EICHMANN
SS-Oberfuehrer Dr. SCHOENGARTH Chief of the Security Police and the SD in the Government General
SS-Sturmbannfuehrer Dr. LANGE Commander of the Security Police and the SD for the General district Latvia, as deputy of the Commander of the Security Police and the SD for the Reich Commissariat "Eastland".

* * *

II. At the beginning of the discussion SS-Obergruppenfuehrer HEYDRICH gave information that the Reich Marshal had appointed him delegate for the preparations for the final solution of the Jewish problem in Europe and pointed out that this discussion had been called for the purpose of clarifying fundamental questions. ...

He said that the Reich Fuehrer-SS and the Chief of the German Police (Chief of the Security Police and the SD) was entrusted with the official handling of the final solution of the Jewish problem centrally without regard to geographic borders.

The Chief of the Security Police and the SD then gave a short report of the struggle which has been carried on against this enemy, the essential points being the following:

a. the expulsion of the Jews from every particular sphere of life of the German people,

   b.   the expulsion of the Jews from the Lebensraum of the German people.

In carrying out these efforts, an increased and planned acceleration of the emigration of Jews from the Reich territory was started, as the only possible present solution.

   By order of the Reich Marshal a Reich Central Office for Jewish emigration was set up in January 1939 and the Chief of the Security Police and SD was entrusted with the management. Its most important tasks were

   a.   to make all necessary arrangements for the preparation for an increased emigration of the Jews,

   b.   to direct the flow of immigration,

   c.   to hurry up the procedure of emigration in each individual case.

The aim of all this being that of clearing the German Lebensraum of Jews in a legal way.

   ... 537 000 Jews were sent out of the country between the day of the seizure of power and the deadline 31 October 1941. ...

* * *

III. Another possible solution of the problem has now taken the place of emigration, i.e. the evacuation of the Jews to the East, provided the Fuehrer agrees to this plan.

   Such activities are, however, to be considered as provisional actions, but practical experience is already being collected which is of greatest importance in relation to the future final solution of the Jewish problem.

   Approx. 11,000,000 Jews will be involved in this final solution of the European problem.

* * *

Under proper guidance the Jews are now to be allocated for labor to the East in the course of the final solution. Able-bodied Jews will be taken in large labor columns to these districts for work on roads, separated according to sexes, in the course of which action a great part will undoubtedly be eliminated by natural causes.

   The possible final remnant will, as it must undoubtedly consist of the toughest, have to be treated accordingly, as it is the product of natural selection, and would, if liberated, act as a bud cell of a Jewish reconstruction (see historical experience).

In the course of the practical execution of this final settlement of the problem, Europe will be cleaned up from the West to the East. Germany proper, including the protectorate Bohemia and Moravia, will have to be handled first because of reasons of housing and other social—political necessities.

The evacuated Jews will first be sent, group by group, into so-called transit-ghettos from which they will be taken to the East.

SS-Obergruppenfuehrer HEYDRICH went on to say that an important provision for the evacuation as such is the exact definition of the group of persons concerned in the matter.

* * *

In Slovakia and Croatia the difficulties arising from this question have been considerably reduced, as the most essential problems in this field have already been brought near to a solution. In Rumania the Government in the meantime has also appointed a commissioner for Jewish questions. In order to settle the question in Hungary it is imperative that an adviser in Jewish questions be pressed upon the Hungarian government without too much delay.

As regards the taking of preparatory steps to settle the question in Italy SS—Obergruppenfuehrer HEYDRICH considers it opportune to contact the chief of the police with a view to these problems.

In the occupied and unoccupied parts of France the registration of the Jews for evacuation can in all probability be expected to take place without great difficulties.

Assistant Under Secretary of State LUTHER in this connection calls attention to the fact that in some countries, such as the Scandinavian states, difficulties will arise if these problems are dealt with thoroughly and that it will be therefore advisable to defer action in these countries. Besides, considering the small numbers of Jews to be evacuated from these countries this deferment means not essential limitation.

On the other hand, the Foreign Office anticipates no great difficulties as far as the South—East and the West of Europe are concerned.

* * *

IV. The implementation of the final solution-problem is supposed to a certain extent to be based on the Nuernberg Laws, in which connection also the solution of the problems presented by the mixed-marriages and the persons of mixed blood is seen to be conditional to an absolutely final clarification of the question.

* * *

Under Secretary of State Dr. BUEHLER stated that it would be welcomed by the Government General [the German occupation authority governing most of Poland] most if the implementation of the final solution of this question could start in the Government General, because the transportation problem there was of no predominant importance and the progress of this action would not be hampered by considerations connected with the supply of labor. The Jews had to be removed as quickly as possible from the territory of the Government General because especially there the Jews represented an immense danger as a carrier of epidemics, and on the other hand were permanently contributing to the disorganization of the economic system of the country through black market operations. Moreover, out of the two and a half million Jews to be affected, the majority of cases was unfit for work.

* * *

Towards the end of the conference the various types of possible solutions were discussed; in the course of this discussion Gauleiter Dr. MEYER as well as Under Secretary of State Dr. BUEHLER advocated the view that certain preparatory measures incidental to the carrying out of the final solution ought to be initiated immediately in the very territories under discussion, in which process, however, alarming the population must be avoided.

With the request to the persons present from the Chief of the Security Police and the SD that they lend him appropriate assistance in the carrying out of the tasks involved in the solution, the conference was adjourned.

7

EXTRACT FROM THE DIARY OF STANISLAV ROZYCKI ON CONDITIONS IN WARSAW GHETTO

1941 OR 1942

The majority are nightmare figures, ghosts of former human beings, miserable destitutes, pathetic remains of former humanity. One if most affected by the characteristic changes which ones sees in their faces: as a result of misery, poor nourishment, the lack vitamins, fresh air, and exercise, the numerous cares, worries, anticipated misfortunes, suffering and sickness, their faces have taken on a skeletal appearance. The prominent bones around their eye sockets, the yellow facial color, the slack pendulous skin, the alarming emaciation and sickliness. And, in addition, this miserable frightened, restless, apathetic and resigned expression like that of a hunted animal. I pass my closest friends without recognizing them and guessing their fate. Many of them recognize me, come up to me and ask curiously how things are "over there" behind the walls—there where there is enough bread, fresh air, freedom to move around, and above all freedom. ...

On the streets children are crying in vain, children who are dying of hunger. They howl, beg, sing, moan, shiver with cold, without underwear, without clothing, without shoes, in rags, sacks, flannel which are bound in strips round the emaciated skeletons, children swollen with hunger, disfigured, half conscious, already completely grown-up at the age of live, gloomy and weary of life. They are like old people and are only conscious of one thing: 'I'm cold', 'I'm hungry'. They have become aware of the most important things in life that quickly. Through their innocent sacrifice and their frightening helplessness the thousands upon thousands of these little beggars level the main accusation against the proud civilization of today. Ten percent of the new generation have already perished: every day and every night hundred of these children die and there is no hope that anybody will put a stop to it.

There are not only children. Young and old people, men and women, bourgeois and proletarians, intelligentsia and business people are all being declassed and degraded They are being gobbled up by the streets on to which they are brutally and ruthlessly thrown. They beg for one month, for two months, for three months—but they all go downhill and die on the street or in hospitals from cold, or hunger, or sickness, or depression. Former human beings whom no one needs fall by the wayside: former citizens, former 'useful members of human society.

I no longer look at people; when I hear groaning and sobbing I go over to the other side of the road; when I see something wrapped in rags shivering with cold stretched out on the ground. I turn away and do not want to look I can't. It's become too much for me. And yet only an hour has passed ...

For various reasons standards of hygiene are terribly poor. Above all, the fearful population density in the streets with which nowhere in Europe can be remotely compared. The fatal over-population is particularly apparent in the streets: people literally rub against each other, it is impossible to pass unhindered through the streets. And then the lack of light, gas, and heating materials. Water consumption is also much reduced; people wash themselves much less and do not have baths or hot water. There are no green spaces, gardens, parks: no clumps of trees and no lawns to be seen. For a year no one has seen a village, a wood, a field, a river or mountain: no one has breathed slightly better air for even a few days this year. Bedding and clothing are changed very rarely because of the lack of soap. To speak of food hygiene would be a provocation and would be regarded as mockery. People eat what is available, however much is available and when it is available. Other principles of nutrition are unknown here. Having said all this, one can easily draw one's own conclusions as to the consequences: stomach typhus and typhus, dysentery, tuberculosis, pneumonia, influenza, metabolic disturbances, the most common digestive illnesses, lack of vitamins and all other illnesses associated with the lack of bread, fresh air, clothing, and heating materials. Typhus is systematically and continually destroying the population. There are victims in every family. On average up to a thousand people are dying each month. In the early morning the corpses of beggars, children, old people, young people and women are lying in every street—the victims of the hunger and the cold. The hospitals are so terribly overcrowded that there are 2–3 patients lying in every bed. Those who do not find a place in a bed lie on the floor in rooms and corridors. The shortage of the necessary medicines in sufficient quantities makes it impossible to treat the sick. Moreover, there is a shortage of food for the sick. There is only soup and tea.

While this cruel struggle for a little bit of bread, for a few meters of living space, for the maintenance of health, energy and life is going on, people are incapable of devoting much energy and strength to intellectual matters. In any case, there are German restrictions and bans. Nothing can be printed, taught or learnt. People are not allowed to organize themselves or exchange cultural possessions. We are cut off from the world and from books. It is not permitted to open libraries and sort out books from other printed materials. We are not allowed to print anything, neither books nor newspapers schools, academic institutions etc. are not permitted to open. There are no cinemas, radio, no contacts with world culture. Nothing reaches us, no products of the human spirit reach us. We have to smuggle is not only foodstuffs and manufactured goods, but also cultural products. For that reason everything which we achieve in this respect is worthy of recognition irrespective of how much there is or what it consists of ...

8

SPEECH ON NECESSITY OF EXTERMINATION

OCTOBER 4, 1943

EXCERPT FROM HEINRICH HIMMLER'S SPEECH TO THE

SS-GRUPPENFÜHRER AT POSEN

In 1941 ... The Russian Army was herded together in great pockets, ground down, taken prisoner. At the time, we did not value the mass of humanity as we value it today: as raw material, as labor. The fact that prisoners died of exhaustion and hunger in tens and hundreds of thousands is by no means regrettable from the standpoint of lost generations but is deplorable now for reasons of lost labor.

* * *

It is basically wrong for us to infuse all our inoffensive soul and spirit, our good nature, and our idealism into foreign peoples. ...

One basic principle must be the absolute rule for the SS man: we must be honest, decent, loyal and comradely to members of our own blood and to nobody else. What happens to a Russian, to a Czech does not interest me in the slightest. What the nations can offer in the way of good blood of our type, we will take, if necessary by kidnapping their children and raising them here with us. Whether nations live in prosperity or starve to death interests me only in so far as we need them as slaves for our Kultur; otherwise, it is of no interest to me. Whether 10,000 Russian females fall down from exhaustion while digging an anti-tank ditch interests me only in so far as the anti-tank

Heinrich Himmler, "Speech on Necessity of Extermination," 1943, pp. 1-4. 1943.

ditch for Germany is finished. We shall never be rough and heartless when it is not necessary, that is clear. We Germans, who are the only people in the world who have a decent attitude towards animals, will also assume a decent attitude towards these human animals. But it is a crime against our own blood to worry about them and give them ideals, thus causing our sons and grandsons to have a more difficult time with them. When somebody comes to me and says, "I cannot dig the anti-tank ditch with women and children, it is inhuman, for it would kill them," then I have to say, "You are a murderer of your own blood because if the anti-tank ditch is not dug, German soldiers will die, and they are sons of German mothers. They are our own blood." That is what I want to instill into the SS and what I believe have instilled into them as one of the most sacred laws of the future. Our concern, our duty is our people and our blood. It is for them that we must provide and plan, work and fight, nothing else. We can be indifferent to everything else. I wish the SS to adopt this attitude to the problem of all foreign, non-Germanic peoples, especially Russians. All else is vain, fraud against our own nation and an obstacle to the early winning of the war.

* * *

When the war is won,—then, as I have already told you, our work will start. ...

If the peace is a final one, we shall be able to tackle our great work of the future. We shall colonize. We shall indoctrinate our boys with the laws of the SS-organization. ... it must be a matter of course that we have children. It must be a matter or course that the most copious breeding should be from this racial super-stratum of the German people. In 20 to 30 years we must really be able to present the whole of Europe with its leading class. If the SS ... run the colony in the East on a grand scale, without any restraint ...

... I hope that our generation will successfully bring it about that every age-group has fought in the East and that every one of our divisions spends a winter in the East every second or third year. Then we never grow soft; then we shall never get SS members who only come to us because it is distinguished or because the black coat will naturally be very attractive in peacetime. Every-one will know that: "If I join the SS, there is the possibility that I might be killed." ... Then we will have a healthy elite for all time. Thus we will create the necessary conditions for the whole Germanic people and the whole of Europe, controlled, ordered and led by us, the Germanic people, to be able, in generations, to stand the test in her battles of destiny against Asia, who will certainly break out again. ...

9

KORHERR REPORT ON NUMBER OF JEWS KILLED

1943

X. BALANCE SHEET FOR THE JEWS IN EUROPE

The total number of Jews in the world was estimated in 1937 in general at around 17 million, of which more than 10 million are found in Europe. They are or were concentrated in Europe especially in the former Polish-Russian territories occupied by Germany between the Baltic Sea and the Gulf of Finland and the Black Sea and the Sea of Azov, as well as in the trading centers and in the Rhine region of central and western Europe and along the coasts of the Mediterranean.

Between 1937 and the beginning of 1943, the number of Jews in Europe is likely to have declined by an estimated 4 million, in part through emigration, in part through excess mortality of the Jews in central and western Europe, in part through the evacuations especially in the völkisch stronger eastern territories, which are calculated here as departure. One must not overlook that only a part of the deaths of Soviet Russian Jews in the occupied eastern territories are recorded here, while those in the rest of European Russia and on the front are not included at all. To this must be added migration streams (unknown to us) of the Jews within Russia into the Asiatic region. The stream of emigration of the Jews out of the European countries outside of German influence is also a largely unknown quantity. All in all, it is likely that since 1933, that is to say, in the first decade of the National Socialist German Machtergreifung, European Jewry is likely to have lost close to half of its numbers.

10

LETTER FROM U. S. SOLDIER HAROLD PORTER ON DAUCHAU

MAY 7, 1945

D ear Mother and Father,

You have, by this time, received a letter mentioning that I am quartered in the concentration camp at Dachau. It is still undecided whether we will be permitted to describe the conditions here, but I'm writing this now to tell you a little, and will mail it later when we are told we can.

It is difficult to know how to begin. By this time I have recovered from my first emotional shock and am able to write without seeming like a hysterical gibbering idiot. Yet, I know you will hesitate to believe me no matter how objective and focused I try to be. I even find myself trying to deny what I am looking at with my own eyes. Certainly, what I have seen in the past few days will affect my personality for the rest of my life.

We knew a day or two before we moved that we were going to operate in Dachau, and that it was the location of one of the most notorious concentration camps, but while we expected things to be grizzly [sic], I'm sure none of us knew what was coming. It is easy to read about atrocities, but they must be seen before they can be believed. To think that I once scoffed at Valtin's book *Out of the Night* as being preposterous! I've seen worse sights than he described.

The trip south from Göttingen was pleasant enough. We passed through Donauworth and Aichach and as we entered Dachau, the country, with the

Source: http://www.archives.gov/exhibits/eyewitness/html.php?section=7

cottages, rivers, country estates and Alps in the distance, was almost like a tourist resort. But as we came to the center of the city, we met a train with a wrecked engine—about fifty cars long. Every car was loaded with bodies. There must have been thousands of them—all obviously starved to death. This was a shock of the first order, and the odor can best be imagined. But neither the sight nor the odor were anything when compared with what we were still to see.

Marc Coyle reached the camp two days before I did and was a guard so as soon as I got there I looked him up and he took me to the crematory. Dead SS troopers were scattered around the grounds, but when we reached the furnace house we came upon a huge stack of corpses piled up like kindling, all nude so that their clothes wouldn't be wasted by the burning. There were furnaces for burning six bodies at once, and on each side of them was a room twenty feet square crammed to the ceiling with more bodies—one big stinking rotten mess. Their faces purple, their eyes popping, and with a hideous grin on each one. They were nothing but bones & skins. Coyle had assisted at ten autopsies the day before (wearing a gas mask) on ten bodies selected at random. Eight of them had advanced T.B., all had typhus and extreme malnutrition symptoms. There were both women and children in the stack in addition to the men.

* * *

Behind the furnaces was the execution chamber, a windowless cell twenty feet square with gas nozzles every few feet across the ceiling. Outside, in addition to a huge mound of charred bone fragments, were the carefully sorted and stacked clothes of the victims—which obviously numbered in the thousands. Although I stood there looking at it, I couldn't believe it. The realness of the whole mess is just gradually dawning on me, and I doubt if it ever will on you.

There is a rumor circulating which says that the war is over. It probably is—as much as it will ever be. ... There was no celebration—it's difficult to celebrate anything with the morbid state we're in.

The Pacific theater will not come immediately for this unit; we have around 36,000 potential and eventual patients here. The end of the work for everyone else is going to be just the beginning for us.

Today was a scorching hot day after several raining cold ones. The result of the heat on the corpses is impossible to describe, and the situation will probably get worse because their disposal will certainly take time.

My arm is sore from a typhus shot so I'm ending here for the present. More will follow later. I have lots to write about now.

Love,

Harold

CHAPTER 6

THE MEDITERRANEAN: NORTH AFRICA, SICILY, AND ITALY

Introduction

This chapter looks at the war in the Mediterranean, North Africa, and Italy from 1940 to the end of the war. Italy under Benito Mussolini entered the war on Germany's side on June 10, 1940, during the last stages of the Battle of France. A small Italian offensive on the border with France failed to gain any ground but at least Mussolini was on the winning side when France fell to Germany. Otherwise the main theater of action for the Italian army was North Africa. Italian forces in Libya soon found themselves in trouble against the British Eighth Army, based in Egypt. Adolf Hitler was obliged to send the German Afrika Korps, under the command of the talented Field Marshal Erwin Rommel to shore up his Italian allies in February 1941. Hitler believed, probably correctly, that the Axis powers did not have the logistical capabilities to conquer Egypt and take the Suez Canal. Italian supply convoys crossing the Mediterranean came under attack from British submarines, surface ships, and air power. Supply trucks moving across the North African desert likewise came under British air attack. To deliver supplies and fuel to front line units, vast amounts of fuel had to be consumed by the supply trucks. Therefore, an enormous logistical effort by the Axis powers in North Africa and the Mediterranean produced a relatively small result at the front. But Rommel was a capable general and by early 1942 the Afrika Korps and its Italian allies were approaching a British defensive position anchored at El Alamein, less than 200 miles west of Cairo. Here the Axis powers were finally stopped.

In mid-August 1942, Winston Churchill appointed General Bernard Montgomery to command the British Eighth Army. Montgomery, or Monty as he came to be known, gained a reputation for being difficult and vainglorious, but he reorganized British defenses and raised the morale of the Eighth Army. Montgomery had the confidence of Churchill and was able to funnel scarce reinforcements and supplies to Egypt. In October 1942, the Eighth Army defeated the depleted Afrika Korps and its Italian allies at the Battle of El Alamein (see Chapter 7), regarded as one of the turning points of the Second World War. In the excerpt from Montgomery's memoir, written after the war (Document 1), what does Montgomery regard as the key to rallying the morale of his troops?

Tank warfare was a major feature of combat in the Second World War. Great tank battles raged across the Eastern front, Western Europe, and, of course, North Africa. British tanker Keith Douglas describes his first-hand experience (Document 2) with tank warfare.

Following defeat at El Alamein, Rommel was forced to retreat the entire distance across North Africa to Tunisia. It proved impossible to form a defensive line in Libya due to the constant danger of being outflanked to the landward side. British resources and air power proved overwhelming. Rommel's retreat was made more urgent by Operation Torch, which began on November 8, 1942. British and American troops landed in Vichy-French controlled Algeria and Morocco, threatening to cut off Rommel from the rear. Although Vichy French forces were quickly subdued, the Allies had landed too far to the west, and Rommel consolidated a defensive position in Tunisia. A prolonged campaign followed over the winter of 1942–1943, featuring a severe American defeat at the Battle of Kasserine Pass, February 1943. The message from Churchill and U.S. president Franklin D. Roosevelt to Soviet premier Joseph Stalin (Document 3) details what went wrong with the hopes raised by Operation Torch. What do you think is the purpose of this message? What does the last sentence tell you about the role of the Eastern front? The remaining Axis armies in Tunisia finally surrendered on May 3, 1943, but only after Rommel had escaped.

The Allies were now free to invade Italy, and on July 9, 1943, British, Canadian, and American troops landed in Sicily (code named Operation Husky). Mussolini was overthrown and temporarily imprisoned in Italy before being rescued by German commandoes. The new Italian regime attempted to change sides, but Hitler sent German forces flooding into Italy, moving down the Italian peninsula to meet the oncoming Allied forces who had crossed over to the Italian mainland after liberating Sicily. The result was a long and bloody campaign in Italy that continued until the end of the war. American, British, and Canadian troops, alongside Italian partisans and additional Allied forces struggled against German troops who made full use of the terrain of the Italian peninsula to fight masterful defensive battles. What does the Joint Planning Staff memoir (Document 4) tell you about Allied hopes for the Italian campaign? Do you think some predictions were overly optimistic? The message from Churchill to the British ambassador in Moscow (Document 5) addresses Soviet complaints that German troops were being withdrawn from the Italian theatre for service on the Eastern front. Given that one purpose of the Italian campaign was to tie down German forces in Italy, what does this message tell you about the progress of the fighting? What difficulties did the Allies face in Italy?

Notable episodes in the Italian campaign included botched Allied amphibious landings at Salerno and Anzio and the long battle to take the German-held Monte Cassino. Rome was liberated by the Allies on June 4, 1944, shortly before D-Day, but the bitter fighting in Italy continued to the very end. The Italian campaign attracted a good deal of criticism from some Allied leaders and historians who have pointed to the enormous cost of the campaign. Critics argue that Allied resources could have been more profitably employed elsewhere, most notably Western Europe. How does Canadian historian G. Nicolson (Document 6) attempt to refute these criticisms? Is his argument convincing?

1

FIELD MARSHAL BERNARD MONTGOMERY MEETS THE EIGHTH ARMY

The Eighth Army consisted in the main of civilians in uniform, not of professional soldiers. And they were, of course, to a man, civilians who read newspapers. It seemed to me that to command such men demanded not only a guiding mind but also a point of focus; or to put it another way, not only a master but a mascot. And I deliberately set about fulfilling this second requirement. It helped, I felt sure, for them to recognize as a person—as an individual—the man who was putting them into battle. To obey an impersonal figure was not enough. They must know who I was. This analysis may sound rather cold blooded, a decision made in the study. And so, in origin, it was: and I submit, rightly so. One had to reason out the best way to set about commanding these men, to bring out their best, and to weld them into an effective and a contented team which could answer the calls I was going to make on them; and these were going to be increasingly arduous. But I read-ily admit that the occasion to become the necessary focus of their attention was also personally enjoyable. For if I were able thereby to give something to them—and it was a sense of unity which I was trying to create—I gained myself from the experience by the way it enabled me to get to know them too, to sense their morale and, as time went on, to feel the affection which they generously extended to me. I started in the Alam Halfa battle by wearing an Australian hat—first of all because it was exceedingly good hat for the desert, but soon because I came to be recognized by it: outside the Australian lines anyway! Later as readers may know, I took a black beret, again for utilitarian reasons in the first place.

And the twin badges in the beret were, in origin, accidental; but I quickly saw their functional result, and what started as a private joke with the tank regiment which gave it to me became in the end the means by which I came to be recognized throughout the desert. I soon learnt that the arrival of the double-badged beret on the battlefield was a help—they knew what I was about, that I was taking an intense and personal interest in their doings, and that I was not just sitting about somewhere in the rear issuing orders. The beret was functional in the way a "brass hat" could never have been. It became, if you like, my signature. It was also very comfortable.

2

British Tanker Keith Douglas on Armoured Warfare at El Alamein[1]

The view from a moving tank is like that in a camera obscura or a silent film—in that since the engine drowns all other noises except explosions, the whole world moves silently. Men shout, vheicles move, aeroplanes fly over, and all soundlessly: the noise of the tank being continuous, perhaps for hours on end, the effect is of silence. It is the same in an aircraft, but unless you are flying low, distance does away with the effect of a soundless pageant. I think it may have been for the fact that for so much of the time I saw it without hearing it, which led me to feel that country into which we were now moving as an illimitably strange land, quite unrelated to real life, like the scenes in 'The Cabinet of Doctor Caligari'. Silence is a strange thing to us who live: we desire it, we fear it, we worship it, we hate it. There is a divinity about cats, as long as they are silent: the silence of the swans gives them an air of legend. The most impressive thing about the dead is their triumphant silence, proof against anything in the world.

A party of prisoners now appeared marching on our left. They were evidently very tired but looked about them with a good deal of interest, particularly at our column. I thought of innumerable pictures of glowering S.S. men in Nazi tanks, and glared at them through my goggles in the hope of looking like part of an inexorable war machine myself. They must have been fairly

---

1 Douglas was later killed in action in France in June 1944, age twenty-four.

impressed with the strength and concentration of our forces by the time they reached their cage at the rear. About two hundred of them passed us, in batches, as we continued our journey. We looked at them with an interest equal to their own. They did not look very fearsome: they were almost all Germans with shapeless green or khaki drill uniforms and floppy peaked caps with a red, white and black bull's eye on them. The desert on either side of the track became more sparsely populated with vehicles, and at length there were nothing but derelicts. The column halted at last, so that my tank stood beside the burnt-out shell of a German Mk.IV Special, with its long gun and rows of little wheels. Most of one side had been torn out, probably by the explosion of its own ammunition. Some charred clothing lay beside it, but not equipment, and there was no sign of the crew. The whole thing made a disconcerting cautionary picture.

On the horizon to our front we could see two vehicles burning fiercely, from which expanding columns of black smoke slanted across the orange sky. We could see shells, visible by their traces as yellow or while lights, sailing in apparently slow curves across our front: they were being fired by tanks on our left, but were landing in dead ground to us. By now the light was ebbing perceptibly and soon the burning derelicts and the shell-traces gleamed against the sky. The traces of enemy shells could be seen flying from beyond the ridge ahead of us. We were now spectators of the closing stages of the day's battles.

3

OPERATION TORCH

MARCH 4, 1943

MESSAGE FROM CHURCHILL AND
ROOSEVELT TO STALIN

The Anglo-American attempt to get to Tunis and Bizerta at a run was abandoned in December because of the strength of the enemy, the impending rainy season, the already sodden character of the ground and the fact the communications stretched 500 miles from Algiers and 160 miles from Bone through bad roads and a week of travelling over single-track French railways. It was only possible to get supplies up to the Army by sea on a small scale owing to the strength of enemy air and submarine attacks. Thus it was not possible to accumulate the petrol or other supplies in the forward areas. Indeed, it was only just possible to nourish the troops already there. The same was true of the air, and improvised airfields became quagmires. When we stopped attacking there were about 40,000 troops in Tunisia apart from Italians and from Rommel who was still in Tripoli. The German force in North Tunisia is now more than double that figure, and they are rushing over every man they can in transport aircraft and destroyers. We suffered some sharp

Winston Churchill and Franklin D. Roosevelt, "Operation Torch," UK National Archives, PREM 3/333/3 Message from Churchill and Roosevelt to Stalin, March 4, 1943. Progress Publishers, 1943.

reverses towards the end of last month but the position has been restored.[1] We hope that the delays caused by this setback will be repaired by the earlier advance of Montgomery's army which should have six divisions (say, 200,000 men) operating from Tripoli with sufficient supplies against the Mareth position by March 19th or perhaps a little earlier.[2] In the North section of Tunisia, however, the ground is still too wet for major operations.

We thought that you would like to know the details of this story although it is on a small scale compared with the tremendous operations over which you preside.

---

1 This is a reference to the American defeat at the Battle of Kasserine Pass, February 19 to 24, 1943.

2 "Mareth position" means the Mareth Line, a network of fortifications originally built by the French in southern Tunisia to defend against an Italian attack from Libya. At this time the Germans were using the line to try to stop the British advance led by General Montgomery.

4

MEDITERRANEAN OPERATIONS

JULY 28, 1943

JOINT PLANNING STAFF MEMOIR

The relevant Trident decisions are:-

a. That forces and equipment should be established in the UK with the object of mounting an operation to secure a lodgement on the Continent with the target date of 1st May, 1944.

b. That the Allied Commander-in-Chief in North Africa should plan such operations in exploitation of Husky as are best calculated to eliminate Italy from the war, and to contain the maximum number of German forces, i.e. so as to assist Russia during the winter and to contribute to the success of (a) above.[1]

---

1 'Trident' refers to an Anglo-American conference in Washington, May 1943. Churchill and Roosevelt both attended. 'Husky' refers to Operation Husky, the invasion of Sicily.

"Mediterranean Operations," UK National Archives, PREM 3/228/5 Joint Planning Staff memoir on Mediterranean Operations, July 28, 1943. Progress Publishers, 1943.

The main arguments which led to this decision to eliminate Italy still stand and indeed have been much reinforced by the success of Husky. They were and still are as follows:-

1. We cannot contemplate our large and battle-trained forces in the Mediterranean standing idle after Husky, while we concentrate solely on preparations for Overlord. So long a period of inaction would allow Germany to concentrate for the defence of France against our invasion, and we should be doing nothing to relieve the pressure on Russia.

2. We had already made a success of Lightfoot and Torch and had seized the initiative in the Mediterranean theatre. Allied bases in this area were now highly developed. As a matter of principle, therefore, we should exploit success in this theatre, rather than divert resources to a theatre where, for the time being, we can do nothing.

3. On the collapse of Italy Germany would be faced with two new commitments:-

    a. The necessity for taking over the garrisons in the Balkans which are economically extremely valuable for her.

    b. The replacement of Italian forces now in France, which would then be threatened by the Allies.

4. Germany would also have to decide whether, in addition to those commitments, she could find the forces to hold on to Northern Italy. Forces to hold this area would have to be at the expense of her already stretched resources elsewhere. Some part of her defensive perimeter would then be left dangerously weak.

5. The liquidation of the Italian fleet would hasten the release of British heavy units to engage the Japanese.

6. The possession of air bases in Italy would be a very great contribution to our whole air strategy. The latter in particular with relation to Overlord, aims at reducing the German fighter strength, and in this, we are not being successful as the German fighter strength is increasing. Airfields in Central, and better still, Northern Italy, offer excellent bases for bombing Southern Europe which is at present virtually undefended and in which lies some 55 percent of the industry on which German fighter strength depends. In addition we should be within effective bombing range of the synthetic oil plants in Southern and Central Germany, the Austrian and Czechoslovakian Armament Works, the Danubian transportation targets, and Ploesti. If our air strategy is to

succeed we must strike at these Southern German aircraft factories and in so doing we should also cause the enemy to set up a defensive system on his Southern perimeter. To accomplish this on lines similar to those necessary in the North-West will be most costly to his already stretched resources of men and technical equipment. In fact he will probably only be able to set up a comparatively simple system. Thus the possession of air bases in Italy would enable us to strike at one half his fighter production and to stretch his whole defensive system thereby paving the way for Overlord by greatly increasing the chances of success of our air strategy.

7. An Italian collapse would weaken the Axis hold in the Aegean. The situation in that area would be more favourable for the entry of Turkey into the war.

8. Our exploitation of an Italian collapse would depend on the redistribution of German forces and on how far she could meet her new commitments, but we should, in any event, be able to increase our supplies to the Resistance Groups in the Balkans. If Germany decided to hold on to Northern Italy she would inevitably be extremely weak in the Balkans, and we could exploit then this situation still further.

9. If Italy collapses, the effect on the German satellites may be profound.

10. In fact, the collapse of Italy would be a military and political disaster to Germany of the first magnitude

The particular arguments relating Mediterranean operations to a cross-Channel invasion of Northern France in 1944, were as follows:-

1. The extra forces Germany would require if Italy collapses can only be found at the expense of resources which are already fully stretched. The result must inevitably react to the advantage either of the Russians or of Overlord, or both.

2. By continuing to engage the Axis land and air forces after Husky we should be refusing Germany the respite she so badly needs before meeting our further blows.

3. The elimination of Italy will reduce the German ability to oppose our Overlord assault. The degree of this reduction will more than offset the limited additional weight of attack which we could hope to mount in the Overlord assault if we relaxed pressure on Italy and withdrew our forces from the Mediterranean.

C.E. Lambe, W. Porter, W. Elliot

5

THE ITALIAN CAMPAIGN

NOVEMBER 7, 1943

MESSAGE FROM CHURCHILL TO AMBASSADOR CLARK-KERR, MOSCOW[1]

The reason why the Italian campaign has flagged is because of the with-drawal of landing-craft in preparation for transit to England in order to set up the Second Front as arranged for Overlord. This meant that the build-up has been slower than was hoped, and also that General Alexander was not able to plan the outflanking amphibious operations on which an advance on the narrow peninsula so largely depends. The exceptionally good weather on the Russian front has carried with it heavy rains in Italy, and the frontal attacks we have had to make with forces not very much stronger than the enemy have necessarily yielded slow progress. Moreover two first-class British divisions, the 50th and 51st, which stood ready in Italy, have been sent home in pursuance of decisions taken at Quadrant in order to build up Overlord.[2]

---

1 Churchill was responding to Soviet complaints that the Germans were moving divisions from the Italian front to the Eastern front to use against the Soviets.

2 'Overlord' refers to the Allied invasion of France. 'Quadrant' was an Anglo-American conference held at Quebec City Canada, August 1943, to discuss future strategy.

Winston Churchill, "The Italian Campaign," UK National Archives, PREM 3/245/8 Letter from Churchill to Ambassador Clark-Kerr, November 7, 1943.

My wish has always been to sustain and press to the utmost the campaign in Italy and to attract to that front and hold upon it as many divisions as possible. I am glad to say that agreement has been reached by the Combined Staffs that no more landing-craft will be withdrawn until December 15. This will enable greater power to be put into the whole of our operations.

You may tell Molotov in strict confidence for Stalin that I am going myself very shortly to this front, and I will do everything in human power to animate the forward movement on which my heart is set.[3] Moreover by making new intense exertions at home I hope to make up, by additional building of landing-craft, for the delay in sending home the others. You should convey all the above verbally from me.

The main German strength in Italy is of course in the North and separated from us by 300 miles. It is from this pool of divisions in the North that the withdrawals back to Southern Russia have been made. Deployed south of Rome there are 10 German divisions, against which we have 12 or 13 of rather greater strength. This is not much of a preponderance for a continuous frontal attack in mountainous country.

---

3 'Molotov' refers to Vyacheslav Molotov, Soviet foreign minister.

6

An Assessment of the Italian Campaign

Canadian Historian G. Nicolson Assesses the Balance Sheet for the Italian Campaign

It remains only to attempt to assess the value of the Allied effort in Italy. The Italian campaign's major contribution to the general victory in Europe may not be denied; but whether equal results might not have been more economically gained had Allied strategy taken a different course is a question which will long be debated. The directive given to General Eisenhower in May 1943, to carry out such operations in exploitation of the conquest of Sicily as would be best calculated "to contain the maximum number of German forces", had remained in effect throughout the campaign. Moreover, as Lord Alexander points out, "The supreme directors of Allied strategy were always careful to see that our strength was never allowed to grow above the minimum necessary for our task." At one time or another during the fighting in Italy they withdrew no less than 21 Allied divisions to benefit other theatres.

Most readers will agree with Lord Alexander that the assistance given the general Allied cause by the operation in Italy reached its peak before the attack on the Gothic Line. Up to that time the campaign had yielded notable strategic gains. The twelve months which followed the invasion of Sicily had deprived Germany of her Axis partner; opened to Allied shipping the important sea

Lt.-Col. G.W.L. Nicholson, "An Assessment of the Italian Campaign," *The Official History of the Canadian Army in the Second World War: Volume Two, The Canadians in Italy, 1943-1945*, pp. 678-681. Queen's Printer, 1957.

route through the Mediterranean to the Middle East and India; gained air bases on the Italian mainland which considerably increased the effectiveness of the great bombing programme against Germany; and enhanced Allied prestige by winning a decisive victory which led to the capture of Rome and set the stage for a successful invasion of Southern France.

None of these strategical considerations can alter the fact that the Allied Armies in Italy had waged and won a hard and well-fought campaign. Always the attacker, they had carried out four major amphibious landings, and three times attacked the enemy with the strength of an Army Group. Fighting much of the time in a country where, in the words of Lord Alexander, "it is generally agreed, a superiority of at least three to one is required for successful offensive operations", their polyglot forces, in which 26 nations were represented, drove the enemy from one position after another up the whole length of the peninsula to complete his destruction on the northern plain. We have noted that the needs of other theatres deprived the Allied commanders in Italy of the use of airborne troops or amphibious forces with which they might have offset the advantages that the narrow and mountainous Italian frontage gave the enemy. That they were forced to advance by attacking through the defensible defiles of restricted valley or narrow coastal plain was the greater challenge to their generalship.

To these successes Canadian troops had made no small contribution. Except for the last two months of the war Canadian formations were engaged in all the major phases of the campaign; when it left Italy the 1st Division had served continuously in the theatre for a longer period than any other division in the Eighth Army. In the long advance from Pachino to the Senio the Canadians had fought against twenty different German divisions. At least four of these—the 1st Parachute, the 29th and 90th Panzer Grenadier and the 26th Panzer Divisions—stand out both for the quality of their performance and the frequency with which they were encountered; for, as we have learned from enemy records, the reported appearance of the Canadians in a given sector was generally the signal for the Germans to commit there the best formations in the theatre.

CHAPTER 7

1942–1943 TURNING POINTS: EL ALAMEIN, STALINGRAD, AND THE ATLANTIC

Introduction

This chapter considers three battles that are considered crucial turning points in the Second World War. All the extracts are written by close participants in these battles.

The Battle of El Alamein (October 22 to November 11, 1942) was a massive offensive by British Commonwealth forces that defeated the German Afrika Korps led by Field Marshal Erwin Rommel and his Italian allies. Heinz Werner Schmidt, who served on Rommel's staff in North Africa, provides an analysis of German failings (Document 1). What does Schmidt consider to be the major reasons for the German defeat? Next read extracts from the memoirs of Field Marshal Bernard Montgomery, who led British and Commonwealth forces at El Alamein and the subsequent North African campaign (Document 2). What is Monty's analysis of the battle? How does it differ from that of Schmidt?

The Battle of Stalingrad (August 23, 1942 to February 2, 1943) is widely regarded as the decisive turning point of the war on the Eastern front. General Vasili Chuikov commanded Soviet Red Army forces in Stalingrad (the 62nd Army) during the worst phases of the fighting. What does Chuikov observe about German tactics and fighting methods (Document 3)? How does he think the Red Army could counter such tactics?

Finally we have four documents relating to the turning of the tide in the Battle of the Atlantic. The Battle of the Atlantic (technically more of a campaign than an actual single battle) was the longest battle of the Second World War, beginning with the sinking of the British passenger liner *SS Athenia* on September 3, 1939, and ending only with the German surrender in 1945. In 1940 British prime minister Winston Churchill wrote to U.S. president Franklin D. Roosevelt about the current situation in the Atlantic (Document 4). As with all documents, pay careful attention to the date. This letter was written before Pearl Harbor and U.S. entry into the war. What is Churchill saying in this letter? What do you think he wants Roosevelt to do?

The Battle of the Atlantic reached its turning point in spring 1943 when a series of developments on the Allied side came together to drastically reduce shipping losses while increasing the number of U-boat sinkings. The report on anti-U-boat warfare by Professor Blackett, a renowned British scientist, points the way to victory for the Allies (Document 5). The final two readings were both written by German participants in the Battle of the Atlantic. Admiral Karl Doenitz headed the German U-boat service (Document 6), and Herbert Werner commanded a U-boat in action (Document 7). What do these three readings tell you about why the Allies won the Battle of the Atlantic?

1

HEINZ WERNER SCHMIDT, WITH THE GERMAN ARMY, ON THE BATTLE OF EL ALAMEIN[1]

OCTOBER 1942

Operation *Lightfoot*—Montgomery's offensive at El Alamein—began on the night of October 23.

The secret of this massed, planned assault had been extraordinarily well kept. It came as a complete surprise, even though indications of an almost immediate offensive had been gathered and assessed by the German Staff during the twenty-four hours before the initial barrage opened.

The Eighth Army had been built up for a 'kill' since August 1; it had been reinforced by 41,000 troops, over 1000 tanks, and 9000 vehicles of various sorts.

The peaceful stars were shaken in their heavens when nearly a thousand guns flashed and roared simultaneously against us that night. Never had this age-old land known so shattering a drum-fire. The earth from the Qattara Depression to the Mediterranean quaked. Far back from the front line, men were jarred to their teeth.

Fifteen minutes of it, and then the firing let up for five minutes. That was just a lull before a renewed storm. Punctually at 10 P.M. the same vast number of guns, plus thousands of tank and infantry weapons, concentrated on our front

---

1   In the original text Schmidt confused Operation Torch and Operation Lightfoot. Operation Torch (began November 8, 1942) refers to Allied landings in Morocco and Algeria, then under the control of Vichy France. Operation Lightfoot was Monty's offensive beginning October 23.

lines. Australians principally, but also Englishmen, Scots, New Zealanders, and South Africans, attacked. The main objective was the Miteiriyeh Ridge. It was occupied on the first night of the battle, but Montgomery did not consolidate his hold on it until after two days of desperate fighting.

The 15th Panzer Division in the north and the 21st in the south lay a short way behind the turmoil of the forward line. They had been split into battle groups in accordance with defensive plans that Rommel had drawn up before he left Africa for medical attention in Germany. In this we made a grave blunder. Rommel had intended that these battle groups should exist independently only during the period preceding an anticipated enemy offensive.

Bayerlein, the Chief of Staff, was on leave. Rommel had to return, unavailingly, to the rescue. On the first day of Montgomery's offensive General Stumme had a heart attack when the unit he was with was attacked by enemy aircraft. Stumme's driver did not even see him fall out of his car on to the Desert. His corpse was found only later.

Central Intelligence in Berlin had told us that the British could not attack before the end of the month.

Hitler telephoned Rommel in hospital in Germany at noon on the second day of the battle and asked him at once to fly back to Africa. The situation was desperate. Rommel had been under treatment for only three weeks and was still ill, but he did not think of saying no. He was airborne before daybreak the following morning, only stopping in Italy to find out what was going on, and particularly to learn whether his forces were getting enough petrol, whether more Panzers were on their way, and whether Kesselring had sent the supplies of *Nebelwerfers*—multiple barreled mortars—which Hitler had promised. He was at Panzer Gruppe Headquarters again a couple of hours after sunset that same night.

I think he knew then that El Alamein was lost: he had found out how short of petrol the Afrika Korps was. He told Bayerlein that we could not win, but he made desperate attempts to retrieve the situation. He was up almost all night planning a counter-attack against Kidney Ridge (Miteiriyeh) in the north. He strove desperately to assemble his Panzer forces in a cohesive whole, as they should have been earlier. The 15th Panzer Division had been practically destroyed, so he summoned the 21st and the Italian Ariete Divisions north, and moved the 90th Light and the Italian Trieste Divisions from their rear areas to protect the front near the sea.

The counter-attack, which Rommel directed in person, was smashed up by our old enemies, the medium bombers and the 25-pounders. He tried again the next day, but was beaten off once more. He lost Panzers he could ill afford—Panzers that would not now be replaced. The 9th Australian Division hammered him farther back.

Montgomery paused to regroup after three days of fighting. (The South Africans, apart from their ubiquitous armoured-car men, had now incidentally completed their main task in the El Alamein battle, and we were not to meet them again until Italy.) At Tel el Aqqaqir the fiercest tank engagement of the battle developed. Both sides suffered heavy losses, but we were the harder hit. Our Panzers were almost annihilated: only a few groups survived.

Montgomery's 'Operation Supercharge'—the new onslaught that followed 'Torch'—was the end at El Alamein. The 21st Panzers had put up their last effective struggle, and, although at one time they almost mastered their old enemies, the British 1st Armoured, they were beaten. Rommel decided to withdraw on the night of November 2–3.

He wirelessed his decision and his reasons to Hitler's headquarters that night. The report was passed to Hitler only the following day: the officer who was on duty when it came through had failed to wake him. (He was reduced in rank.) Hitler raved, and reviled Rommel.

Rommel's retreat was in progress when a wireless signal came from Hitler's H.Q.: 'The situation demands that the positions at El Alamein he held to the last man. A retreat is out of the question. Victory or death! Heil Hitler!' The message bore Hitler's personal signature. For some reason or other, although we were already withdrawing, the signal was circulated to Afrika Korps units.

The ridiculous signal could not improve our morale at that time. Nevertheless, having received it and being obliged to acknowledge it, Rommel could not treat it as non-existent.

Thus, when von Thoma, in command of the Afrika Korps, asked Rommel at the Panzer Gruppe Afrika H.Q. south of El Daba for permission to withdraw to Fuka, Rommel would not endorse the plan but merely gave him authority to act on his own judgment.

Next morning von Thoma gathered information that Tommy had already outflanked the southern wing of the Afrika Korps, and he passed the information up to Rommel. Rommel discredited the information, and said that the formation reported in the south must be a retreating Italian division. Von Thoma went out in a Panzer to check for himself. British tanks pounced upon him, set his Panzer alight, and captured him.

Bayerlein, the Chief of Staff, who went out in search of von Thoma, was also within an ace of capture when he approached to within a few hundred yards and, through his field-glasses, saw von Thoma being rounded up. He scurried back to safety, and succeeded to the command of what was left of the Afrika Korps.

2

Bernard Montgomery on the Battle of El Alamein

A mass of detailed lessons will always emerge from any battle. In the British Army we are inclined to become immersed in details, and we often lose sight of the fundamentals on which the details are based.

There were three distinct phases in this battle, and operations were developed accordingly.

First: The break-in.
This was the battle for position, or the fight for the tactical advantage. At the end of this phase we had to be so positioned and "balanced" that we could begin immediately the second phase. We must in fact have the tactical advantage.

Second: The "dog fight."
I use this term to describe what I knew must develop after the break-in and that was a hard and bloody killing match. During this we had so to cripple the enemy's strength that the final blow would cause the disintegration of his army.

Third: The break out.

This was brought about by a terrific blow directed at a selected spot. During the dog-fight the enemy had been led to believe that the break-out would come in the north, on the axis of the coast road. He was sensitive to such a thrust and he concentrated his Germans in the north to meet it, leaving the Italians to hold his southern flank. We then drove in a hard blow between the Germans and Italians, with a good overlap on the Italian front.

Determined leadership is vital throughout all echelons of command. Nowhere is it more important than in the higher ranks.

Generals who become depressed when things are not going well, who lack the "drive" to get things done, and who lack the resolution, the robust mentality and the moral courage to see their plan through to the end—are useless. They are, in fact, worse than useless—they are a menace—since any sign of wavering or hesitation has immediate repercussions down the scale when the issue hangs in the balance. No battle is ever lost till the general in command thinks it so. If I had not stood firm and insisted that my plan would be carried through, we would not have won at Alamein.

If your enemy stands to fight and is decisively defeated in the ensuing battle, everything is added unto you. Rommel's doom was sounded at Alam Halfa; as Von Mellenthin said, it was the turning point of the desert war. After that, he was smashed in battle at Alamein. He had never been beaten before though had had often had to "nip back to get more petrol." Now he had been decisively defeated. The doom of the Axis forces in Africa was certain—provided we made no more mistakes.

3

Soviet General Vasili Chuikov on the Battle of Stalingrad

The month and a half of fighting which had begun at the other side of the Don on July 23 had taught me a great deal. During this time I had studied the enemy well enough to be able to predict his operational plans.

Pincers driven in depth towards a single point—that was the enemy's main tactic. With superiority in air power and tanks, the enemy was able to penetrate our defences relatively easily, drive in his pincers, and make our units retreat when they seemed to be on the point of being surrounded. No sooner would a stubborn defence or counter-attack stop or eliminate one of the pincers, than another one would appear and try to find a foothold elsewhere.

This was how it had been at the other side of the Don. When the wedge driven by the German 51st Army Corps had been stopped at the River Chir, a second one had appeared in the vicinity of Verkhne-Buzinovka. That was how it had been in the south. When the 64th Army and the Southern Group were beating off attacks from the south and south-west at the beginning of August, a second group approaching the Volga to the north of the city did nothing for a week.

The enemy stuck to the same pattern in his tactics. His infantry went into an attack whole-heartedly only when tanks had already reached the target. The tanks, however, normally went into an attack only when the Luftwaffe was already over the heads of our troops. One had only to break this sequence for an enemy attack to stop and his units to turn back.

Vasili Chuikov, *The Beginning of the Road: The Story of the Battle of Stalingrad*, ed. John Mendelsohn, pp. 70-72. Macgibbon & Kee, 1963.

That was how it had been on the Don, when the 112th Division for several days in succession beat off attacks in the area of Verkhne-Chirskaya and Novomaksimovski. Enemy planes had been afraid to fly too close to our position, as we had a powerful concentration of anti-aircraft artillery here, covering the railway bridge across the Don.

That was how it had been on the River Aksay, when the enemy's tanks were unable to give their infantry any support, so that the infantry was quickly thrown back.

That was how it had been at Plodovitoye and Abganerovo, and in other sectors.

The enemy could not sustain our sudden attacks, particularly by artillery and mortar fire. We had only to organize a good artillery bombardment on an enemy concentration and the Germans would scatter in panic.

The Germans could not stand close fighting; they opened up with their automatic weapons from well over half a mile away, when their bullets could not cover half that distance. They fired simply to keep up their morale. They could not bear us to come close to them when we counter-attacked, soon threw themselves to the ground, and often retreated.

Their communications between infantry, tanks and aeroplanes were good, especially through the use of rockets. They met their aeroplanes with dozens, hundreds of rockets, pin-pointing their positions. Our troops and commanders worked out this signaling system and began to make use of it, frequently leading the enemy to make mistakes.

Analysing the enemy's tactical and operational methods, I tried to find counter-measures and counter-methods. I thought a great deal, in particular, about how to overcome or reduce the importance of German superiority in the air, and its effect on the morale of our troops. I remembered battles against the White Guards and White Poles in the Civil War, when we had to attack under artillery and machine-gun fire, without any artillery support of our own. We used to run up close to the enemy, and his artillery would be unable to take fresh aim and fire on rapidly approaching targets. A short, sharp attack would decide a battle.

I came to the conclusion that the best method of fighting the Germans should be in close battle, applied night and day in different forms. We should get as close to the enemy as possible, so that his air force could not bomb our forward units or trenches. Every German soldier must be made to feel that he was living under the muzzle of a Russian gun, always ready to treat him to a fatal dose of lead.

4

LETTER FROM CHURCHILL TO ROOSEVELT

DECEMBER 8, 1940

PRIME MINISTER WINSTON CHURCHILL OUTLINES BRITAIN'S STRATEGIC OPTIONS FOR 1941 TO PRESIDENT ROOSEVELT

The decision for 1941 lies upon the seas; unless we can establish our ability to feed this Island, to import munitions of all kinds which we need, unless we can move our armies to the various theatres where Hitler and his confederate Mussolini must be met, and maintain them there and do all this with the assurance of being able to carry it on till the spirit of the continental dictators is broken, we may fall by the way and the time needed by the United States to complete her defensive preparations may not be forthcoming. It is therefore in shipping and in the power to transport across the oceans, particularly the Atlantic Ocean, that in 1941 the crunch of the whole war will be found. If on the other hand we are able to move the necessary tonnage to and fro across the salt water indefinitely, it may well be that the application of superior air power to the German homeland and the rising anger of the German and other Nazi-gripped populations will bring the agony of civilization to a merciful and glorious end. But do not let us underrate the task.

Winston Churchill, "Letter from Churchill to Roosevelt, December 7, 1940," UK National Archives, PREM 3/486/1 December 7, 1940.

Our shipping losses, the figure for which in recent months are appended, have been on a scale almost comparable to that of the worst years of the last war. In the 5 weeks ending November 3rd the losses reached a total of 420,300 tons. Our estimation of the annual tonnage which ought to be imported in order to maintain our war effort at full strength is 43,000,000 tons; the tonnage entering in September was only at the rate of 37,000,000 tons and in October at 38,000,000 tons. Were the diminution to continue at this rate it would be fatal, unless indeed immensely greater replenishment than anything present in sight could be achieved in time. Although we are doing all we can to meet this situation by new methods, the difficulty of limiting the losses is obviously much greater than in the last war. We lack the assistance of the French Navy, the Italian Navy and the Japanese Navy, and above all the United States Navy, which was of such vital help to us during the culminating years. The enemy commands the ports all around the northern and western coast of France. He is increasingly basing his submarines, flying boats and combat planes on these ports and on the islands off the French coast. We lack the use of ports or territory in Eire in which to organize our coastal patrols by air and sea. In fact, we have now only one effective passage of entry to the British Isles namely, the northern approach, against which the enemy is increasingly concentrating, reaching ever farther out by U-boat action and long distance bombing. In addition, there have for some months been merchant ship raiders both in the Atlantic and in the Indian Oceans. And now we have powerful warship raiders to contend with as well. We need ships both to hunt down and to escort. Large as are our resources and preparations we do not possess enough.

5

ANTI U-BOAT WARFARE

SUMMARY

The main conclusions arising from the Analysis are as follows—

1. That the present scale of surface ships is adequate to ensure relative safety of convoys only when adequate air cover is also maintained.

2. In the absence of air cover at least double the present escort strength would be necessary.

3. Since the losses in convoys do not seem to increase much, if at all, with the size of the convoys, at least between 20 and 60 ships, the adoption of fewer larger convoys is to be preferred to more small convoys.

4. The extremely high value of V.L.R. aircraft as air cover to shadowed convoys is proved.

Professor Blackett, "Anti-U-boat Warfare," UK National Archives, PREM 3/414/3 February 5, 1943.

Value of Air escort to Convoys

The value of Aircraft to threatened convoys has so far been due to two effects.

1. Aircraft forcing U-boats to operate further out, so making interception more difficult, and also leaving a shorter time for the attack to develop.

2. Aircraft making U-boat attacks more difficult through counter-attack and through forcing then to lose contact by diving.

6

GERMAN ADMIRAL DOENITZ ON THE BATTLE OF THE ATLANTIC

1943

The overwhelming superiority achieved by the enemy defence was finally proved beyond dispute in the operations against the next two convoys, SC130 and HX239. The convoy escorts worked in exemplary harmony with the specially trained 'support groups'. To that must be added the continuous air cover, which was provided by carrier-borne and long-range, shore-based aircraft, most of them equipped with the new radar. There were also new and heavier depth charges and improved means of throwing them. With all this against us it became impossible to carry on the fight against convoys. It was only bit by bit that I received definite details of the losses we had suffered in the action against these two convoys, and among the boats on passage, particularly in the Bay of Biscay, off Iceland and the focal areas in the North Atlantic. Losses had suddenly soared. By May 22 we had already lost thirty-one U-boats since the first of the month, a frightful total, which came as a hard and unexpected blow; for, notwithstanding the very much more powerful enemy anti-submarine forces in operation in this fourth year of war, an increase in U-boat losses had not until this moment been perceptible.

Karl Doenitz, *Memoirs: Ten Years and Twenty Days*, pp. 340-341. Copyright © 1959 by Greenhill Books. Reprinted with permission.

Of the monthly average number of boats at sea, the percentage of losses had been:

1939 ....17.5%
1940 ....13.4%
1941 ....11.4%
1942 January—June 3.9%
1942 July—December ...8.9%
1943 January—March ...9.2%

It will be seen that losses during the first months of war were relatively the highest we suffered. To this, technical weaknesses and the inexperience of the crews had contributed. Our lowest losses were incurred in the first half of 1942, during the operation in American waters, where anti-U-boat defence was weak.

If these two periods are omitted, our average monthly losses work out at 11.2 per cent of the boats at sea. In the first half of 1942 therefore our losses were proportionately below the average.

Since the beginning of 1943 U-boat operations had been concentrated more and more against convoys. This is reflected in the ratio between total sinkings and sinkings of ships in convoy. In the first half of 1942 ships in convoy represented 39 percent of the total sinkings; in the first three months of 1943, however, the figure rose to 75 per cent. Operations against convoys are nevertheless much more difficult and more dangerous than attacks on solitary ships in far distant waters. Yet, in spite of the fact that the number of U-boats detailed to work against convoys had been vastly increased, the losses incurred rose only slightly from 8.9 per cent to 9.2 per cent and they certainly constituted no warning indication of the sudden soaring of the rate of losses which we now experienced.

In the submarine war there had been plenty of setbacks and crises. Such things are unavoidable in any form of warfare. But we had always overcome them because the fighting efficiency of the U-boat arm had remained steady. Now, however, the situation had changed. Radar, and particularly radar location by aircraft, had to all practical purposes robbed the U-boats of their power to fight on the surface. Wolf-pack operations against convoys in the North Atlantic, the main theatre of operations and at the same time the theatre in which air cover was strongest, were no longer possible. They could only be resumed if we succeeded in radically increasing the fighting power of the U-boats.

This was the logical conclusion to which I came, and I accordingly withdrew the boats from the North Atlantic. On May 24 I ordered them to proceed, using the utmost caution, to the area south-west of the Azores.

We had lost the Battle of the Atlantic.

7

U-boat Commander Herbert Werner on the Battle of the Atlantic[1]

1943

On December 18, two days after the end of our patrol, the crew was presented to the Commanding Admiral, who showered us with praise and medals. As he fastened another Iron Cross to my chest, it reminded me of all my friends in their iron coffins. By that sunny day in December of 1943, nearly all of the old guard of the Atlantic front had been eliminated, and many newcomers from the German ports were being hacked to bits in the Norwegian Sea before they could achieve their operational goals. The Mediterranean, too, was a deadly battleground. The latest boat to fall victim was U-593 under command of Kelbling, the one-time "guest commander" aboard U-557. His successful career was terminated just after he had torpedoed a British escort near the North African coast. American destroyers caught up with his boat and sent her down to the bottom.

What our U-boats had not achieved in four years—supremacy on the seas—the Allies had attained in a matter of seven months. Their all-out drive to sweep the seas clean of U-boats was almost an accomplished fact. Only a small force of U-boats was afloat after the bloody massacres in summer and fall. As of the December, the Allies had destroyed 386 of our boats, of which 237 had been sunk in 1943 alone.

CHAPTER 8

BOMBERS AND THE BOMBED

Introduction

Europe's major powers developed substantial air forces to fight the First World War, steadily improving aircraft performance and using airplanes to observe and attack enemy forces, as well as each other, and to bomb enemy factories, ports, and cities. Continued research and development after the war produced a host of important technological developments, including more powerful engines and flush-riveted all-metal construction. These facilitated the development of both commercial and military aviation, which improved considerably in speed, range, and carrying capacity in the 1930s. Interwar air power theorists promised that aviation would revolutionize warfare. The most prominent of them, Giulio Douhet, argued in *Command of the Air* (1921) that destroying an enemy's industrial capacity by aerial bombing would produce victory in future wars (Document 1). Bereft of industry to sustain its military forces, an enemy would have no choice but to surrender. Douhet also suggested that bombing would terrorize the civilian population whose members would demand their government make peace to save them from the horrors of continued bombing.

In summer 1940, following the conquest of France, German leaders applied Douhet's theories in the Battle of Britain. Anticipating the German air campaign, British prime minister Winston Churchill exhorted Britons to "break Hitler's air weapon" and "so bear ourselves that, if the British Empire and its

Commonwealth last for a thousand years, men will still say, 'This was their finest hour'" (Document 2). After sustained air attacks on Royal Air Force (RAF) and air defense installations failed to destroy the Royal Air Force, the Germans shifted their focus to bombing cities. Losses to British air defenses and RAF fighters, praised by Churchill (Document 3), were so heavy that the Germans switched to bombing at night, targeting first London and then other cities, among them Coventry, a city with little military importance, which suffered a devastating raid on November 14, 1940 (Document 4). German bombing inflicted substantial damage and killed more than 50,000 British civilians, but failed to break their will or force Britain's surrender.

Despite Germany's failure, British leaders launched a similar bombing campaign against German cities, which the Americans joined after they entered the war. Like the Germans, the British bombed at night. The Americans, who hoped to cripple German industry by accurately hitting precise targets, bombed during the day. Four-engine American and British heavy bombers carried several times the bomb load of the two-engine medium bombers on which Germany relied throughout the war and inflicted devastating damage on several dozen German cities. Nonetheless, Josepeh Goebbles, Germany's propaganda minister, encouraged Germans to embrace this total war and see revenge on their enemies (Document 5). A few weeks later, British and American bombers targeted Hamburg in a series of raids, which ignited a firestorm on July 28, 1943. The fires burned out much of the city and killed more than 40,000 civilians (Document 6)." After the war, American scholars studied the effects of the bombing campaigns and issued the multivolume Strategic Bombing Survey (Document 7) that detailed their findings. Its 208 studies and reports concluded that although bombing had contributed to Allied victory, it had not been decisive. Similarly, bombing hurt enemy morale but did not destroy it.

As conventional bombing continued, the United States, aided by an international host of scientists, worked to develop an atomic bomb, an idea first proposed to President Franklin D. Roosevelt by famed physicist Albert Einstein at the behest of Enrico Fermi and other nuclear scientists (Document 8). Einstein himself never worked on the bomb, which was completed in summer 1945 and tested near Alamogordo, New Mexico, on July 16, 1945.

Americans applied their experience bombing Germany to bombing Japan and American incendiary raids had already devastated several dozen Japanese cities and killed about 200,000. Debates continue to this day as to how much warning the Americans should have given the Japanese, the targets on which to drop the bombs, and the terms of surrender to demand from

Japan. In the Potsdam Declaration, the United States warned Japan it would face "unprecedented destruction" if it failed to surrender (Document 9). Less than two weeks later on August 6, an American bomber dropped at atomic bomb on Hiroshima, killing more than 100,000 people and leveling much of the Japanese city. Three days later, the United States struck Nagasaki with its second atomic bomb (a third was being assembled). Despite efforts by the U.S. government to restrict information on the atomic bomb, the magnitude and horror the atomic bombings was presented in U.S. newspapers (Document 10). The debate over the decision to drop the bomb is contentious and shows no sign of abating. The last two selections of this chapter showcase the opposing camps. President Harry Truman justified his decision to use the bomb by arguing it would shorten the war and thus save lives (Document 11). Historian Gar Alperovitz, though, argues that other factors led to the use of the atomic bomb, particularly fears of the Soviet Union (Document 12).

1

"The Magnitude of Aerial Offensives"

Some conception of the magnitude aerial offensives may reach in the future is essential to an evaluation of the command of the air, a conception which the World War can clarify for us in part.

Aerial bombs have only to fall on their target to accomplish their purpose; hence their construction does not require as much metal as is needed in artillery shells. If bombs containing high explosives require a large amount of metal in proportion to their internal charge in order to ensure an effective explosion, the proportion of metal in bombs containing incendiaries or poison gases may be reduced to a minimum. We may be not far off if we figure roughly the proportion of metal in them at 50 per cent of their total weight. The construction of aerial bombs does not call for high-grade steel, other special metals, nor for precision work. What it does demand is that the active ingredients of the bombs—the explosives, incendiaries, and poison gases—have the maximum efficacy, and that research be directed to this end.

Aerial bombardment can certainly never hope to attain the accuracy of artillery fire; but this is an unimportant point because such accuracy is unnecessary. Except in unusual cases, the targets of artillery fire are designed to withstand just such fire; but the targets of aerial bombardment are ill-prepared to endure such onslaught. Bombing objectives should always be large; small targets are unimportant and do not merit our attention here.

Giulio Douhet,"Magnitude of Aerial Offensives," *Command of the Air*, trans. Dino Ferrarri, pp. 19-23. U.S. Air Force, 1998.

The guiding principle of bombing actions should be this: the objective must be destroyed completely in one attack, making further attack on the same target unnecessary. Reaching an objective is an aerial operation which always involves a certain amount of risk and should be undertaken once only. The complete destruction of the objective has moral and material effects, the repercussions of which may be tremendous. To give us some idea of the extent of these repercussions, we need only envision what would go on among the civilian population of congested cities once the enemy announced that he would bomb such centers relentlessly, making no distinction between military and nonmilitary objectives.

In general, aerial offensives will be directed against such targets as peacetime industrial and commercial establishments; important buildings, private and public; transportation arteries and centers; and certain designated areas of civilian population as well. To destroy these targets three kinds of bombs are needed—explosive, incendiary, and poison gas—apportioned as the situation may require. The explosives will demolish the target, the incendiaries set fire to it, and the poison-gas bombs prevent fire fighters from extinguishing the fires.

Gas attacks must be so planned as to leave the target permeated with gas which will last over a period of time, whole days, indeed, a result which can be attained either by the quality of the gases used or by using bombs with varying delayed-action fuses. It is easy to see how the use of this method, even with limited supplies of explosive and incendiary bombs, could completely wreck large areas of population and their transit lines during crucial periods of time when such action might prove strategically invaluable.

* * *

As a matter of fact, this same offensive power, the possibility of which was not even dreamed of fifteen years ago, is increasing daily, precisely because the building and development of large, heavy planes goes on all the time. The same thing is true of new explosives, incendiaries, and especially poison gases. What could an army do faced with an offensive power like that, its lines of communication cut, its supply depots burned or blown up, its arsenals and auxiliaries destroyed? What could a navy do when it could no longer take refuge in its own ports, when its bases were burned or blown up, its arsenals and auxiliaries destroyed? How could a country go on living and working under this constant threat, oppressed by the nightmare of imminent destruction and death? How indeed! We should always keep in mind that aerial offensives can be directed not only against objectives of least physical resistance, but against those of least moral resistance as well. For instance, an infantry regiment in a shattered trench may still be capable of some resistance even after losing two-thirds of its effectives; but when the working personnel of a factory sees one of its machine shops destroyed, even with a minimum loss of life, it quickly breaks up and the plant ceases to function.

All this should be kept in mind when we wish to estimate the potential power of aerial offensives possible even today. To have command of the air means to be in a position to wield offensive power so great it defies human imagination. It means to be able to cut an enemy's army and navy off from their bases of operation and nullify their chances of winning the war. It means complete protection of one's own country, the efficient operation of one's army and navy, and peace of mind to live and work in safety. In short, it means to be in a position to win. To be defeated in the air, on the other hand, is finally to be defeated and to be at the mercy of the enemy, with no chance at all of defending oneself, compelled to accept whatever terms he sees fit to dictate.

This is the meaning of the "command of the air."

2

"Their Finest Hour"

June 18, 1940

The disastrous military events which have happened during the past fortnight have not come to me with any sense of surprise. ... I made it perfectly clear then that whatever happened in France would make no difference to the resolve of Britain and the British Empire to fight on, "if necessary for years, if necessary alone." During the last few days we have successfully brought off the great majority of the troops we had on the line of communication in France; and seven-eighths of the troops we have sent to France since the beginning of the war-that is to say, about 350,000 out of 400,000 men-are safely back in this country. Others are still fighting with the French, and fighting with considerable success in their local encounters against the enemy. We have also brought back a great mass of stores, rifles and munitions of all kinds which had been accumulated in France during the last nine months.

* * *

This brings me, naturally, to the great question of invasion from the air, and of the impending struggle between the British and German Air Forces. It seems quite clear that no invasion on a scale beyond the capacity of our land forces to crush speedily is likely to take place from the air until our Air Force has been definitely overpowered. In the meantime, there may be raids by parachute troops and attempted descents of airborne soldiers. We should be able

Winston Churchill, "Their Finest Hour," The Churchill Centre, pp. 6231-6238. 1974.

to give those gentry a warm reception both in the air and on the ground, if they reach it in any condition to continue the dispute. But the great question is: Can we break Hitler's air weapon? Now, of course, it is a very great pity that we have not got an Air Force at least equal to that of the most powerful enemy within striking distance of these shores. But we have a very powerful Air Force which has proved itself far superior in quality, both in men and in many types of machine, to what we have met so far in the numerous and fierce air battles which have been fought with the Germans. In France, where we were at a considerable disadvantage and lost many machines on the ground when they were standing round the aerodromes, we were accustomed to inflict in the air losses of as much as two and two-and-a-half to one. In the fighting over Dunkirk, which was a sort of no-man's-land, we undoubtedly beat the German Air Force, and gained the mastery of the local air, inflicting here a loss of three or four to one day after day. Anyone who looks at the photographs which were published a week or so ago of the re-embarkation, showing the masses of troops assembled on the beach and forming an ideal target for hours at a time, must realize that this re-embarkation would not have been possible unless the enemy had resigned all hope of recovering air superiority at that time and at that place.

* * *

There remains, of course, the danger of bombing attacks, which will certainly be made very soon upon us by the bomber forces of the enemy. It is true that the German bomber force is superior in numbers to ours; but we have a very large bomber force also, which we shall use to strike at military targets in Germany without intermission. I do not at all underrate the severity of the ordeal which lies before us; but I believe our countrymen will show themselves capable of standing up to it, like the brave men of Barcelona, and will be able to stand up to it, and carry on in spite of it, at least as well as any other people in the world. Much will depend upon this; every man and every woman will have the chance to show the finest qualities of their race, and render the highest service to their cause. For all of us, at this time, whatever our sphere, our station, our occupation or our duties, it will be a help to remember the famous lines: He nothing common did or mean, Upon that memorable scene.

* * *

If Hitler can bring under his despotic control the industries of the countries he has conquered, this will add greatly to his already vast armament output. On the other hand, this will not happen immediately, and we are now assured of immense, continuous and increasing support in supplies and munitions of all kinds from the United States; and especially of aeroplanes and pilots from the Dominions and across the oceans coming from regions which are beyond the reach of enemy bombers.

* * *

What General Weygand called the Battle of France is over. I expect that the Battle of Britain is about to begin. Upon this battle depends the survival of Christian civilization. Upon it depends our own British life, and the long continuity of our institutions and our Empire. The whole fury and might of the enemy must very soon be turned on us. Hitler knows that he will have to break us in this Island or lose the war. If we can stand up to him, all Europe may be free and the life of the world may move forward into broad, sunlit uplands. But if we fail, then the whole world, including the United States, including all that we have known and cared for, will sink into the abyss of a new Dark Age made more sinister, and perhaps more protracted, by the lights of perverted science. Let us therefore brace ourselves to our duties, and so bear ourselves that, if the British Empire and its Commonwealth last for a thousand years, men will still say, "This was their finest hour."

3

"The Few"

August 20, 1940

The great air battle which has been in progress over this Island for the last few weeks has recently attained a high intensity. It is too soon to attempt to assign limits either to its scale or to its duration. We must certainly expect that greater efforts will be made by the enemy than any he has so far put forth. Hostile air fields are still being developed in France and the Low Countries, and the movement of squadrons and material for attacking us is still proceeding. It is quite plain that Herr Hitler could not admit defeat in his air attack on Great Britain without sustaining most serious injury. If after all his boastings and bloodcurdling threats and lurid accounts trumpeted round the world of the damage he has inflicted, of the vast numbers of our Air Force he has shot down, so he says, with so little loss to himself; if after tales of the panic-stricken British crushed in their holes cursing the pluto-cratic Parliament which has led them to such a plight—if after all this his whole air onslaught were forced after a while tamely to peter out, the Fuhrer's reputation for veracity of statement might be seriously impugned. We may be sure, therefore, that he will continue as long as he has the strength to do so, and as long as any preoccupations he may have in respect of the Russian Air Force allow him to do so.

On the other hand, the conditions and course of the fighting have so far been favorable to us. I told the House two months ago that, whereas in France our fighter aircraft were wont to inflict a loss of two or three to one upon the

Winston Churchill, "The Few," *Winston S. Churchill, The Complete Speeches*, ed. Robert Rhodes James, pp. 6260-6268. 1974.

Germans, and in the fighting at Dunkirk, which was a kind of no-man's-land, a loss of about three or four to one, we expected that in an attack on this Island we should achieve a larger ratio. This has certainly come true. It must also be remembered that all the enemy machines and pilots which are shot down over our Island, or over the seas which surround it, are either destroyed or captured; whereas a considerable proportion of our machines, and also of our pilots, are saved, and soon again in many cases come into action.

* * *

The gratitude of every home in our Island, in our Empire, and indeed throughout the world, except in the abodes of the guilty, goes out to the British airmen who, undaunted by odds, unwearied in their constant challenge and mortal danger, are turning the tide of the World War by their prowess and by their devotion. Never in the field of human conflict was so much owed by so many to so few. All hearts go out to the fighter pilots, whose brilliant actions we see with our own eyes day after day; but we must never forget that all the time, night after night, month after month, our bomber squadrons travel far into Germany, find their targets in the darkness by the highest navigational skill, aim their attacks, often under the heaviest fire, often with serious loss, with deliberate careful discrimination, and inflict shattering blows upon the whole of the technical and war-making structure of the Nazi power. On no part of the Royal Air Force does the weight of the war fall more heavily than on the daylight bombers, who will play an invaluable part in the case of invasion and whose unflinching zeal it has been necessary in the meanwhile on numerous occasions to restrain.

We are able to verify the results of bombing military targets in Germany, not only by reports which reach us through many sources, but also, of course, by photography. I have no hesitation in saying that this process of bombing the military industries and communications of Germany and the air bases and storage depots from which we are attacked, which process will continue upon an ever-increasing scale until the end of the war, and may in another year attain dimensions hitherto undreamed of, affords one at least of the most certain, if not the shortest, of all the roads to victory. Even if the Nazi legions stood triumphant on the Black Sea, or indeed upon the Caspian, even if Hitler was at the gates of India, it would profit him nothing if at the same time the entire economic and scientific apparatus of German war power lay shattered and pulverized at home.

4

1000 Left Dead or Injured in Coventry, Ancient English City, in Worst Nazi Air Raid of War

Coventry, England. Nov 15—German bombers have blasted the heart out of this once peaceful city in the English Midlands with a dusk to dawn raid which turned parts of the city into an inferno and left at least 1000 dead and injured.

Coventry's beautiful and famous brownstone cathedral is a smoking wreck. Only its big main spire, 303 feet high, remains standing. All the rest of the medieval structure, started in 1373 and completed in 1450, lies in a tangle of broken stone and crumpled debris.

FALL OF SMOKE

In a quick dash tonight into the still burning sector of the stricken town, a vital industrial center, I scrambled over great piles of brick and stone.

Coventry was like a scene out of Hades between dusk and dawn while German raiders dumped their bombs in ceaseless relays.

A full moon shone, but its brilliance was dimmed by a pall of smoke and the glare of fire from the burning buildings.

Alfred Wall, "1000 Left Dead or Injured In Coventry, Ancient English City, in Worst Nazi Air Raid of War," *Ellensburg Daily Record, Nov 15, 1940*, pp. 1-2. Copyright © 1940 by Wright's Media. Reprinted with permission.

Today there are at least 1,000 dead and injured, numberless victims buried under vast piles of wreckage, fires licked through the town and the 14th century cathedral, with its 303-foot spire, was but one of many buildings in ruins.

Scarcely a street escaped the pounding of the raiders. It was the worst continuous attack experienced by any city—including London—since the siege of Britain began.

All night long, the narrow streets where Lady Godiva rode on her horse nearly 1,000 years ago trembled and crumbled with the thunder of diving planes, the scream of bombs and their explosions and the roar of anti-aircraft cannonade.

HOSPITALS HIT

Searchlights stabbed vainly through the shroud of smoke in an attempt to spot the raiders. Rifles and machine guns crackled as the city's defenders tried to shoot scores of flares out of the sky.

At least two hospitals were hit. There were casualties in one; in another, all the glass was blown from the operating theater.

Store after store was damaged, but authorities said that supplies were not affected materially and that there would be no food shortage.

The aeronautical expert of the press association also said the Germans "failed lamentably" to hit military targets.

Several other Midlands towns were raided, and in one, 24 houses were demolished, 150 damaged extensively and a bomb dropped on a school shelter full of people.

AWFUL EXPERIENCE

In Coventry tonight frenzied men tore at piles of brickwork and concrete covering the bodies of their women and children.

The first thing they did was to halt a frightened caravan of refugees seeking safety in the country.

The awful experience of the night before was written in the pinched white faces that peered at the minister's limousine from trucks, wagons, and automobiles.

Royal Air Force pilots took fire hoses from the hands of firemen reeling with fatigue and played streams of water on the smouldering heaps of rubble which are all that remain of some of Britain's finest examples of Tudor architecture.

Two policemen, Fred Rollins and William Timms, were among the hero dead of the night before. They worked for hours amid falling bombs, rescuing women and children trapped by debris, survivors said.

At dawn factory workers from night shifts burrowed into the smoking wreckage of their homes, shouting names of their wives and children and calling "We're coming ... we're coming!"

One young man recovered a body and then tunneled into the wreckage, his hands torn and bleeding, to pull out another—his wife.

Four persons literally numbed by the shock of the explosions were found in an air raid shelter and told that they were officially "missing." They nodded vaguely and continued to sit there, despite pleas of welfare workers that they come out.

5

Joseph Goebbles Calls for Total War

June 5, 1943

So if we at home have to make sacrifices in *this* war, at least we know *what they're for.* In so far as food is concerned, however, it seems to me that they are bearable in comparison with the sacrifices which the population in the areas hit by air raids have had to make almost *night after night* for the past *weeks* and *months.* [Applause] Our enemies are attacking their goods and belongings and their lives with *brutal cynicism* in an attempt to wear down their morale. They even *admit it quite openly.* It will be to their *eternal shame* that in this attempt they have destroyed German cultural treasures. But they want to do more. They are waging war against the *morale* of our nation; they are killing civilians, *old people, women and children*, and are barely trying any longer to cover their infamous bloody terror with a cloak of humanity. A few days ago, the Church of England stated hypocritically that English bombs no longer discriminate between men, women and children. [Booing] This statement seems, however, almost too meek when compared with the infernal outbursts of *hatred and triumph* which can be found in the London *Jew* papers.

We present-day Germans are not the kind of people who seek indulgence from an enemy who is out to destroy us. We know that against British-US bomb terror there is only one effective *remedy: counter-terror.* [Applause] Today there is but one thought in the minds of the whole of the German people: *to repay the enemy in his own kind.* [Applause] Far be it from us to boast or

Völkischer Beobachter, "Joseph Goebbles Calls for Total War," *Nazism, 1919-1945, Vol. 4: The German Home Front in World War II*, ed. and trans. Jeremy Noakes, pp. 500. Copyright © 1998 by Liverpool University Press. Reprinted with permission.

threaten. We merely take note. *Every English comment today* which considers the bombing of German women, old people and children an entirely humane or even Christian method of conquering the German nation *will one day be a welcome argument in our reply to these villainies.* [Applause] The British people have no cause to triumph. They will have to pay for the bill marked up by its leaders by order of those Jews who instigated and spurred them into their bloody crimes.

The enemy can make dust and ashes of our houses; but this makes the hearts of our population burn with *hatred*, but not to burn to ashes. One day the hour of retribution will come. ...

6

WITNESS ON HAMBURG FIRESTORM

AUGUST 24, 1943

MATHILDE WOLFF-MÖNCKEBERG'S DESCRIBES THE AFTERMATH OF THE HAMBURG FIRESTORM

During the night of Tuesday-Wednesday there was yet another terror attack, such a heavy one that it seemed to me even more horrifying than the one we had had on Saturday. After the siren had gone, there was only a little shooting at first, then all was quiet and we thought it was over. But then it started as if the whole world would explode. The light went out immediately and we were in darkness, then a tiny flickering light. We sat with wet towels over nose and mouth and the noise from one direct hit after another was such that the entire house shook and rattled, plaster spilling from the walls and glass splintering from the windows. Frau Leiser fainted and lay on the floor, her sweet baby was frozen with fear, nobody uttered a sound, and families grabbed each other by the hands and made for the exit. Never have I felt the nearness of death so intensely, never was I so petrified with fear. With every expansion we thought the house would come down on top of us, that the end was there; we choked with the smell of burning, we were blinded by sudden flashes of fire. And the stillness.

The following morning Maria reported that all women and children had to be evacuated from the city within six hours. There was no gas, no electricity, not a drop of water, neither the lift nor the telephone was working. It is hard to imagine the panic and chaos. Each one for himself, only one idea: flight. We too—W. raced to the police station for our exit permits. There were endless queues, but our permits were issued because we had a place to go to. But how could we travel? No trains could leave from Hamburg because all the stations had been gutted ... There were no trams, no Underground, no rail-traffic to the suburbs.

Most people loaded some belongings on carts, bicycles, prams, or carried things on their backs, and started on foot, just to get away, to escape. A long stream of human beings flooded along the Sierichstrasse, thousands were prepared to camp out, anything rather than stay in this catastrophic inferno in the city. During the night the suburbs of Hamm, Hammerbrock, Rothenburgsort and Barmbeck had been almost razed to the ground. People who had fled from collapsing bunkers and had got stuck in huge crowds in the streets had burning phosphorus poured over them, rushed into the next air raid shelter and were shot in order not to spread the flames. In the midst of the fire and the attempts to quench it, women had their babies in the streets. Parents and children were separated and torn apart in this frightful upheaval of surging humanity and never found each other again. It must have been indescribably gruesome. Everyone had just one thought: to get away. We tried vainly for some kind of vehicle. Most people in our house made hasty impromptu arrangements, carrying bits and pieces into the cellar, and we also towed away a few things. Since nobody could cook, communal kitchens were organized. But wherever people gathered together, more unrest ensued. People wearing party badges had them torn off their coats and there were screams of "Let's get that murderer." The police did nothing. We had another alarm during the night, but only a short one. Maria stayed the night with us because she had had such an awful time in the bunker with the heat and the stink, collapsing people, drunkenness and over aggression, howling children everywhere.

7

U.S. STRATEGIC BOMBING SURVEY

1945

Allied air power was decisive in the war in Western Europe. Hindsight inevitably suggests that it might have been employed differently or better in some respects. Nevertheless, it was decisive. In the air, its victory was complete. At sea, its contribution, combined with naval power, brought an end to the enemy's greatest naval threat—the U-boat; on land, it helped turn the tide overwhelmingly in favor of Allied ground forces. Its power and superiority made possible the success of the invasion. It brought the economy which sustained the enemy's armed forces to virtual collapse, although the full effects of this collapse had not reached the enemy's front lines when they were overrun by Allied forces. It brought home to the German people the full impact of modern war with all its horror and suffering. Its imprint on the German nation will be lasting.

SOME SIGNPOSTS

1. The German experience suggests that even a first class military power—rugged and resilient as Germany was—cannot live long under full-scale and free exploitation of air weapons over the heart of its territory. By the beginning of 1945, before the invasion of the homeland itself,

"U.S. Strategic Bombing Survey," 1945, pp. 17-18.

244

Germany was reaching a state of helplessness. Her armament production was falling irretrievably, orderliness in effort was disappearing, and total disruption and disintegration were well along. Her armies were still in the field. But with the impending collapse of the supporting economy, the indications are convincing that they would have had to cease fighting—any effective fighting—within a few months. Germany was mortally wounded.

2. The significance of full domination of the air over the enemy—both over its armed forces and over its sustaining economy—must be emphasized. That domination of the air was essential. Without it, attacks on the basic economy of the enemy could not have been delivered in sufficient force and with sufficient freedom to bring effective and lasting results.

3. As the air offensive gained in tempo, the Germans were unable to prevent the decline and eventual collapse of their economy. Nevertheless, the recuperative and defensive powers of Germany were immense; the speed and ingenuity with which they rebuilt and maintained essential war industries in operation clearly surpassed Allied expectations. Germany resorted to almost every means an ingenious people could devise to avoid the attacks upon her economy and to minimize their effects. Camouflage, smoke screens, shadow plants, dispersal, underground factories, were all employed. In some measure all were helpful, but without control of the air, none was really effective. Dispersal brought a measure of immediate relief, but eventually served only to add to the many problems caused by the attacks on the transportation system. Underground installations prevented direct damage, but they, too, were often victims of disrupted transportation and other services. In any case, Germany never succeeded in placing any substantial portion of her war production underground ...

4. The mental reaction of the German people to air attack is significant. Under ruthless Nazi control they showed surprising resistance to the terror and hardships of repeated air attack, to the destruction of their homes and belongings, and to the conditions under which they were reduced to live. Their morale, their belief in ultimate victory or satisfactory compromise, and their confidence in their leaders declined, but they continued to work efficiently as long as the physical means of production remained. The power of a police state over its people cannot be underestimated.

5. The importance of careful selection of targets for air attack is emphasized by the German experience. The Germans were far more concerned over attacks on one or more of their basic industries and services—their oil, chemical, or steel industries or their power or transportation networks—than they were over attacks on their armament industry or the city areas. The most serious attacks were those which destroyed the industry or service which most indispensably served other industries. The Germans found it clearly more important to devise measures for the protection of basic industries and services than for the protection of factories turning out finished products.

6. The German experience showed that, whatever the target system, no indispensable industry was permanently put out of commission by a single attack. Persistent re-attack was necessary.

7. In the field of strategic intelligence, there was an important need for further and more accurate information, especially before and during the early phases of the war. ...

8. Among the most significant of the other factors which contributed to the success of the air effort was the extraordinary progress during the war of Allied research, development, and production. As a result of this progress, the air forces eventually brought to the attack superiority in both numbers and quality of crews, aircraft, and equipment. Constant and unending effort was required, however, to overcome the initial advantages of the enemy and later to keep pace with his research and technology. It was fortunate that the leaders of the German Air Force relied too heavily on their initial advantage. For this reason they failed to develop, in time, weapons, such as their jet-propelled planes, that might have substantially improved their position. There was hazard, on the other hand, in the fact that the Allies were behind the Germans in the development of jet propelled aircraft. The German development of the V weapons, especially the V-2, is also noteworthy.

9. The achievements of Allied air power were attained only with difficulty and great cost in men, material, and effort. Its success depended on the courage, fortitude, and gallant action of the officers and men of the aircrews and commands. It depended also on a superiority in leadership, ability, and basic strength. These led to a timely and careful training of pilots and crews in volume; to the production of planes, weapons, and supplies in great numbers and of high quality; to the securing of

adequate bases and supply routes; to speed and ingenuity in development; and to cooperation with strong and faithful Allies. The failure of any one of these might have seriously narrowed and even eliminated the margin.

Of the Future

The air war in Europe was marked by continuous development and evolution. This process did not stop on VE-day; great strides have been made since in machines, weapons, and techniques. No greater or more dangerous mistake could be made than to assume that the same policies and practices that won the war in Europe will be sufficient to win the next one—if there should be another. ...

The great lesson to be learned in the battered towns of England and the ruined cities of Germany is that the best way to win a war is to prevent it from occurring. That must be the ultimate end to which our best efforts are devoted. It has been suggested—and wisely so—that this objective is well served by insuring the strength and the security of the United States. The United States was founded and has since lived upon principles of tolerance, freedom, and good will at home and abroad. Strength based on these principles is no threat to world peace. Prevention of war will not come from neglect of strength or lack of foresight or alertness on our part. Those who contemplate evil and aggression find encouragement in such neglect. Hitler relied heavily upon it.

* * *

The air has become a highway which has brought within easy access every point on the earth's surface—a highway to be traveled in peace, and in war, over distances without limit at ever increasing speed. ... The outstanding significance of the air in modern warfare is recognized by all who participated in the war in Europe or who have had an opportunity to evaluate the results of aerial offensive. ... Speed, range, and striking power of the air weapons of the future, as indicated by the signposts of the war in Europe must—specifically—be reckoned with in any plans for increased security and strength. The combination of the atomic bomb with remote-control projectiles of ocean-spanning range stands as a possibility which is awesome and frightful to contemplate.

8

Albert Einstein's Letter to President Roosevelt on Atomic Weapons

August 2, 1939

Sir:

Some recent work by E. Fermi and L. Szilard, which has been communicated to me in manuscript, leads me to expect that the element uranium may be turned into a new and important source of energy in the immediate future. Certain aspects of the situation which has arisen seem to call for watchfulness and, if necessary, quick action on the part of the administration. I believe therefore that it is my duty to bring to your attention the following facts and recommendations:

In the course of the last four months it has been made probable—through the work of Joliot in France as well as Fermi and Szilard in America—that it may become possible to set up a nuclear chain reaction in a large mass of uranium, by which vast amounts of power and large quantities of new radium like elements would be generated. Now it appears almost certain that this could be achieved in the immediate future.

This new phenomenon would also lead to the construction of bombs, and it is conceivable—though much less certain—that extremely powerful bombs of a new type may thus be constructed. A single bomb of this type, carried by boat and exploded in a port, might very well destroy the whole port together with some of the surrounding territory. However, such bombs might very well prove to be too heavy for transportation by air.

Albert Einstein, "Albert Einstein's Letter to President Roosevelt on Atomic Weapons," pp. 1-2. 1939.

The United States has only very poor [illegible] of uranium in moderate quantities. There is some good ore in Canada and the former Czechoslovakia, while the most important source of Uranium is Belgian Congo.

In view of this situation you may think it desirable to have some permanent contact maintained between the Administration and the group of physicists working on chain reactions in America. One possible way of achieving this might be for you to entrust with this task a person who has your confidence and who could perhaps serve in an unofficial capacity. His task might comprise the following:

a. To approach Government Departments, keep them informed of the further development, and out forward recommendations for Government action, giving particular attention to the problem of uranium ore for the United States;

b. To speed up the experimental work, which is at present being carried on within the limits of the budgets of University laboratories, by providing funds, if such funds be required, through his contacts with private persons who are willing to make a contribution for this cause, and perhaps also by obtaining the co-operation of industrial laboratories which have the necessary equipment.

I understand that Germany has actually stopped the sale of uranium from the Czechoslovakian mines, which she has taken over. That she should have taken such early action might perhaps be understood on the ground that the son of the German Under-Secretary of State, Von Weishlicker [sic], is attached to the Kaiser Wilheim Institute in Berlin where some of the American work on uranium is now being repeated.

Yours very truly,

Albert Einstein

9

POTSDAM DECLARATION

JULY 26, 1945

1. We, the President of the United States, the President of the National Government of the Republic of China and the Prime Minister of Great Britain, representing the hundreds of millions of our countrymen, have conferred and agree that Japan shall be given an opportunity to end this war.

2. The prodigious land, sea and air forces of the United States, the British Empire and of China, many times reinforced by their armies and air fleets from the west are poised to strike the final blows upon Japan. This military power is sustained and inspired by the determination of all the Allied nations to prosecute the war against Japan until she ceases to resist.

3. The result of the futile and senseless German resistance to the might of the aroused free peoples of the world stands forth in awful clarity as an example to the people of Japan. The might that now converges on Japan is immeasurably greater than that which, when applied to the resisting Nazis, necessarily laid waste to the lands, the industry and the method of life of the whole German people. The full application of our military power, backed by our resolve, *will* mean the inevitable and complete destruction of the Japanese armed forces and just as inevitably the utter devastation of the Japanese homeland.

Harry S. Truman, Winston Churchill, and Chiang Kai-Shek, "Potsdam Declaration, July 26, 1945," *U.S. Department of State, A Decade of American Foreign Policy: Basic Documents, 1941-49*, pp. 1-2. 1945.

4. The time has come for Japan to decide whether she will continue to be controlled by those self-willed militaristic advisers whose unintelligent calculations have brought the Empire of Japan to the threshold of annihilation, or whether she will follow the path of reason.

5. Following are our terms. We will not deviate from them. There are no alternatives. We shall brook no delay.

6. There must be eliminated for all time the authority and influence of those who have deceived and misled the people of Japan into embarking on world conquest, for we insist that a new order of peace, security and justice will be impossible until irresponsible militarism is driven from the world.

7. Until such a new order is established *and* until there is convincing proof that Japan's war-making power is destroyed, points in Japanese territory to be designated by the Allies shall be occupied to secure the achievement of the basic objectives we are here setting forth.

8. The terms of the Cairo Declaration shall be carried out and Japanese sovereignty shall be limited to the islands of Honshu, Hokkaido, Kyushu, Shikoku and such minor islands as we determine.

9. The Japanese military forces, after being completely disarmed, shall be permitted to return to their homes with the opportunity to lead peaceful and productive lives.

10. We do not intend that the Japanese shall be enslaved as a race or destroyed as a nation, but stern justice shall be meted out to all war criminals, including those who have visited cruelties upon our prisoners. The Japanese government shall remove all obstacles to the revival and strengthening of democratic tendencies among the Japanese people. Freedom of speech, of religion, and of thought, as well as respect for the fundamental human rights shall be established.

11. Japan shall be permitted to maintain such industries as will sustain her economy and permit the exaction of just reparations in kind, but not those industries which would enable her to re-arm for war. To this end, access to, as distinguished from control of raw materials shall be permitted. Eventual Japanese participation in world trade relations shall be permitted.

12. The occupying forces of the Allies shall be withdrawn from Japan as soon as these objectives have been accomplished and there has been established in accordance with the freely expressed will of the Japanese people a peacefully inclined and responsible government.

13. We call upon the Government of Japan to proclaim now the unconditional surrender of all the Japanese armed forces, and to provide proper and adequate assurances of their good faith in such action. The alternative for Japan is prompt and utter destruction.

10

HIROSHIMA TOTALLY RUINED, LIFE IS WIPED OUT

SPOKANE DAILY CHRONICLE

AUGUST 8, 1945

Guam, Aug. 8. (AP)—One Superfort, dropping one atomic bomb, "completely destroyed" 60 per cent of Hiroshima, important Japanese military base—and General Spaatz warned the enemy today that more B-29s are ready to drop more of the world's most destructive explosive on his cities.

Four and one-tenth of Hiroshima's built-up area of 6.9 square miles was totally wiped out and five unidentified military targets were destroyed by the single bomb, Spaatz announced today in a communiqué giving the first official report of Monday's raid. Additional damage was revealed outside the destroyed section by reconnaissance photographs, on which the communiqué was based.

However, the harbor area of Hiroshima—population about 343,000—appears to have been barely touched by the tremendous concussion of the new explosive.

In contrast, the wrecked heart of the city appears to have been devastated with awful thoroughness—as is a giant bulldozer had swept up buildings and houses and dumped them into a river.

The concussion of fire effect was so overpowering that several firebreaks and seven streams—one firebreak about three city blocks wide—failed to stop the conflagration.

Hiroshima, about the size of Memphis, Tenn., or San Antonio, Texas, was tightly congested. This probably contributed to the degree of destruction.

Few Structure Left

In the heart of the city a few concrete structures remain standing, like bleak sentinels over a scene of ruin. They are believed to be air raid shelters. Although they were not destroyed, photographs indicate they were burned out.

Two small fires were burning when the photographs were taken in the afternoon. The bomb was dropped at 9:15 am Japanese time.

An expert at the United States army strategic air force headquarters said there was no comparison between the fire caused by the atomic bomb and normal conflagrations. When Yokohama was burned by incendiaries, he said, it looked as if smoke pots were burning throughout the city. At Hiroshima, a white plume of smoke rose thousands of feet into the air. Crewmen of the B-29 which dropped the bomb said it rose 40,000 feet.

At the base of this high-necked mushroom was a cloudlike accumulation which was believed to be dust blown into the air by the tremendous concussion. Similar dust clouds were created in Europe by British four ton bombs.

* * *

In that one, swift, devastating strike, a B-29 piloted by Col. Paul W. Tibbets Jr., wrought as great damage as normally is inflicted by a lage force of the sky giants. Tibbets' Superfort, 10 miles from the scene and several miles high, itself was rocked as if an anti-aircraft shell had burst close by.

Although all crew members were wearing dark glasses, the "visual impact" of the explosives' great flash was so tremendous that some cried "my God" in sheer amazement. Only three men on the bomber had known of their secret mission.

Spaatz, although disclosing results of the world's greatest weapon, made this initial announcement simply in these words:

"Reconnaissance photographs made over Hiroshima on the morning of August 6 show that 4.1 square miles, of 60 percent of the city's built-up area of 6.9 miles were completely destroyed by the atomic bombing mission. Five major industrial targets with this area were destroyed. Additional damage was shown outside the completely destroyed area."

11

HARRY TRUMAN RECOUNTS HIS DECISION TO DROP ATOMIC BOMBS ON JAPAN

At Potsdam, as elsewhere, the secret of the atomic bomb was kept closely guarded. We did not extend the very small circle of Americans who knew about it. Churchill naturally knew about the atomic bomb project from its very beginning, because it had involved the pooling of British and American technical skill.

On July 24 I casually mentioned to Stalin that we had a new weapon of unusual destructive force. The Russian Premier showed no special interest. All he said was that he was glad to hear it and hoped we would make "good use of it against the Japanese."

A month before the test explosion of the atomic bomb the service Secretaries and the Joint Chiefs of Staff had laid their detailed plans for the defeat of Japan before me for approval. There had apparently been some differences of opinion as to the best route to be followed, but these had evidently been reconciled, for when General Marshall had presented his plan for a two-phase invasion of Japan, Admiral King and General Arnold had supported the proposal heartily.

The Army plan envisaged an amphibious landing in the fall of 1945 on the island of Kyushu, the southernmost of the Japanese home islands. This would be accomplished by our Sixth Army, under the command of General Walter Krueger. The first landing would then be followed approximately four months later by a second great invasion, which would be carried out by our Eighth and Tenth Armies, followed by the First Army transferred from Europe, all of which would go ashore in the Kanto plains area near Tokyo. In all, it had been estimated that it would require until the late fall of 1946 to bring Japan to her knees.

This was a formidable conception, and all of us realized fully that the fighting would be fierce and the losses heavy. But it was hoped that some of Japan's forces would continue to be preoccupied in China and others would be prevented from reinforcing the home islands if Russia were to enter the war.

There was, of course, always the possibility that the Japanese might choose to surrender sooner. Our air and fleet units had begun to inflict heavy damage on industrial and urban sites in Japan proper. Except in China, the armies of the Mikado had been pushed back everywhere in relentless successions of defeats.

Acting Secretary of State Grew had spoken to me in late May about issuing a proclamation that would urge the Japanese to surrender but would assure them that we would permit the Emperor to remain as head of the state. Grew backed this with arguments taken from his ten years' experience as our Ambassador in Japan, and I told him that I had already given thought to this matter myself and that it seemed to me a sound idea.

* * *

It was my decision then that the proclamation to Japan should be issued from the forthcoming conference at Potsdam. This, I believed, would clearly demonstrate to Japan and to the world that the Allies were united in their purpose. By that time, also, we might know more about two matters of significance for our future effort: the participation of the Soviet Union and the atomic bomb. We knew that the bomb would receive its first test in mid-July. If the test of the bomb was successful, I wanted to afford Japan a clear chance to end the fighting before we made use of this newly gained power. If the test should fail, then it would be even more important to us to bring about a surrender before we had to make a physical conquest of Japan. General Marshall told me that it might cost half a million American lives to force the enemy's surrender on his home grounds.

* * *

My own knowledge of these developments had come about only after became President, when Secretary Stimson had given me the full story. He had told me at that time that the project was nearing completion and that a bomb could be expected within another four months. It was at his suggestion, too, that I had then set up a committee of top men and had asked them to study with great care the implications the new weapon might have for us.

* * *

It was their recommendation that the bomb be used against the enemy as soon as it could be done. They recommended further that it should be used without specific warning and against a target that would clearly show its devastating strength. I had realized, of course, that an atomic bomb explosion would inflict damage and casualties beyond imagination. On the other hand, the scientific advisers of the committee reported, "We can propose no technical demonstration likely to bring an end to the war; we see no acceptable alternative to direct military use." It was their conclusion that no technical demonstration they might propose, such as over a deserted island, would be likely to bring the war to an end. It had to be used against an enemy target.

The final decision of where and when to use the atomic bomb was up to me. Let there be no mistake about it. I regarded the bomb as a military weapon and never had any doubt that it should be used. The top military advisers to the President recommended its use, and when I talked to Churchill he unhesitatingly told me that he favored the use of the atomic bomb if it might aid to end the war.

* * *

In deciding to use this bomb I wanted to make sure that it would be used as a weapon of war in the manner prescribed by the laws of war. That mean at I wanted it dropped on a military target. I had told Stimson that the bomb should be dropped as nearly as possible upon a war production center of prime military importance.

* * *

Four cities were finally recommended as targets: Hiroshima, Kokura, Niigata, and Nagasaki. They were listed in that order as targets for the first attack. The order of selection was in accordance with the military importance of these cities, but allowance would be given for weather conditions at the time of the bombing. Before the selected targets were approved as proper for military purposes, I personally went over them in detail with Stimson, Marshall, and Arnold, and we discussed the matter of timing and the final choice of the first target.

General Spaatz, who commanded the Strategic Air Forces, which would deliver the bomb on the target, was given some latitude as to when and on which of the four targets the bomb would be dropped. ...

* * *

On August 9 the second atom bomb was dropped, this time on Nagasaki. We gave the Japanese three days in which to make up their minds to surrender, and the bombing would have been held off another two days had weather permitted. During those three days we indicated that we meant business. On August 7 the 20th Air Force sent out a bomber force of some one hundred and thirty B-29's, and on the eighth it reported four hundred and twenty B-29's in day and night attacks. The choice of targets for the second atom bomb was first Kokura, with Nagasaki second. The third city on the list, Niigata, had been ruled out as too distant. By the time Kokura was reached the weather had closed in, and after three runs over the spot without a glimpse of the target, with gas running short, a try was made for the second choice, Nagasaki. There, too, the weather had closed in, but an opening in the clouds gave the bombardier his chance, and Nagasaki was successfully bombed.

This second demonstration of the power of the atomic bomb apparently threw Tokyo into a panic, for the next morning brought the first indication that the Japanese Empire was ready to surrender.

12

ATOMIC DIPLOMACY

Perhaps the most remarkable aspect of the decision to use the atomic bomb is that the President and his senior political advisers do not seem ever to have shared Eisenhower's "grave misgivings." As we have seen, they simply assumed that they would use the bomb, never really giving serious consideration to not using it. Hence, to state in a precise way the question "Why was the atomic bomb used?" is to as why senior political officials did not seriously question its use as Eisenhower did.

The first point to note is that the decision to use the weapon did not derive from overriding military considerations. Despite Truman's subsequent statement that the weapon "saved millions of lives," Eisenhower's judgment that it was "completely unnecessary" as a measure to save lives was almost certainly correct. This is not a matter of hindsight; before the atomic bomb was dropped each of the Joint Chiefs of Staff advised that it was highly likely that Japan could be forced to surrender "unconditionally," without use of the bomb and without an invasion. Indeed, this characterization of the position taken by the senior military advisers is a conservative one.

General Marshall's June 18 appraisal was the most cautiously phrased advice offered by any of the Joint Chiefs: "The impact of Russian entry on the already hopeless Japanese may well be the decisive action levering them into capitulation." Admiral Leahy was absolutely certain there was no need for the bombing to obviate the necessity of an invasion!" His judgment after the

Gar Alperovitz, *Atomic Diplomacy: Hiroshima and Potsdam: The Use of the Atomic Bomb and the American Confrontation with Soviet Power*, pp. 237-240, 242. Copyright © 1994 by Pluto Press. Reprinted with permission.

fact was the same as his view before the bombing: "It is my opinion that the use of this barbarous weapon at Hiroshima and Nagasaki was of no material assistance in our war against Japan. The Japanese were already defeated and ready to surrender..."

* * *

The military appraisals made before the weapons were used have been confirmed by numerous post-surrender studies. The best known is that of the United States Strategic Bombing Survey. The Survey's conclusion is unequivocal: "Japan would have surrendered even if the atomic bombs had not been dropped, even if Russia had not entered the war, and even if no invasion had been planned or contemplated."

That military considerations were not decisive is confirmed—and illuminated—by the fact that the President did not even ask the opinion of the military adviser most directly concerned. General MacArthur, Supreme Commander of Allied Forces in the Pacific, was simply informed of the weapon shortly before it was used at Hiroshima." Before his death he stated on numerous occasions that, like Eisenhower, he believed the atomic bomb was completely unnecessary from a military point of view."

Although military considerations were not primary, as we have seen, unquestionably political considerations related to Russia played a major role in the decision; from at least mid-May American policy makers hoped to end the hostilities before the Red Army entered Manchuria. For this reason they had no wish to test whether Russian entry into the war would force capitulation—as most thought likely— long before the scheduled November invasion. Indeed, they actively attempted to delay Stalin's declaration of war.

* * *

If indeed the "second consideration" involved in the bombing of Hiroshima and Nagasaki was the desire to impress the Russians, it might explain the strangely ambiguous statement by Truman that not only did the bomb end the war, but it gave the world "a chance to face the facts?" It would also accord with Stimson's private advice to McCloy: "We have got to regain the lead and perhaps do it in a pretty rough and realistic way. We have coming into action a weapon which will be unique. Now the thing [to do is] let our actions speak for themselves?" Again, it would accord with Stimson's statement to Truman that the "greatest complication" would occur if the President negotiated with

Stalin before the bomb had been "laid on Japan." It would tie in with the fact that from mid-May strategy toward all major diplomatic problems was based upon the assumption the bomb would be demonstrated. Finally, it might explain why none of the highest civilian officials seriously questioned the use of the bomb as Eisenhower did; for, having reversed the basic direction of diplomatic strategy because of the atomic bomb, it would have been very difficult indeed for anyone subsequently to challenge an idea which had come to dominate all calculations of high policy.

CHAPTER 9

HOME FRONT

Introduction

More than half the adult populations of the major Axis and Allied powers became involved in the war efforts in some way: serving in the military, working in war-related industries, supporting coast or air defense, and assisting in many other capacities. This chapter details efforts on the home front, and how people coped with the rigors of war. Many goods were rationed or in short supply, including gasoline, rubber, and foods ranging from meat and eggs to fresh fruit. Canned meat, epitomized by Spam, became a staple in many households. Food was particularly scarce in parts of Russia, and for people living under German occupation or trapped in besieged cities such as Leningrad (today's St. Petersburg) who struggled to survive on starvation diets.

Germany's Nazi government changed its school curriculum to encourage militarism and racism. Dissidents, both in Germany and in the nations it conquered, were treated ruthlessly. Before the war, Nazi leaders altered school curriculums to ensure they promoted the Nazi state and spread its propaganda, particularly history teachers (Document 1). Resistance was fiercely punished, particularly in Nazi-occupied Poland where General Hand Frank ordered draconian and collective punishment for any resistance (Document 2). Despite the risks they faced, some Germans resisted Nazi rule, among them the members of the White Rose, a group of students at the University of Munich led by siblings Hans and Sophie Scholl who distributed leaflets condemning

Nazi atrocities, including the mass murder of Jews on the Eastern front in Russia (Document 3). Caught by the Gestapo in February 1943, most of his members were executed following short trials.

Fighting Nazi Germany forced many Americans to confront racism within their own society, a process encouraged by African American leaders who launched the "Double V Campaign," which called for victory against both Nazism abroad and racism at home. A planned march on Washington by A. Philip Randolph to protest wage inequities (Document 4) convinced President Franklin D. Roosevelt to take action, and he banned discrimination in war work (Document 5). Elizabeth Gurley Flynn similarly encouraged women to participate in the war effort and hoped to use war to reduce sexism and open work and career opportunities for women during and after the war (Document 6). Although job opportunities opened for African Americans and women, anti-Japanese sentiment, already strong along the west coasts of the United States and Canada, surged. President Franklin Roosevelt issued Executive Order 9066 (Document 8) on February 19, 1942. It authorized government officials to relocate more than 120,000 people of Japanese ancestry, more than half of whom were U.S. citizens away from areas of military importance. They spent much of the war in concentration camps.

Although Japan's government promised to liberate East Asians from European rule and establish a Great East Asia Co-Prosperity Sphere, Japan's leaders treated the Asian peoples they conquered as inferior. The Japanese Army routinely committed atrocities in China, such as the 1937 Nanking Massacre. The Japanese Army also forced tens of thousands of Asian women, mostly from China, Korea, and the Philippines, into brothels to serve the sexual needs of its soldiers, the account of one of whom, Kim Dae-il, appears in this chapter (Document7).

Speaking in mid-1942, Japanese Prime Minister Tojo Hideki, celebrated Japan's stunning, victories in the first months of 1942 (Document 9). Although Japan had suffered serious defeats at the Battles of Coral Sea (May 4–8) and Midway (June 4–7), Tojo concealed these from the Japanese people and instead called them to redouble their efforts to defeat Britain and the United States, and bring the war with China, then in its eleventh year, to a successful conclusion.

1

Nazi Guidelines for Teaching History

1938

The German nation in its essence and greatness, in its fateful struggle for internal and external identity is the subject of the teaching of history. It is based on the natural bond of the child with his nation and, by interpreting history as the fateful struggle for existence between the nations, has the particular task of educating young people to respect the great German past and to have faith in the mission and future of their own nation and to respect the right of existence of other nations. The teaching of history must bring the past alive for the young German in such a way that it enables him to understand the present, makes him feel the responsibility of every individual for the nation as a whole and gives him encouragement for his own political activity. It will thereby awaken in the younger generation that sense of responsibility towards ancestors and grandchildren which will enable it to let its life be subsumed in eternal Germany.

* * *

A new understanding of the German past has emerged from the faith of the National Socialist movement in the future of the German people. The teaching of history must come from this vital faith, it must fill young people with the awareness that they belong to a nation which of all the European nations had the longest and most difficult path to its unification but now, at the beginning of a new epoch, can look forward to what is coming full of confidence. [...]

The certainty of a great national existence [...] is for us based [...] at the same time on the clear recognition of the basic racial forces of the German nation which are always active and indestructibly enduring. Insight into the permanence of the hereditary characteristics and the merely contingent significance of environment facilitates a new and deep understanding of historical personalities and contexts.

* * *

The course of history must not appear to our young people as a chronicle which strings events together indiscriminately, but, as in a play, only the important events, those which have a major impact on life, should be portrayed in history lessons. It is not only the successful figures who are important and have an impact on life, but also the tragic figures and periods, not only the victories, but also the defeats. But it must always show greatness because in greatness, even when it intimidates, the eternal law is visible. Only a sentient grasp of great deeds is the precondition for an understanding of historical contexts; the powerless and insignificant have no history.

2

DECREE FOR THE COMBATING OF VIOLENT ACTS IN THE GENERAL GOVERNMENT [POLAND]

1939

1. Anyone who commits a violent act against the German Reich or the German sovereign authority in the Government General will receive the death penalty.

2. Anyone who willfully damages equipment belonging to the German authorities, objects which serve the work of the authorities, or installations which are for the benefit of the public will receive the death penalty.

3. Anyone who encourages or incites disobedience to the decrees or regulations issued by the German authorities will receive the death penalty.

4. Anyone who commits a violence act against a German because of his membership in the German nation will receive the death penalty.

5. Anyone who willfully commits arson and thereby damages the property of a German will receive the death penalty.

Nazism 1919-1945, Volume 3: Foreign Policy: War and Racial Extermination: A Documentary Reader, ed. and trans. Jeremy Noakes and Geoffrey Pridham, pp. 307. Copyright © 2001 by Liverpool University Press. Reprinted with permission.

6. Those who incite or aid such acts will be punished in the same way as the persons who commit them. Attempted acts will be punished in the same was as those which have been committed. ...

7. Anyone who conspires to commit such a crime as those contained in Sections 1–5, enters into serious discussion of such crimes, offers to commit such a crime, or anyone who accepts such an offer will receive the death penalty.

8. Anyone who receives information about the intention to commit a crime such as those contained in Sections 1–5 and fails to report it to the authorities or to the person who is threatened at once, or in time for the crime to be prevented will receive the death penalty. ...

9. (2) Anyone who receives information about he unauthorized possession of a weapon by another person and fails to inform the authorities immediately will receive the death penalty.

3

THE FIFTH BROADSHEET OF THE WHITE ROSE

A CALL TO ALL GERMANS!

The war is approaching its destined end. As in the year 1918, the German government is trying to focus attention exclusively on the growing threat of submarine warfare, while in the East the armies are constantly in retreat and invasion is imminent in the West. Mobilization in the United States has not yet reached its climax, but already it exceeds anything that the world has ever seen. It has become a mathematical certainty that Hitler is leading the German people into the abyss. *Hitler cannot win the war; he can only prolong it.* The guilt of Hitler and his minions goes beyond all measure. Retribution comes closer and closer.

But what are the German people doing? They will not see and will not listen. Blindly they follow their seducers into ruin. *Victory at any price!* is inscribed on their banner. "I will fight to the last man," says Hitler—but in the meantime the war has already been lost.

Germans! Do you and your children want to suffer the same fate that befell the Jews? Do you want to be judged by the same standards as your traducers? Are we to be forever the nation which is hated and rejected by all mankind? No. Dissociate yourselves from National Socialist gangsterism. Prove by your deeds that you think otherwise. A new war of liberation is about to begin. The better part of the nation will fight on our side. Cast off the cloak of indifference

Inge Scholl, "The Fifth Broadsheet of the White Rose," *The White Rose: Munich 1942-1943*, trans. Arthur R. Schultz, pp. 1-2. Copyright © 1983 by Wesleyan University Press. Reprinted with permission.

you have wrapped around you. Make the decision *before it is too late*! Do not believe the National Socialist propaganda which has driven the fear of Bolshevism into your bones. Do not believe that Germany's welfare is linked to the victory of National Socialism for good or ill. A criminal regime cannot achieve a German victory. Separate yourselves *in time* from everything connected with National Socialism. In the aftermath a terrible but just judgment will be meted out to those who stayed in hiding, who were cowardly and hesitant.

What can we learn from the outcome of this war—this war that never was a national war?

The imperialist ideology of force, from whatever side it comes, must be shattered for all time. A one-sided Prussian militarism must never again be allowed to assume power. Only in large-scale cooperation among the nations of Europe can the ground be prepared for reconstruction. Centralized hegemony, such as the Prussian state has tried to exercise in Germany and in Europe, must be cut down at its inception. The Germany of the future must be a federal state. At this juncture only a sound federal system can imbue a weakened Europe with a new life. The workers must be liberated from their condition of down-trodden slavery under National Socialism. The illusory structure of autonomous national industry must disappear. Every nation and each man have a right to the goods of the whole world!

Freedom of speech, freedom of religion, the protection of individual citizens from the arbitrary will of criminal regimes of violence—these will be the bases of the New Europe.

Support the resistance. Distribute the leaflets!

* * *

Source of English translation: Inge Scholl. "The Fifth Broadsheet of the White Rose" from The White Rose: Munich 1942–1943. © 1983 by Inge Aicher-Scholl and reprinted by permission of Wesleyan University Press.

4

A. Philip Randolph Proposes a March on Washington

January 1941

PROGRAM OF THE MARCH ON WASHINGTON MOVEMENT

1. We demand, in the interest of national unity, the abrogation of every law which makes a distinction in treatment between citizens based on religion, creed, color, or national origin. This means an end to Jim Crow in education, in housing, in transportation and in every other social, economic, and political privilege. Especially, we demand, in the capital of the nation, an end to all segregation in public places and in public institutions.

2. We demand legislation to enforce the Fifth and Fourteenth Amendments guaranteeing that no person shall be deprived of life, liberty or property without due process of law, so that the full weight of the national government may be used for the protection of life and thereby may end the disgrace of lynching.

3. We demand the enforcement of the Fourteenth and Fifteenth Amendments and the enactment of the Pepper Poll Tax bill so that all barriers in the exercise of suffrage are eliminated.

A. Philip Randolph, "A. Philip Randolph Proposes March on Washington, January 1941," 1941.

4. We demand the abolition of segregation and discrimination in the army, navy, marine corps, air corps, and all other branches of national defense.

5. We demand an end to discrimination in jobs and job training. Further, we demand that the F.E.P.C. be made a permanent administrative agency of the U.S. Government and that it be given power to enforce its decisions based on its findings.

6. We demand that federal funds be withheld from any agency which practices discrimination in the use of such funds.

7. We demand colored and minority group representation on all administrative agencies so that these groups may have recognition of their democratic right to participate in formulating policies.

8. We demand representation for the colored and minority racial groups on all missions, political and technical, which will be sent to the peace conference so that the interests of all people everywhere may be fully recognized and justly provided for in the post-war settlement.

5

EXEC ORDER 8802, PROHIBITION OF DISCRIMINATION IN THE DEFENSE INDUSTRY

JUNE 25, 1941

EXECUTIVE ORDER 8802: REAFFIRMING POLICY OF FULL PARTICIPATION IN THE DEFENSE PROGRAM BY ALL PERSONS, REGARDLESS OF RACE, CREED, COLOR, OR NATIONAL ORIGIN, AND DIRECTING CERTAIN ACTION IN FURTHERANCE OF SAID POLICY

WHEREAS it is the policy of the United States to encourage full participation in the national defense program by all citizens of the United States, regardless of race, creed, color, or national origin, in the firm belief that the democratic way of life within the Nation can be defended successfully only with the help and support of all groups within its borders; and

WHEREAS there is evidence that available and needed workers have been barred from employment in industries engaged in defense production solely because of considerations of race, creed, color, or national origin, to the detriment of workers' morale and of national unity:

Franklin D. Roosevelt, "Exec Order 8802, Prohibition of Discrimination in the Defense Industry," 1941.

NOW, THEREFORE, by virtue of the authority vested in me by the Constitution and the statutes, and as a prerequisite to the successful conduct of our national defense production effort, I do hereby reaffirm the policy of the United States that there shall be no discrimination in the employment of workers in defense industries or government because of race, creed, color, or national origin, and I do hereby declare that it is the duty of employers and of labor organizations, in furtherance of said policy and of this order, to provide for the full and equitable participation of all workers in defense industries, without discrimination because of race, creed, color, or national origin;

And it is hereby ordered as follows:

1. All departments and agencies of the Government of the United States concerned with vocational and training programs for defense production shall take special measures appropriate to assure that such programs are administered without discrimination because of race, creed, color, or national origin;

2. All contracting agencies of the Government of the United States shall include in all defense contracts hereafter negotiated by them a provision obligating the contractor not to discriminate against any worker because of race, creed, color, or national origin;

3. There is established in the Office of Production Management a Committee on Fair Employment Practice, which shall consist of a chairman and four other members to be appointed by the President. The Chairman and members of the Committee shall serve as such without compensation but shall be entitled to actual and necessary transportation, subsistence and other expenses incidental to performance of their duties. The Committee shall receive and investigate complaints of discrimination in violation of the provisions of this order and shall take appropriate steps to redress grievances which it finds to be valid. The Committee shall also recommend to the several departments and agencies of the Government of the United States and to the President all measures which may be deemed by it necessary or proper to effectuate the provisions of this order.

6

ELIZABETH GURLEY FLYNN ENCOURAGES WOMEN TO SUPPORT THE WAR

We American women, like the Chinese, British, and Soviet women, will work till we drop and fight till we die to defend our beautiful country and our democratic liberties from the brutish ideology of the Nazis. We are not called upon to engage in actual military action. But in mortal crisis, as the heroic Soviet girl Liudmila Pavlichenko, became a crack sniper; as Ma-Lu, the young Chinese girl, led a Japanese regiment to death over a mined bridge; as the strong Basque women hurled the fascists into the sea; as the Czech, Dutch, and French women patriots carry on guerilla warfare to resist the Nazi masters, so will we take arms, if necessary, in the spirit of Molly Pitcher and Harriet Tubman.

Today it is more useful and just as heroic to *make arms* for our fighting forces and our brave allies. Our main tasks are on the home front. Eighteen people are required to work to keep one fighter on the field, at sea, or in the air. Women's work is manifold today. It includes industry, civilian defense, politics, the labor unions, and as trained auxiliaries to the armed forces. General H. H. Kitchener said in the last war: "If the women of either side should stop their war work, that side would lose." This is even more evident today. The women of our nation are essential to winning the war. They are the reservoir of labor. In ever-increasing numbers women will be called out

Elizabeth Gurley Flynn, *Women in the War*, pp. 11-23. 1942.

of the kitchen onto the assembly line. It is a matter of patriotism, necessity, and arithmetic. Women are cheerfully answering the call.

* * *

In England over five million women have entered industry and auxiliary war service. Over 50,000 are employed on the railroads. Thirty million women are on the home front behind the dauntless Soviet battle lines—in agriculture and industry, including coal mines, steel plants, and on ships. We women will not lag behind our Allied sisters in working while our men fight. Soviet women today inspire the women of the whole world by their work and bravery.

* * *

All women who want war jobs should register with the U.S. Employment Service. Do not be disheartened if you are not called immediately. All who volunteer for our armed forces are not called at once. One's turn will come more quickly if qualifications and experience are on record. State what you want to do and apply for training. Prepare for a job while you wait for it. We must grasp new opportunities firmly and demand to be made able to meet the requirements.

Prejudices break down in a national crisis. Women and the Negro people must be given the right to show their mettle as workers. Work is not *man's* versus women's, any more than it is white's versus Negro's or *native born's* versus foreign born's, or Christian's versus Jew's. Such a characterization as "male, white, Christian, native born" is typically Nazi, repugnant to American concepts of democracy. Women's role in industry, like that of the Negro people, is not of a temporary nature.

* * *

The Negro people and women must have permanent access to all jobs and professions. This is democracy. To deny it is to disrupt national unity and cripple production in a critical war period. Victory is at stake.

Women, white and Negro, will not sit at home with folded hands. They want to "do something" to help their fighting sons, brothers, husbands, fathers. Pearl Harbor widows set a heroic example when they went to work as a group in California airplane plant. Old and young, married and single, mothers, yes, and grandmothers—are busy at all kinds of jobs today. They test tanks and machine guns at Army proving grounds; ferry airplanes from factories to fields; run stores, farms, hotels, gas stations. They work in banks, copper smelters, Army warehouses, canneries grinding diamonds for tools, as mechanics in the Navy yards, on bombers and tanks, at wood turning, in aluminum plants, on shells, at ship building, parachute rigging, servicing and repairing planes, as guards for plants, assembling carburetor parts, at air-traffic control, as streetcar conductors, in the electrical industries as assemblers, welders, inspectors, loading detonators, making guns and bullets, building Jeeps, making glass for planes. These are just a few random samples of the *Victory girls at work.*

* * *

Child care is a major issue in our country today. The unions who sponsor it and the congressmen who fight for further appropriations will win the ardent support of women. ...

* * *

Housing is another major need of workers in war production centers. The Manpower Commission could far more readily move labor forces around the country if this problem were adequately met. New workers coming into cities like Oakland, San Diego, Buffalo, and Bridgeport are worn out by lack of accommodations, and then their cost of living is doubled.

Women are even more sensitive to bad housing conditions than men are because they carry the burden of domestic duty after a day's work. Homes are working places to them. Let a woman worker come home to a modern, comfortable government project house with all facilities for a quick bath, a dinner already prepared in the Frigidaire or partly cooked in an electric stove—and the world looks different to her. Workers who live in these houses are happy. The only trouble is, there are too few of them ...

To summarize—the vital needs of American women workers to help win the war are as follows:

1. Equal opportunity to work for all women (Negro and white) at all occupations

2. Adequate training for jobs, under government and union supervision

3. Equal pay for equal work.

4. Safe and sanitary shop conditions.

5. Equal membership, protection by, and participation in labor unions.

6. Child-care centers, with federal funds and supervision.

7. Adequate modern housing

7

Interview with Kim Dae-il

Kim Dae-il discusses the lives of "Comfort Women"

I am Kim Dae-il, born July 7, 1916, in Sariwon, Hwang-hae Province. I vividly remember the experience I suffered as a "comfort woman" although it was such a long time ago.

I remember the time when we traveled from Korea to Shimonoseki, Japan. Mr. Fukuda, a Japanese military first lieutenant, said, "This is Japan. From now on, you must not speak Korean. Your new and only name is "Shizue." The word "comfort women" is used nowadays, but it was called *teishintai,* or volunteer corps, in those days. So, forty of us "volunteers" were taken to Manchuria. Each of us was assigned a number for identification, and a small space of four feet by six with one *tatami,* a Japanese straw mattress, for the floor. These cubicles were built by the military construction corps.

So we were made sex slaves and were forced to service 40 to 50 soldiers each day. One time a soldier sat on top of the stomach of a pregnant "comfort woman" who was almost full term. Apparently this act induced labor. As a baby started to appear, he stabbed both the infant and the mother and exclaimed, "Hey these *senjing* (dirty Koreans) are dead. Come and see.

"Interview with Kim Dae-il," *Comfort Women Speak: Testimony of Sex Slaves of the Japanese Military*, ed. Sang-mie Choi Schellstede, pp. 25-27. Copyright © 2000 by Holmes & Meier.

It was a common practice for soldiers to manhandle us, but the soldiers of the Sixth Army Division from Kyushu were the worst. They would frequently beat us. One day a drunken soldier walked into my cubicle, stuck his bayonet on the *tatami* mat, and yelled at me, "You must have heard of the Sixth Division. I am the one. I will kill you if you do not do as I say."

Some of them were too impatient to wait their turns for sex. They would yell, "Hey, hurry up, and come out now." A few even intruded into my cubicle and tried to mount me before the previous soldier could remove himself from me.

I often fainted after serving so many soldiers, 50 or so. The next soldier in line came in, and holding a lighted cigarette close to my nose, made me inhale the smoke to wake me up. He then stuck the lit cigarette into my vagina, spreading my two legs apart. He laughed and clapped his hands for having done this.

One time another drunken soldier came in and continued drinking in my cubicle. He then stabbed the lower part of my body and shouted, "Hey, this *senjing* (a dirty Korean) is dying. He then screamed, *"Kono yaro!"* (damn you!) and stabbed a few more times on my lower abdomen. I became crippled for life from these wounds."

8

Executive Order No. 9066: Japanese Relocation

February 19, 1942

Authorizing the Secretary of War to Prescribe Military Areas

Whereas the successful prosecution of the war requires every possible protection against espionage and against sabotage to national-defense material, national-defense premises, and national-defense utilities ...

Now, therefore, by virtue of the authority vested in me as President of the United States, and Commander in Chief of the Army and Navy, I hereby authorize and direct the Secretary of War, and the Military Commanders whom he may from time to time designate, whenever he or any designated Commander deems such action necessary or desirable, to prescribe military areas in such places and of such extent as he or the appropriate Military Commander may determine, from which any or all persons may be excluded, and with respect to which, the right of any person to enter, remain in, or leave shall be subject to whatever restrictions the Secretary of War or the appropriate Military Commander may impose in his discretion. The Secretary of War is hereby authorized to provide for residents of any such area who are excluded therefrom, such transportation, food, shelter, and other accommodations as may be necessary, in the judgment of the Secretary of War or the said Military Commander, and until other arrangements are made, to accomplish

Franklin D. Roosevelt, "Executive Order No. 9066: Japanese Relocation," 1942, pp. 1-2.

the purpose of this order. The designation of military areas in any region or locality shall supersede designations of prohibited and restricted areas by the Attorney General under the Proclamations of December 7 and 8, 1941, and shall supersede the responsibility and authority of the Attorney General under the said Proclamations in respect of such prohibited and restricted areas.

I hereby further authorize and direct the Secretary of War and the said Military Commanders to take such other steps as he or the appropriate Military Commander may deem advisable to enforce compliance with the restrictions applicable to each Military area hereinabove authorized to be designated, including the use of Federal troops and other Federal Agencies, with authority to accept assistance of state and local agencies.

I hereby further authorize and direct all Executive Departments, independent establishments and other Federal Agencies, to assist the Secretary of War or the said Military Commanders in carrying out this Executive Order, including the furnishing of medical aid, hospitalization, food, clothing, transportation, use of land, shelter, and other supplies, equipment, utilities, facilities, and services.

This order shall not be construed as modifying or limiting in any way the authority heretofore granted under Executive Order No. 8972, dated December 12, 1941, nor shall it be construed as limiting or modifying the duty and responsibility of the Federal Bureau of Investigation, with respect to the investigation of alleged acts of sabotage or the duty and responsibility of the Attorney General and the Department of Justice under the Proclamations of December 7 and 8, 1941, prescribing regulations for the conduct and control of alien enemies, except as such duty and responsibility is superseded by the designation of military areas hereunder.

9

BROADCAST BY JAPANESE PRIME MINISTER HIDEKI TOJO ON JAPAN'S WAR EFFORT

JULY 27, 1942

Truly seven months have passed since the beginning of the Greater East Asia war and the people have reaffirmed their conviction of ultimate victory more than ever. ... To begin with, 11 years have passed since the outbreak of the Manchurian Incident, and during this period we have overcome various difficulties and surmounted obstacles through the Manchurian Incident, the China Continent, and moreover the various fronts in Greater East Asia, the various changes in the Pacific, the prosecution of the war today, and in the extension of the Imperial Crown as far as our eye can reach. At this time, I join with you in expressing my heartfelt appreciation to the indomitable fighting spirit and superiority of the men and officers of the Imperial forces that are accounting for repeated and successive victories and in offering our reverent respects to the souls of the war dead who have passed away during the performance of their duties in the furtherance of Greater East Asia. ...

Recently our naval forces have carried out an attack on the enemy stronghold of Midway and have annihilated the remnant aircraft carrier force, and at the same time our forces in the northern Pacific carried out an attack on America's northernmost fortifications of Dutch Harbor ... in the Aleutians, and thus our forces have established strategic positions of solid rock foundation. In regard to the southern regions, Sydney of northern Australia and Madagascar in the Indian Ocean have been included among the objectives of our attacks. ... Our Imperial forces are pressing the enemy in the China

Foreign Broadcast Monitoring Service, FCC, "Tojo on Japanese war effort, July 1942," Ibiblio. 1942.

Continent, in the Pacific, and in (Australia) and at the same time carrying out rapid and concrete progress in the construction of a new order so that the various races may extend their part in the co-prosperity sphere. The various races in the southern regions have understood our true intentions and are gladly extending their cooperation. ...

* * *

The shining countries of Germany and Italy have made considerable preparations and ... are achieving brilliant war results in all theaters of war [and are] inflicting tremendous losses on the sea transportation conditions of both America and Britain ... As a result, the life of America and Britain is rapidly vanishing. ...

... Following this course, I should like to mention on this occasion what the government expects of the people.

The first is the strengthening of the spiritual consolidation of the people. The thoughts of the soldiers at the front are filled with memories of their native land and the protection of the home front. These thoughts can overcome the grief encountered during the performance of patriotic service ... behind the glorious achievements of war results lie the spiritual consolidation of the people behind the home front. This point must never be forgotten by the people. ...

The second is that the government is carrying out policies only necessary under the wartime situation. The world situation today is undergoing changes with bewildering rapidity, and in coping with the rapid and radical changes and in meeting the needs of the armed forces the question of peace and order internally must be dealt with most adequately and must be settled most speedily. ... This has been exemplified by the supply of needed men sent throughout the Greater East Asia sphere with government duties to perform. ...

Third is the establishment of a strong security of the people's living conditions. In order to fight through the war to victory, it is exceedingly important to expand the strength of the armed forces and to establish security in the living conditions on a minimum basis, while carrying out a policy to protect the home front through the efforts of the people at home. As a policy the government is expending every effort in the increase of production of foodstuffs, fuel, materials, and other fields, as well as in the firm establishment of a wartime national structure. It is of primary importance that the living conditions of the people be made completely secure and undoubtedly there will be some inconvenience imposed on the people. Among the belligerent nations today there is no other country where living conditions are more blessed than the present conditions existing in Japan. ...

Fourth is the successful increased production, which is vital for the strengthening of the military ... in order to exterminate British and American power. ...

The fifth is the immediate reformation of education. In carrying through the war, education plays an important part, but in order to spread the influence of education, it will depend on the spirit with which it is carried out. ... In winning this great war over Britain and America, and in order to establish a new Greater East Asia with trained leaders as the backbone, men of fine characters who are fit to carry out the various tasks must be trained. ...

At this time, when the nation is confronted with an unprecedented crisis, national structures applicable in the southern regions must be established with some enthusiasm on the part of the people. On this day of 2602 year since the founding of the Japanese Empire, it is of great importance that the people throughout the nation unite into a ball and go forward in order to spread the Imperial Way throughout the world. ... the people must strive toward the establishment of a new world order and at the same time must establish peace. We must by all means complete our sacred mission of this war.

... Total effort must be collected in the form of total strength and I believe the objective of the Greater East Asia war will be realized with certainty. At the conclusion I wish to thank you again for the cooperation you have extended thus far and I beg of you to extend your continued efforts. I pray for your health. I wish to conclude my talk.

CHAPTER 10

Wartime Diplomacy, Conferences, and the Grand Alliance

Introduction

Diplomatic activity does not cease upon the outbreak of war. Diplomats do not sit out the war and wait for the postwar peace conference. Wartime coalitions have to be strengthened and neutral powers have to be persuaded to enter the war on the right side. The documents in this chapter focus on the diplomatic aspects of the Second World War.

First, review the text of the Tripartite Alliance between Germany, Italy, and Japan, signed on September 27, 1940 (Document 1). What are the terms of this alliance? Do you think the terms of this treaty will make for a close alliance during the war?

Next, we have the text of the Soviet-Japanese Neutrality Pact of April 13, 1941 (Document 2), one of the forgotten documents of the war. Japan and Russia had a long history of hostility. Japan had defeated Russia in the Russo-Japanese War of 1904–1905, and Japan had intervened against the Communists in the Russian Civil War. Border clashes followed the Japanese conquest of Manchuria in 1931, culminating in a heavy Japanese defeat during the Nomonhan border war of August 1939. Why would these two countries now decide to sign a neutrality pact? Again, pay close attention to the date, and think about subsequent events in 1941. What benefit does each signatory gain from this pact?

The Anglo-Soviet Agreement of July 12, 1941 (Document 3) was signed during the early phases of Operation Barbarossa. What are the signatories trying to accomplish with this text?

The Atlantic Charter was signed by Winston Churchill and Franklin D. Roosevelt on August 14, 1941 (Document 4), when the United States was not yet in the war. This document is often seen as a statement of Allied war aims. What are the Allies fighting for? Do you see any continuities with Woodrow Wilson's Fourteen Points in Chapter 1?

Germany declared war on the United States on December 11, 1941 (Document 5). Why, according to the Germans, are they going to war with the United States? Refer back to the terms of the Tripartite Alliance to consider whether Hitler had any obligation to go to war with the United States following the Japanese attack on Pearl Harbor.

The Declaration of the United Nations of January 1, 1942 (Document 6) marks the first use of the term "United Nations." What continuities do you see with the Atlantic Charter?

The British-Soviet Treaty of May 26, 1942 (Document 7) was meant to follow up on the two countries' agreement of 1941. What are the terms of this treaty? What are the benefits to the two signatories?

Next, we have an exchange of letters between Churchill, Joseph Stalin, and Roosevelt concerning the destruction of convoy P.Q. 17 (Document 8). Read the full document to understand what happened to the convoy. Allied lend-lease shipments to Russia were regarded as crucial to keeping the USSR in the war. Can you understand the point of view of each of the three Allied leaders? How does the tone of these letters differ from the public statements in the rest of this chapter? What do these letters tell you about the nature of coalition warfare?

The Allies met at the Casablanca Conference of January 1943. In their letter to Stalin, Roosevelt and Churchill outline the strategy of the western Allies for 1943 (Document 9). How did their plans actually unfold later that year? Do you detect any hidden tensions between the western Allies and Stalin? How do you think Stalin would receive this letter? What do you think were Churchill and Roosevelt's intentions in sending this letter? How does the public communique differ from the letter to Stalin?

Similar questions could be asked about the communique from the Anglo-American Quebec Conference of August 1943 (Document 10). What differences and similarities do you see from the Casablanca Conference documents?

In the reading from the Moscow Conference of October 1943 (Document 11), what continuities do you see with earlier documents in this chapter? What is the purpose of the statement on atrocities?

The final reading concerns the Tehran Conference of late 1943 (Document 12). How do the Allies propose to win the war? What is their strategy for 1944? How closely did events subsequently adhere to their plan?

1

The Tripartite Alliance

September 27, 1940

The governments of Germany, Italy and Japan, considering it as a condition precedent of any lasting peace that all nations of the world be given each its own proper place, have decided to stand by and co-operate with one another in regard to their efforts in greater East Asia and regions of Europe respectively wherein it is their prime purpose to establish and maintain a new order of things calculated to promote the mutual prosperity and welfare of the peoples concerned.

Furthermore, it is the desire of the three governments to extend co-operation to such nations in other spheres of the world as may be inclined to put forth endeavours along lines similar to their own, in order that their ultimate aspirations for world peace may thus be realized.

Accordingly, the governments of Germany, Italy and Japan have agreed as follows:

Article One: Japan recognizes and respects the leadership of Germany and Italy in the establishment of a new order in Europe.

Article Two: Germany and Italy recognize and respect the leadership of Japan in the establishment of a new order in greater East Asia.

Article Three: Germany, Italy and Japan agree to co-operate in their efforts on aforesaid lines. They further undertake to assist one another with all political, economic and military means when one of the three contracting

"The Tripartite Alliance, September 27, 1940," The Avalon Project. 1940.

parties is attacked by a power not involved in the European war or in the Chinese-Japanese conflict.

Article Four: With the view to implementing the present pact, joint technical commissions, members which are to be appointed by the respective governments of Germany, Italy and Japan will meet without delay.

Article Five: Germany, Italy and Japan affirm that the aforesaid terms do not in any way affect the political status which exists at present as between each of the three contracting powers and Soviet Russia.

Article Six: The present pact shall come into effect immediately upon signature and shall remain in force 10 years from the date of its coming into force. At the proper time before expiration of said term, the high contracting parties shall at the request of any of them enter into negotiations for its renewal.

2

SOVIET-JAPANESE NEUTRALITY PACT

APRIL 13, 1941

The Presidium of the Supreme Soviet of the USSR and His Majesty the Emperor of Japan, guided by the desire to strengthen peaceful and friendly relations between the two countries, have decided to conclude a pact of neutrality. ...

Article 1. Both contracting parties undertake to maintain peaceful and friendly relations between themselves and mutually to respect the territorial integrity and inviolability of the other contracting party.

Article 2. Should one of the contracting parties become the object of hostilities on the part of one or several third Powers, the other contracting party will observe neutrality throughout the entire duration of the conflict.

Article 3. The present pact comes into force from the day of its ratification by both contracting parties and shall remain valid for five years. Should neither of the contracting parties denounce the pact one year before the expiration of that term, it will be considered automatically prolonged for the following five years.

"The Soviet-Japanese Neutrality Pact, April 13, 1941," *Soviet Documents on Foreign Policy*. 1941.

3

ANGLO-SOVIET AGREEMENT

JULY 12, 1941

His Majesty's Government in the United Kingdom and the Government of the Union of Soviet Socialist Republics have concluded the present Agreement and declare as follows:

1. The two Governments mutually undertake to render each other assistance and support of all kinds in the present war against Hitlerite Germany.

2. They further undertake that during this war they will neither negotiate nor conclude an armistice or treaty of peace except by mutual agreement.

"Anglo-Soviet Agreement, July 12, 1941," The Avalon Project. 1941.

4

THE ATLANTIC CHARTER

AUGUST 14, 1941

The President of the United States of America and the Prime Minister, Mr. Churchill, representing His Majesty's Government in the United Kingdom, being met together, deem it right to make known certain common principles in the national policies of their respective countries on which they base their hopes for a better future for the world.

First, their countries seek no aggrandizement, territorial or other;

Second, they desire to see no territorial changes that do not accord with the freely expressed wishes of the peoples concerned;

Third, they respect the right of all peoples to choose the form of government under which they will live; and they wish to see sovereign rights and self government restored to those who have been forcibly deprived of them;

Fourth, they will endeavor, with due respect for exiting obligations, to further the enjoyment by all States, great or small, victor or vanquished, of access, on equal terms, to the trade and raw materials of the world which are needed for their economic prosperity;

Fifth, they desire to bring about the fullest collaboration between all nations in the economic field with the object of securing, for all, improved labor standards, economic advancement and social security;

Sixth, after the final destruction of Nazi tyranny, they hope to see established a peace which will afford to all nations the means of dwelling in safety within

Franklin D. Roosevelt and Winston Churchill, "The Atlantic Charter, August 14, 1941," The Avalon Project. 1941.

their own boundaries, and which will afford assurance that all the men in all lands may live out their lives in freedom from fear and want;

Seventh, such a peace should enable all men to traverse the high seas and oceans without hindrance;

Eighth, they believe that all the nations of the world, for realistic as well as spiritual reasons must come to the abandonment of the use of force. Since no future peace can be maintained if land, sea or air armaments continue to be employed by nations which threaten, or may threaten, aggression outside of their frontiers, they believe, pending the establishment of a wider and permanent system of general security, that the disarmament of such nations is essential. They will likewise aid and encourage all other practicable measures which will lighten for peace-loving peoples the crushing burden of armaments.

5

GERMAN DECLARATION OF WAR ON THE UNITED STATES

DECEMBER 11, 1941

The Government of the United States, having violated in the most flagrant manner and in ever increasing measure all rules of neutrality in favor of the adversaries of Germany and having continually been guilty of the most severe provocations toward Germany ever since the outbreak of the European war, provoked by the British declaration of war against Germany on September 3, 1939, has finally resorted to open military acts of aggression.

On September 11, 1941, the President of the United States publicly declared that he had ordered the American Navy and Air Force to shoot on sight at any German war vessel. In his speech of October 27, 1941, he once more expressly affirmed that this order was in force. Acting under this order, vessels of the American Navy, since early September 1941, have systematically attacked German naval forces. Thus, American destroyers, as for instance the Greer, the Kearney and the Reuben James, have opened fire on German submarines according to plan. The Secretary of the American Navy, Mr. Knox, himself confirmed that American destroyers attacked German submarines.

Furthermore, the naval forces of the United States, under order of their Government and contrary to international law have treated and seized German merchant vessels on the high seas as enemy ships.

The German government therefore establishes the following facts:

Although Germany on her part has strictly adhered to the rules of international law in her relations with the United States during every period of the

Joachim von Ribbentrop, "German Declaration of War on the United States, December 11, 1941," The Avalon Project, pp. 1-2. 1941.

present war, the Government of the United States from initial violations of neutrality has finally proceeded to open acts of war against Germany. The Government of the United States has thereby virtually created a state of war.

The German Government, consequently, discontinues diplomatic relations with the United States of America and declares that under these circumstances brought about by President Roosevelt Germany too, as from today, considers herself as being in a state of war with the United States of America.

Accept, Mr. Charge d'Affaires, the expression of my high consideration.

December 11, 1941.

Ribbentrop.

6

DECLARATION BY THE UNITED NATIONS

JANUARY 1, 1942

The Governments signatory hereto,

Having subscribed to a common program of purposes and principles embodied in the Joint Declaration of the President of the United States of America and the Prime Minister of the United Kingdom of Great Britain and Northern Ireland dated August 14, 1941, known as the Atlantic Charter.

Being convinced that complete victory over their enemies is essential to defend life, liberty, independence and religious freedom, and to preserve human rights and justice in their own lands as well as in other lands, and that they are now engaged in a common struggle against savage and brutal forces seeking to subjugate the world,

Declare:

1. Each Government pledges itself to employ its full resources, military of economic, against those members of the Tripartite Pact and its adherents with which such government is at war.

2. Each Government pledges itself to cooperate with the Governments signatory hereto and not to make a separate armistice or peace with the enemies.

"Declaration by the United Nations, January 1, 1942," The Avalon Project. 1942.

The foregoing declaration may be adhered to by other nations which are, or which may be, rendering material assistance and contributions in the struggle for victory of Hitlerism.

Original signatories: The United States, Great Britain, the USSR, China, Australia, Belgium, Canada, Costa Rica, Cuba, Czechoslovakia, Dominican Republic, El Salvador, Greece, Guatemala, Haiti, Honduras, India, Luxembourg, Netherlands, New Zealand, Nicaragua, Norway, Panama, Poland, South Africa, Yugoslavia.

7

British-Soviet Treaty

May 26, 1942

His Majesty the King of Great Britain, Ireland and British Dominions beyond the Seas, Emperor of India, and the Presidium of the Supreme Council of the Union of the Soviet Socialist Republics:

Desiring to confirm the stipulations of the agreement between His Majesty's Government in the United Kingdom and the Government of the Union of the Soviet Socialist Republics for joint action in the war against Germany signed at Moscow, July 12, 1941, and to replace them by formal treaty;

Desiring to contribute after the war to the maintenance of peace and to the prevention of further aggression by Germany or the States associated with her in acts of aggression in Europe;

Desiring, moreover, to give expression to their intention to collaborate closely with one another as well as with the other United Nations at the peace settlement and during the ensuing period of reconstruction on a basis of the principles enunciated in the declaration made August 14, 1941, by the President of the United States of America and the Prime Minister of Great Britain, to which the Government of the Union of Soviet Socialist Republics has adhered;

Desiring finally to provide for mutual assistance in the event of attack upon either high contracting party by Germany or any of the States associated with her in acts of aggression in Europe;

Have decided to conclude a treaty for that purpose ...

"British-Soviet Treaty, May 26, 1942," The Avalon Project, pp. 1-3. 1942.

PART ONE

ARTICLE I

In virtue of the alliance established between the United Kingdom and the Union of Soviet Socialist Republics, the high contracting parties mutually undertake to afford one another military and other assistance and support of all kinds in war against Germany and all those States which are associated with her in acts of aggression in Europe.

ARTICLE II

The high contracting parties undertake not to enter into any negotiations with the Hitlerite Government or any other government in Germany that does not clearly renounce all aggression intentions, and not to negotiate or conclude, except by mutual consent, any armistice or peace treaty with Germany or any other State associated with her in acts of aggression in Europe.

PART TWO

ARTICLE III

1. The high contracting parties declare their desire to unite with other like-minded States in adopting proposals for common action to preserve peace and resist aggression in the post-war period.

2. Pending adoption of such proposals, they will after termination of hostilities take all measures in their power to render impossible the repetition of aggression and violation of peace by Germany or any of the States associated with her in acts of aggression in Europe.

ARTICLE IV

Should either of the high contracting parties during the postwar period become involved in hostilities with Germany or any of the States mentioned in Article III, Section 2, in consequence of the attack by that State against that party, the other high contracting party will at once give to the contracting party so involved in hostilities all military and other support and assistance in his power.

This article shall remain in force until the high contracting parties, by mutual agreement, shall recognize that it is superseded by adoption of proposals contemplated in Article III, Section I. In default of adoption of such proposals, it shall remain in force for a period of twenty years and thereafter until terminated by either high contracting party as provided in Article VIII.

ARTICLE V

The high contracting parties, having regard to the interests of security of each of them, agree to work together in close and friendly collaboration after re-establishment of peace for the organization of security and economic prosperity in Europe.

They will take into account the interests of the United Nations in these objects and they will act in accordance with the two principles of not seeking territorial aggrandizement for themselves and of non-interference in the internal affairs of other States.

ARTICLE VI

The high contracting parties agree to render one another all possible economic assistance after the war.

ARTICLE VII

Each contracting party undertakes not to conclude any alliance and not to take part in any coalition directed against the other high contracting party.

ARTICLE VIII

The present treaty is subject to ratification in the shortest possible time and instruments of ratification shall be exchanged in Moscow as soon as possible.

It comes into force immediately on the exchange of instruments of ratification and shall thereupon replace the agreement between the Government of the Union of the Soviet Socialist Republics and His Majesty's Government in the United Kingdom signed at Moscow July 12, 1941.

Part One of the present treaty shall remain in force until the re-establishment of peace between the high contracting parties and Germany and the powers associated with her in acts of aggression in Europe.

Part Two of the present treaty shall remain in force for a period of twenty years. Thereafter, unless twelve months' notice has been given by either party to terminate the treaty at the end of the said period of twenty years, it shall continue in force until twelve months after either high contracting party shall have given notice to the other in writing of his intention to terminate it.

8

Convoy PQ 17 Recriminations

Message from Churchill to Roosevelt

July 14, 1942

Only four ships have reached Archangel with five more precariously in the ice off Nova Zembla out of the thirty-three included in convoy PQ Seventeen. If half had got through we should have persevered, but with only about a quarter arriving the operation is not good enough. For instance of nearly six hundred tanks in PQ Seventeen little over one hundred have arrived and nearly five hundred were lost. This cannot help anybody except the enemy. The Admiralty cannot see what better protection can be devised, nor can they hazard battleships east of Bear Island. Stark agrees with Admiralty view and that all possible was done by us last time. *Washington* has already been withdrawn for her task in the Pacific.[1]

We therefore advise against running PQ Eighteen which must start eighteenth at the latest. If it were composed only of our merchant ships we should certainly not send them, but no fewer than twenty-two are your own American ships. We should therefore like to know how you feel about it.

Future prospects of supplying Russia by this northern route are bad. Murmansk has been largely burnt out and there are several signs of an impending German attack upon it. By the time that perpetual daylight gives place to

---

1   Admiral Harold Stark was Commander of US Naval Forces in Europe. *Washington* was an American North Carolina class battleship.

Winston Churchill, Joseph Stalin and Franklin D. Roosevelt, "Convoy PQ 17 Recriminations," UK National Archives, PREM 3/393/38. 1942.

the dark period, Archangel will be frozen.[2] Some additional supplies may be passed over the Basra route.[3] This is being pressed, but it will not amount to much. Thus Russia is confronted at this anxious moment with a virtual cutting off of the Northern Sea communications. We await your answer before explaining things to Stalin, and meanwhile the convoy is continuing to load and assemble.

Allied shipping losses in the seven days ending July 13 including the Russian convoys were reported at not far short of four hundred thousand tons for this one week, a rate unexampled in either this war or the last, and if maintained evidently beyond all existing replacement plans.

MESSAGE FROM STALIN TO CHURCHILL

JULY 23, 1942

I received your message on 18th July. Two conclusions could be drawn from it. First, the British government refuses to continue the sending of war materials to the Soviet Union via the Northern route. Second, in spite of the agreed communique concerning the urgent tasks of creating a second front in 1942 the British government postpones this matter until 1943.

Our naval experts consider then reasons put forward by the British naval experts to justify the cessation of convoys to the Northern ports of the USSR to be wholly unconvincing. They are of the opinion that with good will and readiness to fulfill the contracted obligations these convoys could be regularly undertaken and heavy losses could be inflicted on the enemy. Our experts also find it difficult to understand and to explain the order given by the Admiralty that the escorting vessels of the P.Q. 17 convoy should return whereas the cargo boats should disperse and try to reach the Soviet ports one by one without any protection at all.[4] Of course I do not think that regular convoys

2 Perpetual daylight hours during the summer months in the Arctic allowed for round-the-clock German U-boat and air attacks. However, the Germans were hesitant to use major surface assets such as the battleship *Tirpitz*.

3 Churchill is referring to a transport route through modern Iraq and Iran into southern Russia.

4 Fearful of an attack by the German battleship *Tirpitz* (which failed to materialize) the British Admiralty had ordered the P.Q. 17 escort vessels to return home and the cargo ships to try to reach the Russian ports on their own. This only made matters easier for the Germans.

to the Soviet Northern ports could be effected without risk or losses. In any case I never expected that the British Government will stop despatch of war materials to us just at the very moment when the Soviet Union in view of the serious situation on the Soviet-German front require these materials more than ever. It is obvious that the transport via Persian Gulf could in no way compensate for the cessation of convoys to the Northern ports.

With regard to the second question, i.e., the question of creating a second front in Europe, I am afraid it is not being treated with the seriousness it deserves. Taking fully into account the present position on the Soviet-German front I must state in the most emphatic manner that the Soviet government cannot acquiesce in the postponement of a second front until 1943.

I hope you will not feel offended that I expressed frankly and honestly my own opinion as well as the opinion of my colleagues on the questions raised in your message.

MESSAGE FROM ROOSEVELT TO CHURCHILL

JULY 29, 1942

I agree with you that your reply to Stalin must be handled with great care. We have got always to bear in mind the personality of our ally and the very difficult and dangerous situation that confronts him. No one can be expected to approach the war from a world point of view whose country has been invaded. I think we should try to put ourselves in his place.

I think he should be told, in the first place, quite specifically that we have determined upon a course of action in 1942. I think that without advising him of the precise nature of our proposed operations the fact that they are going to be made should be told him without any qualifications.

While I think that you should not raise any false hopes in Stalin relative to the northern convoy, nevertheless I agree with you that we should run one if there is any possibility of success, in spite of the great risk involved.[5]

---

5   Convoy P.Q. 18 reached Archangel later in September 1942. While the convoy lost 13 out of 41 ships, the escort vessels sunk three U-boats and shot down 40 German aircraft.

9

THE CASABLANCA CONFERENCE

JANUARY 1943

TELEGRAM FROM ROOSEVELT AND CHURCHILL TO STALIN

JANUARY 25, 1943

1. We have been in conference with our military advisers and have decided the operations which are to be undertaken by American and British forces in the first nine months of 1943. We wish to inform you of our intentions at once. We believe these operations, together with your powerful offensive, may well bring Germany to her knees in 1943. Every effort must be made to accomplish this purpose.

2. We are in no doubt that our correct strategy is to concentrate on the defeat of Germany, with a view to achieving early and decisive victory in the European theatre. At the same time, we must maintain sufficient pressure on Japan to retain the initiative in the Pacific and the Far East, sustain China, and prevent the Japanese from extending their aggression to other theatres such as your Maritime Provinces.

3. Our main desire has been to divert strong German land and air forces from the Russian front and to send to Russia the maximum flow of supplies. We shall spare no exertion to send you material assistance by every available route.

4. Our immediate intention is to clear the Axis out of North Africa and set up the naval and air installations to open:-

   1. An effective passage through the Mediterranean for military traffic; and

   2. An intensive bombardment of important Axis targets in Southern Europe.

5. We have made the decision to launch large-scale amphibious operations in the Mediterranean at the earliest possible moment. The preparation for these operations is now underway and will involve a considerable concentration of forces, including landing craft and shipping in Egyptian and North African ports. In addition we shall concentrate in the United Kingdom a strong American land and air force. These, combined with the British forces in the United Kingdom, will prepare themselves to re-enter the Continent of Europe as soon as practicable. These concentrations will certainly be known to our enemies, but they will not know where or when, or on what scale we propose to strike. They will therefore be compelled to divert both land and air forces to all the shores of France, the Low Countries, Corsica, Sardinia, Sicily, the heel of Italy, Yugoslavia, Greece, Crete and the Dodecanese.

6. In Europe we shall increase the Allied Bomber offensive from the U.K. against Germany at a rapid rate and, by midsummer, it should be more than double its present strength. Our experiences to date have shown that the day bombing attacks result in destruction and damage to large numbers of German Fighter Aircraft. We believe that an increased tempo and weight of daylight and night attacks will lead to greatly increased material and morale damage in Germany and rapidly deplete German fighter strength. As you are aware, we are already containing more than half the German Air Force in Western Europe and the Mediterranean. We have no doubt that our intensified and diversified bombing offensive, together with the other operations which we are undertaking, will compel further withdrawals of German air and other forces from the Russian front.

7. In the Pacific it is our intention to eject the Japanese from Rabaul within the next few months and thereafter to exploit success in the general direction of Japan. We also intend to increase the scale of our operations in Burma in order to reopen our channel of supply to China. We intend to increase our air force in China at once. We shall not, however, allow our operations against Japan to jeopardize our capacity to take

advantage of every opportunity that may present itself for the decisive defeat of Germany in 1943.

8. Our ruling purpose is to bring to bear upon Germany and Italy the maximum forces by land, sea and air which can be physically applied.

Conference Communiqué

January 24 1943

For ten days the Combined Staffs have been in constant session meeting two or three times a day, and recording progress at intervals to the President and the Prime Minister. The entire field of the war was surveyed theatre by theatre throughout the world and all resources were marshalled for the more intense prosecution of the war by sea, land and air. Nothing like this prolonged discussion between two Allies has ever taken place before. Complete agreement was reached between the leaders of the two countries and their respective Staffs upon the war plans and enterprises to be undertaken during the campaign of 1943 against Germany, Italy and Japan with a view to drawing the utmost advantage from the markedly favourable turn of events at the close of 1942.

Premier Stalin was cordially invited to meet the President and the Prime Minister, in which case the meeting would have been held very much further to the East. He was, however, unable to leave Russia at this time on account of the great offensive which he himself, as Commander-in-Chief is directing.

The President and the Prime Minister realized to the full the enormous weight of the war which Russia is successfully bearing along her whole land front, and their prime object has been to draw as much of the weight as possible off the Russian armies by engaging the enemy as heavily as possible at the best selected points.

Premier Stalin has been fully informed of the military proposals.

The President and the Prime Minister have been in communication with Generalissimo Chiang Kai Shek. They have apprised him of the measures which they are undertaking to assist him in China's magnificent and unrelaxing struggle for the common cause.

The occasion of the meeting between the President and the Prime Minister made it opportune to invite General Giraud to confer with the Combined Chiefs of Staff and to arrange for a meeting between him and General de Gaulle. The two Generals have been in close consultation.

The President and the Prime Minister and the Combined Staffs having completed their plans for the offensive campaigns of 1943, have now separated in order to put them into active and concerted execution.

Although the term 'unconditional surrender' does not appear in the final communiqué, Roosevelt confirmed to journalists a few days later that the Allies had in fact decided at Casablanca that the war would only be ended by an 'unconditional surrender' of the Axis powers.

10

THE QUEBEC CONFERENCE

AUGUST 21, 1943

Secret and personal to Marshal Stalin from the United States Government and His Majesty's Government in the United Kingdom.

In our conference at Quebec, just concluded, we have arrived at the following decision as to military operations to be carried out during 1943 and 1944.

The bomber offensive against Germany will be continued on a rapidly increased scale from bases in the United Kingdom and Italy. The objective of this attack will be to destroy German air combat strength, to dislocate the German military, industrial and economic system, and to prepare the way for a cross channel invasion.

A large-scale buildup of American forces in the United Kingdom is now underway. It will provide an initial assault force of British and American divisions for cross channel operations. A bridgehead in the continent once secured will be reinforced steadily by additional American troops at the rate of from three to five divisions per month. This operation will be the primary British and American ground and air effort against the Axis.

The war in the Mediterranean is to be pressed vigorously. Our objective in that area will be the elimination of Italy from the Axis alliance, and the occupation of that country as well as Sardinia and Corsica as bases for operations against Germany.

"The Quebec Conference, August 21, 1943," The Avalon Project, pp. 1-3. 1944.

Our operations in the Balkans will be limited to the supply of Balkan Guerrillas by air and sea transport, to minor raids by Commandos, and to the bombing of strategic objectives.

We shall accelerate our operations against Japan in the Pacific and in Southeast Asia. Our purposes are to exhaust Japanese air, naval, and shipping resources, to cut the Japanese communications and to secure bases from which to bomb Japan proper.

11

THE MOSCOW CONFERENCE

OCTOBER 1943

JOINT FOUR-NATION DECLARATION

The governments of the United States of America, United Kingdom, the Soviet Union and China;

United in their determination, in accordance with the declaration by the United Nations of January, 1942, and subsequent declarations, to continue hostilities against those Axis powers with which they respectively are at war until such powers have laid down their arms on the basis of unconditional surrender;

Conscious of their responsibility to secure the liberation of themselves and the peoples allied with them from the menace of aggression;

Recognizing the necessity of insuring a rapid and orderly transition from war to peace and of establishing and maintaining international peace and security with the least diversion of the world's human and economic resources for armaments;

Jointly declare:

1. That their united action, pledged for the prosecution of the war against their respective enemies, will be continued for the organization and maintenance of peace and security.

"The Moscow Conference, October 1943," The Avalon Project, pp. 1-4. 1943.

2. That those of them at war with a common enemy will act together in all matters relating to the surrender and disarmament of that enemy.

3. That they will take all measures deemed by them to be necessary to provide against any violation of the terms imposed upon the enemy.

4. That they recognize the necessity of establishing at the earliest practicable date a general international organization, based on the principle of the sovereign equality of all peace-loving states, and open to membership by all such states, large and small, for the maintenance of international peace and security.

5. That for the purpose of maintaining international peace and security pending the re-establishment of law and order and the inauguration of a system of general security they will consult with one another and as occasion requires with other members of the United Nations, with a view to joint action on behalf of the community of nations.

6. That after the termination of hostilities they will not employ their military forces within the territories of other states except for the purposes envisaged in this declaration and after joint consultation.

7. That they will confer and cooperate with one another and with other members of the United Nations to bring about a practicable general agreement with respect to the regulation of armaments in the post-war period. ...

STATEMENT ON ATROCITIES

SIGNED BY PRESIDENT ROOSEVELT, PRIME MINISTER CHURCHILL AND PREMIER STALIN.

The United Kingdom, the United States and the Soviet Union have received from many quarters evidence of atrocities, massacres and cold-blooded mass executions which are being perpetrated by Hitlerite forces in many of the countries they have overrun and from which they are now being steadily expelled. The brutalities of Nazi domination are no new thing, and all peoples or territories in their grip have suffered from the worst form of government by terror. What is new is that in their desperation the recoiling Hitlerites and Huns are redoubling their ruthless cruelties. This is now evidenced with particular clearness by monstrous crimes on the territory of the Soviet Union which is being liberated from Hitlerites, and on French and Italian territory.

Accordingly, the aforesaid three Allied powers, speaking in the interest of the thirty-two United Nations, hereby solemnly declare and give full warning of their declaration as follows:

At the time of granting of any armistice to any government which may be set up in Germany, those German officers and men and members of the Nazi party who have been responsible for or have taken a consenting part in the above atrocities, massacres and executions will be sent back to the countries in which their abominable deeds were done in order that they may be judged and punished according to the laws of these liberated countries and of free governments which will be erected therein. Lists will be compiled in all possible detail from all these countries having regard especially to invaded parts of the Soviet Union, to Poland and Czechoslovakia, to Yugoslavia and Greece including Crete and other islands, to Norway, Denmark, Netherlands, Belgium, Luxembourg, France and Italy.

Thus, Germans who take part in wholesale shooting of Polish officers or in the execution of French, Dutch, Belgian or Norwegian hostages or Cretan peasants, or who have shared in slaughters inflicted on the people of Poland or in territories of the Soviet Union which are now being swept clear of the enemy, will know they will be brought back to the scene of their crimes and judged on the spot by the peoples whom they have outraged.

Let those who have hitherto not imbrued their hands with innocent blood beware lest they join the ranks of the guilty, for most assuredly the three Allied powers will pursue them to the uttermost ends of the earth and will deliver them to their accusors in order that justice may be done.

The above declaration is without prejudice to the case of German criminals whose offenses have no particular geographical localization and who will be punished by joint decision of the government of the Allies.

12

THE TEHRAN CONFERENCE

NOVEMBER 28 TO DECEMBER 1, 1943

DECLARATION OF THE THREE POWERS

DECEMBER 1, 1943

We, the President of the United States, the Prime Minister of Great Britain, and the Premier of the Soviet Union, have met these four days past, in this, the Capital of our Ally, Iran, and have shaped and confirmed our common policy.

We express our determination that our nations shall work together in war and in the peace that will follow.

As to war—our military staffs have joined in our round table discussions, and we have concerted our plans for the destruction of the German forces. We have reached complete agreement as to the scope and timing of the operations to be undertaken from the east, west and south.

The common understanding which we have here reached guarantees that victory will be ours.

And as to peace—we are sure that our concord will win an enduring Peace. We recognize fully the supreme responsibility resting upon us and all the United Nations to make a peace which will command the goodwill of the overwhelming mass of the peoples of the world and banish the scourge and terror of war for many generations.

"The Tehran Conference, 1943," The Avalon Project, pp. 1-3. 1943.

With our Diplomatic advisors we have surveyed the problems of the future. We shall seek the cooperation and active participation of all nations, large and small, whose peoples in heart and mind are dedicated, as are our own peoples, to the elimination of tyranny and slavery, oppression and intolerance. We will welcome them, as they may choose to come, into a world family of Democratic Nations.

No power on earth can prevent our destroying the German armies by land, their U-boats by sea, and their war plants from the air.

Our attack will be relentless and increasing.

Emerging from these cordial conferences we look with confidence to the day when all peoples of the world may live free lives, untouched by tyranny, and according to their varying desires and their own consciences.

We came here with hope and determination. We leave here, friends in fact, in spirit and in purpose.

Roosevelt, Churchill and Stalin

Signed at Tehran, December 1, 1943

MILITARY CONCLUSIONS OF THE
TEHRAN CONFERENCE

1. Agreed that the Partisans in Yugoslavia should be supported by supplies and equipment to the greatest possible extent, and also by commando operations.

2. Agreed that, from the military point of view, it was most desirable that Turkey should come into the war on the side of the Allies before the end of the year.

3. Took note of Marshal Stalin's statement that if Turkey found herself at war with Germany, and as a result Bulgaria declared war on Turkey or attacked her, the Soviet would immediately be at war with Bulgaria. The Conference further took note that this fact could be explicitly stated in the forthcoming negotiations to bring Turkey into the war.

4. Took note that Operation OVERLORD would be launched during May 1944, in conjunction with an operation against southern France. The

latter operation would be undertaken in as great a strength as availability of landing-craft permitted. The Conference further took note of Marshal Stalin's statement that the Soviet forces would launch an offensive at about the same time with the object of preventing the German forces from transferring from the Eastern to the Western Front.

5. Agreed that the military staffs of the Three Powers should henceforward keep in close touch with each other in regard to the impending operations in Europe. In particular it was agreed that a cover plan to mystify and mislead the enemy as regards these operations should be concerted between the staffs concerned.

CHAPTER 11

BALKAN DIVERSION AND THE EASTERN FRONT, 1941–1945

Introduction

Having failed to subdue Britain in the fall of 1940, Adolf Hitler turned his attention to the USSR. The invasion of the Soviet Union was planned for summer 1941, but in the spring of that year Hitler was distracted by events on the Balkan peninsula. In late October 1940, the Italian army invaded Greece from bases in Albania, which had been occupied by the Italians since 1939. The Greek army not only put up a remarkable defense but launched a counterattack that pushed the invaders back into southern Albania. British and Commonwealth ground forces and British Spitfire fighter squadrons arrived in Greece in March 1941, marking the return of British armed forces to the European continent for the first time in almost a year. Furthermore, a *coup d'état* in Yugoslavia in late March 1941 overthrew the pro-Nazi government of that country. Hitler could not embark upon Operation Barbarossa (the invasion of the USSR) as long as his southern flank was destabilized and his oil supplies in Romania threatened. In early April, German tank panzer divisions swept into Yugoslavia from staging grounds in Austria, Hungary, Bulgaria, and Romania. The poorly led and ill-equipped Yugoslav army quickly collapsed and the Germans conquered Yugoslavia for the loss of only about 150 fatalities. The Germans then stormed south into Greece. Despite British urgings, the Greeks were unable to shorten their defensive lines. Greece was overrun by the Germans and again British and Commonwealth forces were expelled from the continent. In the final act of the Balkan campaign, the Germans carried out a daring, if costly, airborne invasion of the Greek island of Crete. According to the British War Office 1941 analysis of the Battle of Crete (Document 1), why did the Germans win?

Germany unleashed Operation Barbarossa in the early morning hours of June 22, 1941. Almost 3.6 million German and Axis troops, organized into three Army Groups, invaded the USSR along a front stretching from the Baltic Sea in the north to the Black Sea in the south. The Germans achieved operational surprise and inflicted devastating defeats on the Soviet Red Army. Nevertheless, the Soviets should not have been taken by surprise. Soviet premier Joseph Stalin chose to ignore intelligence warnings of a German troop buildup on the Soviet frontier. Stalin also ignored a message sent to him by British prime minister Winston Churchill in early April 1941 (Document 2). Churchill's information was based on Ultra decrypts of secret German codes. Do you think Churchill was being too careful with his words? Do you see why he was being so cautious? Why do you think Stalin ignored all these warnings?

The next two readings focus on Operation Barbarossa. The first is an account written Marshal Bagramian of the Red Army (Document 3). How does Bagramian describe the opening phases of the war in the East? Why, according to this author, were the Germans so successful? The next excerpt by Guderian is taken from his postwar memoir, *Panzer Leader* (Document 4). How does his account differ from that of Bagramian? Why does Guderian think the Germans were successful, at least initially? The extract from Guderian continues into late summer 1941, when the Germans were facing increasing difficulties in the USSR. What does Guderian think of Hitler's decision making? Do you think Guderian is being entirely truthful in his account?

Soviet losses in the early phases of Barbarossa were catastrophic. In terms of territory, the Soviets lost the Baltic states, the eastern half of Poland taken in 1939, plus most of Ukraine and modern Belarus. The Soviets of course also lost all the agricultural and industrial resources in those territories. Leningrad was subjected to a brutal siege that lasted 900 days and was not lifted until the end of January 1944. The Red Army lost more than 3.3 million soldiers taken prisoner plus uncounted thousands of tanks and aircraft.

All the more astonishing, therefore, was the German defeat at the Battle of Moscow in December 1941. The German defeat cannot simply be attributed to cold weather. Archival research since the end of the Cold War has produced recent historical accounts that emphasize the extent to which the Red Army outfought the German army at the Battle of Moscow.[1] The Red Army adapted to German tactics and successfully countered them, although much remained to be learned and Soviet losses remained heavy throughout the war.

Hitler was reluctant to attack Moscow directly again in 1942, feeling the Soviets were too strong in that sector. Instead he turned his attention to the southern section of the line where Soviet defenses were weaker. The German offensive in summer 1942 focused on the Soviet oil industry in south Russia and the city of Stalingrad on the Volga. Capturing Stalingrad would have severed the Red Army from its oil supplies in the south. The resulting Battle of Stalingrad concluded in a decisive German defeat (see Chapter 7).

The reading from the British Joint Intelligence Sub-Committee is dated June 1, 1942 (Document 6) and assesses options for both sides during the summer campaign. The extracts included here form the conclusion of the report. The document conveys the sense that the war on the Eastern front was approaching a decisive stage. Do you think some of the predictions were overly optimistic? Why would this be the case? What would be the consequences of a Soviet (Russian) collapse in 1942? What does this tell you about the importance of the Eastern front?

The Germans launched their last major offensive (codenamed Operation Citadel) on the Eastern front in summer 1943. The result was the Battle of Kursk, which resulted in another German defeat, although Soviet losses were unnecessarily heavy. According to Guderian's analysis of the Kursk battle (Document 5), why did the Germans lose? What were the long term consequences of Kursk?

The long Red Army campaign from the heart of the USSR to Berlin stands as a remarkable military accomplishment, although the cost in lives was staggering. Historian Kristian Ungvary assesses the consequences of the Soviet success at the Battle of Budapest from late 1944 to early 1945 (Document 7). Why do you think we hear so little about the Eastern front?

Our final extract describes a shocking encounter between Soviet troops and members of the Hitler Youth (child soldiers) during the Battle of Berlin (Document 8). It is taken from General Vasil I. Chuikov's account of the Battle of Berlin, which ended the war in Europe in May 1945. How does Chuikov characterize the Nazi war effort at this stage?

---

1   See, for example, D. M. Glantz, *Reborn Colossus: The Red Army at War, 1941–1943* (Lawrence: University Press of Kansas, 2005); or Alexander Hill, *The Red Army and the Second World War* (Cambridge, UK: Cambridge University Press, 2017).

1

THE BRITISH WAR OFFICE ON THE BATTLE OF CRETE

The methods used by the Germans to attack and capture CRETE may be summarized under the following heading;-

1. Several days' aerial reconnaissance preceded the attack, followed by dive-bombing attacks on aerodromes and defences, the main effort being directed against MALEME aerodrome, on the two days before the attack was launched.

2. The landing of parachutists in three separate areas—MALEME, RETIMO and HERAKLION—with the object of capturing aerodromes and causing dispersion of the defence. Parachutist landings were immediately followed by the arrival of air-borne troops, which were landed on the beaches, when it was found that parachutists alone had failed to capture the aerodrome at MALEME.

3. The use of parachutists to attack our positions and artillery from the rear.

4. Fighter protection for parachutists.

5. Intensive dive-bombing of aerodromes, A.A. defences, ground positions and shipping, between the airborne landings.

"The Battle of Crete," United Kingdom National Archives, War Office 106/3240 M05, The Battle of Crete, 1941, May-June 1941.

6. Exploitation to the full of any local success, regardless of losses. This occurred only at MALEME. The parachutist detachments at RETIMO and HERAKLION were not considerably reinforced, the intention being that they should maintain their positions in these areas and exploit their nuisance value in the main effort continued at MALEME. There is reason to believe that airborne troops were diverted from RETIMO and HERAKLION to MALEME as soon as the smallest degree of success became apparent there. In consequence the aerodrome was captured and then made secure from our artillery fire.

7. An efficient system of signaling from ground to air to facilitate the timely arrival of reinforcements, ammunition and supplies. German troops were also equipped with W/T sets enabling them to establish and maintain touch with other groups, thus facilitating co-operation between groups landed for the execution of a particular operation.

Apart from the troops-carrying aircraft, some use was made of gliders. It is believed that gliders were used mainly as an operational experiment, and that the results were not altogether successful, for, so far as can be judged from reports received, their use ceased after the first two or three days. No reliable information is as yet available of the number used, the number towed by each aircraft or of their carrying capacity in men and equipment.

The outstanding conclusions to date show that air superiority is vital for the success of a purely airborne attack and subsequent consolidation, and that in defence fighter aircraft are essential for dealing with air transports and for protection against dive-bombing.

2

CHURCHILL'S WARNING TO STALIN

MESSAGE FROM CHURCHILL TO STAFFORD CRIPPS,

BRITISH AMBASSADOR TO MOSCOW

APRIL 3, 1941

Following from me to M. Stalin, provided it can be personally delivered by you:-

I have information from a trusted agent that when the Germans thought they had got Yugoslavia in the net, that is to say, after 20th March, they began to move three out of the five Panzer Divisions from Roumania to Southern Poland. The moment they heard of the Serbian revolution this movement was countermanded. Your Excellency will readily appreciate the significance of these facts.

MESSAGE FROM ANTHONY EDEN, BRITISH FOREIGN SECRETARY, TO CRIPPS

APRIL 4, 1941.

If your reception gives you opportunity of developing the argument, you might point out that this change in German military dispositions surely implies that Hitler, through the action of Yugoslavia, has now postponed his previous plans for threatening the Soviet Government. If so, it should be possible for Soviet Government to use this opportunity to strengthen their own position.

Winston Churchill and Anthony Eden, "Churchill's Warning to Stalin, April 3, 1941," PREM 3/403/7 April 3, 1941.

This delay shows that the enemy forces are not unlimited, and illustrates the advantages that will follow anything like a united front.

MESSAGE FROM CHURCHILL TO EDEN

OCTOBER 14, 1941.

This was the only message before the attack that I sent Stalin direct. It had to be somewhat cryptic, in view of the deadly character of the information contained. Its brevity, the exceptional character of the communication, the fact that it came from the Head of the Government and was to be delivered personally to the Head of the Russian Government by the Ambassador were all intended to give it special significance and arrest Stalin's attention.[1]

---

1   This note was prompted by the fact that Stalin, complained to the British later that summer that he had never been warned of an impending German attack.

3

OPERATION BARBAROSSA

THE SOVIET VIEW

JUNE 21, 1941

TESTIMONY BY RED ARMY MARSHAL I. KH. BAGRAMIAN

On June 21, with the onset of darkness, the border guards and army intelligence noticed a great stir along the other side of the border; quite clearly one could hear the rumble of tanks and the noise of tractors. It was not hard for experienced fighting men to guess what such activity meant! In addition to everything else, at about midnight a German soldier in the 222nd Infantry Regiment, 74th Infantry Division, deserted to our side in the zone of the 5th Army west of Vladmir-Volynskii. When he learned that the attack on the Soviet Union was to begin at 4:00 a.m., he slipped quietly into the water and swam across the border river at the risk of being shot by German security forces or Soviet border guards. ... The deserter reported that everything was ready for an attack which was to begin at 4:00 a.m. The chief of the border outpost reported it through channels. The message was so important that General Khomenko, chief of border troops of the Ukraine, was routed out of bed. He immediately reported to his superiors in Moscow and informed the commander of the military district. Everyone's reaction to the message was, "But isn't this a provocation?" Naturally the district military council did not dare without Moscow's sanction to issue an order to put into operation the plan for covering the state border. Only General M.I. Potapov, Commander of the 5th Army, who had also learned about the deserter, decided not long before the attack to put his corps on the alert. Therefore, they had at their disposal somewhat more time to prepare to meet the enemy. At their own risk, the commanding officers of the 41st and 87th Rifle Divisions, stationed right at the border, also brought their units to combat readiness.

At 2:30 a.m. the communications center in Tarnopol' began receiving a telegram, in which the People's Commissar and the Chief of the General Staff warned that "a surprise attack by the Germans may possibly take place on June 22–23, 1941." The task of our troops was not to yield to any provocations. It was categorically demanded that commanders of border military districts hold their troops "in complete combat readiness to meet a possible surprise attack by the Germans and their allies." The telegram also outlined measures for bringing the troops to combat readiness, and the commanders of the military districts were instructed to carry the measures out. But at 3:45 the war had already begun. The moment it became known that Hitler's hordes had treacherously invaded our territory, Kirponos *(commander of the Kiev military district)* with the approval of the military council member and the chief of staff, ordered the following telegram sent to the Armies: "Put the Kiev Special Military District Plan No. 41 into operation. Open the sealed special orders."

If only this command had been issued twenty-four hours earlier! It is not difficult to imagine that then the Hitlerite hordes which attacked our country would have run up against an organized and firm defense by the cover troops right at the border. If the aggressor's troops had managed to break through our defense in any direction, in a short time they would have come under an organized counterattack by second echelon troops from our interior. If the war had begun this way, the German troops would hardly have been able to push so swiftly and deeply into our territory. Unfortunately, the war began differently.

The first German air attacks were unleashed on Kiev and other large cities in the Ukraine and on the most important airfields in our military district. The military council immediately reported to Moscow what had happened and what steps had been taken.

The commander and the chief of staff started to put order into troop control, trying as quickly as possible to impart a more organized character to the combat actions of the Army Group's cover troops and air force. After receiving the order to push the invading German units back over the state boundary line, divisions of first echelon cover troops headed for the state border under relentless enemy bombing.

While sealed orders were being opened at headquarters of the Armies and orders were being issued to the troops about putting into operation the plan for covering the border, the German air force was making a second series of attacks, this time on the troops and airfields closest to the border. These attacks, which caught the majority of the units still at their permanent stations, led to the first serious losses among troops located in the border zone.

The fact that German planes had gained supremacy in the air from the very start of the invasion was particularly alarming. The military district air force lost 180 planes in the first German air strikes. Our troops, which had started towards the frontiers, did not have adequate cover against air attacks. Only small isolated groups of fighter planes broke through the German air umbrella to support them.

4

OPERATION BARBAROSSA

ACCOUNT OF GERMAN GENERAL HEINZ GUDERIAN

On the fateful day of June 22nd, I went at 02.10 hrs. to my Group command post which was located in an observation tower south of Bohukaly, 9 miles north-west of Brest-Litovsk. It was still dark when I arrived there at 03.10 hrs. At 03.15 hrs. our artillery opened up. At 03.40 hrs. the first dive-bomber attack went in. At 04.15 hrs. advance units of the 17th and 18th Panzer Division began to cross the Bug. At 04.45 hrs. the leading tanks of the 18th Panzer Division forded the river. For this they were equipped with the waterproofing that had been tested for *Operation Sea-lion*, which enabled them to move through 13 feet of water.

At 06.50 hrs. I crossed the Bug in an assault boat in the neighbourhood of Kolodno. My command staff, consisting of two armoured wireless trucks, a number of cross-country vehicles and some motorcyclists, followed at 08.30 hrs. I began by following the tank tracks of 18th Panzer Division and soon reached the bridge over the Lesna, whose capture was important for the advance of XLVII Panzer Corps; there I found nobody except some Russian pickets. The Russians took to their heels when they saw my vehicles. Two of my orderly officers set off after them, against my wishes; unfortunately they both lost their lives as a result.

At 10.25 hrs. the leading tank company reached the Lesna and crossed the bridge. Next to arrive was the divisional commander, General Nehring. I accompanied the 18th Panzer in their advance until mid-afternoon. At 16.30

Heinz Guderian, *Panzer Leader*, pp. 153-154, 189-190. Copyright © 1950 by Random House LLC. Reprinted with permission.

hrs. I returned to the bridgehead at Kolodno and from there I went at 18.30 hrs. to my command post.

We had managed to take the enemy by surprise along the entire Panzer Group front. To the south of Brest-Litovsk the XXIV Panzer Corps had captured the bridges over the Bug intact. To the north-west of the fortress our bridges were being built according to plan. The enemy, however, soon recovered from his initial surprise and put up a tough defense in his prepared positions. The important citadel of Brest-Litovsk held out with remarkable stubbornness for several days thus depriving us of the use of the road and rail communications across the Bug and Muchaviec.

The conference with Hitler *(August 4, 1941)* took place in Novy Borissov, at the headquarters of Army Group Centre. Those present were Hitler and Schmundt, Field-Marshal von Bock, Hoth and myself, as well as a representative of the *OHK*, Colonel Heusinger, the Chief of the Operations Department. We were each given the opportunity to express our views and we did this alone so that no man might know what his predecessor might have said. But Field Marshal-Marshal von Bock, Hoth and I shared the opinion that a continuation of the offensive towards Moscow was of vital importance. Hoth reported that the earliest date by which his Panzer Group could resume its advance was August 20th; the date I gave for my Group was the 15th. Then Hitler assembled the whole company together and began himself to speak. He designated the industrial area around Leningrad as this primary objective. He had not yet decided whether Moscow or Ukraine would come next. He seemed to incline toward the latter target for a number of reasons: first, Army Group South seemed to be laying the groundwork for a victory in that area: secondly, he believed that the raw materials and agricultural produce of the Ukraine were necessary to Germany for the further prosecution of the war: and finally he thought it essential that the Crimea, 'that Soviet aircraft carrier operating against the Rumanian oilfields,' be neutralised. He hoped to be in possession of Moscow and Kharkov by the time winter began. No decisions were reached on this day concerning those problems of strategy which we regarded as most important.

The conference then began to discuss more detailed questions. The important point for my Panzer Group was a decision not to evacuate the Elnya salient, since it was not yet known whether this salient might not still be needed as a jumping-off point for an attack towards Moscow. I stressed the fact that our tank engines had become very worn as a result of the appalling dust; in consequence they must be replaced with all urgency if any more large-scale tank operations were to be carried out during the current year. It was also essential that replacements be provided for our tank casualties from current production. After a certain amount of humming and hawing Hitler promised to supply 300 new tank engines for the whole Eastern Front, a figure I described as totally inadequate. As for new tanks, we were not to get any, since Hitler intended to retain them all at home for the equipping of newly set-up formations. In the ensuing argument I stated that we could only cope with the Russians' great numerical superiority in tanks if our tank losses were rapidly made good again. Hitler then said: 'If I had known that the figures for Russian tank strength which you gave in your book were in fact true ones, I would not—I believe—ever have started this war.' He was referring to my book *Achtung! Panzer!,* published in 1937, in which I had estimated Russian tank strength at that time as 10,000; both the Chief of the Army General Staff, Beck, and the censor had disagreed with this statement. It had cost me a lot of trouble to get that figure printed; but I had been able to show that intelligence reports at the time spoke of 17,000 Russian tanks and that my estimate was therefore, if anything, a very conservative one. To imitate the ostrich in political matters has never been a satisfactory method of avoiding danger; yet this is what Hitler, as well as his more important political, economic and even military advisers, chose to do over and over again. The consequences of this deliberate blindness in the face of hard facts were devastating; and it was we who now had to bear them.

5

BRITISH INTELLIGENCE ANALYSIS OF THE EASTERN FRONT

JUNE 1, 1942

We think it unlikely, however, that by August a decisive success by either side will have been achieved. Between August and September, however, events may move to a climax. Both sides will have suffered severe casualties. The German Air Force may be reduced from a total operational strength of 5,800 aircraft on all fronts to some 4,500 aircraft, a force which will have to be maintained practically on a 'factory to unit basis'. The German High Command may at about this time be faced with the problem of whether to throw in their last reserves even to the extent of dangerously denuding occupied countries in the hope of bringing about a complete Russian defeat before the winter or to conserve their resources to meet the growing Anglo-American threat in the West. The margin between success or failure may be very narrow, and it may be touch and go which of the two adversaries collapses first.[1]

If the Germans realize that they cannot avoid another winter campaign in Russia and are faced with the threat of Anglo-American invasion in the West, they may collapse with unexpected rapidity as they did in 1918.

On the other hand, we cannot rule out the possibility of Russia collapsing. Should she do so, the Germans would, during the winter, after making provision for the garrisoning of Russia and other occupied territories, be able to build up to meet a threatened Anglo-American invasion of the Continent

---

1   PREM 3/395/13 Joint Intelligence Sub-Committee analysis of the Eastern front, 1942.

"British Intelligence Analysis of the Eastern Front, June 1, 1942," PREM 3/395/13 Joint Intelligence Sub-Committee Analysis of the Eastern Front, 1942.

next spring a force of some 2,500 aircraft and a field army on the 1st April, 1943, of some 30–50 divisions, including 5–10 armoured and 5–10 motorised, rising to 50–60 divisions including some 20 armoured and 20 motorised, by 1st June 1943. Subject to conditions then prevailing, a part of this force could be employed by the Germans for offensive operations in the Middle East.

6

General Guderian Assesses the Consequences of the Battle of Kursk

July 1943

While these events in the South were bringing the war ever closer to Germany, in the East Hitler launched an offensive which was both inadequately planned and carried out. From the area of Bielgorod in the south ten panzer, one panzergrenadier, and seven infantry divisions attacked, while in the north seven panzer, two panzergrenadier, and nine infantry divisions went in from the area west of Orel. Everything that the German Army could muster in the way of attacking strength was committed in this offensive; Hitler had himself correctly said in Munich that it must not fail, since even a return to our original positions would spell defeat. It is not yet clear how Hitler was eventually persuaded to launch this attack. It seems likely that pressure by the Chief of the Army General Staff was the deciding factor.

The attack began on July 5th. Our tactics were those that had been used many times before against the Russians, who as a result knew exactly what to expect. Hitler had two alternative plans: one to attack through Sevsk against the most advanced part of the Russian salient, the other to break through and roll up the Russian front south-east of Kharkov. He had scrapped both these plans in favour of the Zeitzler plan which involved a double envelopment of the Russian salient in the Tim area with the purpose of regaining the initiative on the Eastern Front.

I visited both the attacking fronts during the time between the 10th and the 15th of July; I went first to the southern and then to the northern area, and talked to tank commanders on the spot. I there gained an insight into the course that events were taking, the lack of our men's experience in the attack and the weaknesses of our equipment. My fears concerning the premature commitment of the Panthers were justified. Also the ninety Porsche Tigers, which were operating with Model's army, were incapable of close-range fighting since they lacked sufficient ammunition for their guns, and this defect was aggravated by the fact that they possessed no machine gun. Once they had broken into the enemy's infantry zone they literally had to go quail shooting with cannons. They did not manage to neutralize, let alone destroy, the enemy rifles and machine-guns, so that the infantry was unable to follow up behind them. By the time they reached the Russian artillery they were on their own. Despite showing extreme bravery and suffering unheard-of casualties, the infantry of Weidling's division did not manage to exploit the tanks' success. Model's attack bogged down after some 6 miles. In the south our successes were somewhat greater but not enough to seal off the salient or force the Russians to withdraw. The Russian counter-attack began on July 15th towards Orel, the defence of which weakened our offensive. The town had to be evacuated on August 4th. On the same day Bielgorod fell.

Up to this time the Susha-Oka position to the north-east of Orel had weathered every storm. This was the defensive line that I had chosen in December 1941 for my Second Panzer Army and into which I had withdrawn that army. This had been the reason for my quarrel with Hitler which Field-Marshal von Kluge had made use of in order to bring about my dismissal.

By the failure of *Citadel* we had suffered a decisive defeat. The armoured formations, reformed and re-equipped with so much effort, had lost heavily both in men and in equipment and would now be unemployable for a long time to come. It was problematical whether they could be rehabilitated in time to defend the Eastern Front; as for being able to use them in defence of the Western Front against the Allied landings that threatened for next spring, this was even more questionable. Needless to say, the Russians exploited their victory to the full. There were to be no more periods of quiet on the Eastern Front. From now on the enemy was in undisputed possession of the initiative.

7

HISTORIAN KRISZTIAN UNGVARY ASSESSES THE COST OF THE SIEGE OF BUDAPEST

1944–1945

The battle for Budapest is remembered in history as one of the bloodiest city sieges of the Second World War in Europe. According to Soviet statistics, the Red Army's casualties in the struggle for the capital and in associated actions—including those against the German relief efforts—amounted to 240,056 wounded and 80,026 dead. The latter figure represents half of all the Soviets who died within the current—post-1946—Hungarian borders, meaning that every other Soviet soldier killed in Hungary gave his life for Budapest. The losses of matériel were of a similar order. In the 108 days of the Budapest operations—dating the siege, as the Soviets did, from 29 October 1944—Malinovsky's 2nd Ukrainian Front and Tolbukhin's 3rd Ukrainian Front lost a total of 135,100 small arms, 1,766 tanks and assault guns, 4,127 pieces of heavy artillery, and 293 aircraft. In Soviet statistics the total losses of the 2nd Ukrainian Front (29 October 1944 to 13 February 1945) and the 3rd Ukrainian Front (12 December 1944 to 13 February 1945) are attributed to the Budapest operation, even if they occurred in the Ercsi, Hatvan, or Nagybajom region. Thus it is extremely difficult to compare the losses of the two sides, particularly as figures given for those of the Germans and Hungarians during the operations in question are only approximate.

According to my own calculations, 25 percent of all Soviet casualties connected with Budapest stemmed from the relief attempts, 55 percent from the battle for the city itself, and 20 percent from actions that, in German and

Hungarian records, are not directly associated with the capital. For operations within the territory of Hungary (as defined by the Trianon Treaty) the Hero of the Soviet Union medal was awarded to 382 individuals. Among the 276 awards referring to specific locations, operations in and around Budapest—particularly for the Danube crossing at Ersci, with 115 awards—account for a surprisingly large proportion.

The number of German and Hungarian military casualties can only be estimated, because we do not know whether any Hungarians are included in the figures given for the relief attempts (making a possible difference of up to 10 percent). The total cannot have exceeded 60 percent of the Soviet casualties, even though practically the whole garrison was killed or wounded. The picture is further complicated by the fact that between November 1944 and the closure of the encirclement, numerous units were withdrawn from, and others moved to, the capital. Based on the available incomplete war reports and my own calculations, a total of some 137,000 Hungarian and German casualties (approximately 26,000 wounded, 48,000 dead, and 63,000 taken prisoner) compares with some 280,000 Soviet and Roman casualties (approximately 202,000 wounded, 70,000 dead, and 8,000 taken prisoner).

The diversion of Soviet troops to Budapest enabled the Germans to maintain their crumbling positions elsewhere in Hungary for some time. Even after Christmas 1944 they held the front line in Transdanubia only because the capital tied down substantial Soviet forces which they could not have matched. As the arrival of reinforcements enhanced the strength of the German front lines, the importance of Budapest as a fortress to be defended at all costs rapidly declined. In any case, the defenders, because of supply problems, even lacked the potential combat strength commensurate to their numbers; by the end of the first few weeks, for example, they had no heavy arms left. After the failure of the relief attempts it became clear that the stabilization of the front until the end of December would be paid for by the entire equipment of four German divisions and nearly 100,000 German and Hungarian soldiers, who could never be replaced.

The German command therefore could expect to profit from the siege only for a brief period. Nevertheless, it adhered to the same strategy to the very end. Three times enormous German reserves were concentrated for a counterattack but were preempted by the Soviets. The actions of these huge forces either remained largely defensive or miscarried because of lack of fuel, as in the last German offensive, when tanks had to be blown up to prevent them from falling into Soviet hands.

On 25 September 1944 the number of divisions thrown by the German Army Group South into the Hungarian theater of war was 14 (including 4 panzer divisions), with 277 tanks and assault guns (of which 192 were deployable and 85 under repair). By 10 January 1945 these numbers had increased to 28 divisions (including 9 panzer divisions), with 1,796 tanks and assault guns (772 deployable, 1024 under repair). These increases reflect the growing importance the Germans attached to Hungary, and appear even more significant if one remembers that during the period in question four German divisions were completely annihilated and vanished from the battle order. In March 1945 half the German panzer divisions on the eastern front (about 30 percent of the total) were operating in Hungary, even though Soviet troops were already within 60 kilometers of Berlin.

Although the Red Army finally succeeded in its objective, the siege, from the Soviet point of view, amounted to a series of defeats. Malinovsky's attempt to take the city failed four times: each time—on 7 November, in the third week of November, and in the first and last weeks of December 1944—the date had to be changed because the supreme command's orders were impracticable. Malinovsky himself was furious about the protracted fighting: "If I weren't obliged to account for your head in Moscow, I'd have you hanged in the main square of Buda," he roared at Pfeffer-Wildenbruch when he was at last able to interrogate him. The delay in the capture of the capital made it impossible to release sufficient Soviet forces for an effective stand against the Germans; typically, in early February 1945, when the Germans had only begun to move their 6th Panzer Army to Hungary, most Soviet units were still depleted as a result of the Konrad operations. Major-General Shtemenko, chief of the Red Army's general staff in 1945, admits in his memoirs that the Soviet "plans to reach Vienna by the end of December and southern Germany in March were upset mainly by the lengthy siege of the Hungarian capital."

Battles for towns and cities differ in various respects from other types. In open-field battles one side generally collapses relatively early, while street battles may last weeks or months. One factor making the defenders' task in a city relatively easy is that utilities break down only gradually, enabling both soldiers and civilians to persevere despite the agony. Another factor is that the attackers have much greater difficulty finding their way in the confusing mass of buildings. Central control often ceases, and the operations disintegrate into dozens of small-scale actions, led by the commanders of units between 50 and 250 soldiers. The effectiveness of heavy weapons is greatly reduced, and the defense must usually be overcome in hand-to-hand fighting. In Leningrad, for example, the garrison did not capitulate even after hundreds of thousands had starved or frozen to death. The rebels in the Warsaw ghetto were able to resist the German flamethrowers, bomber aircraft, and tanks for more than 30 days, although they had only small arms. And even American-style carpet bombing failed to obliterate the entire population of Germany's big cities.

As the attackers advance in a city, the fighting intensifies. The defenders' strength temporarily increases because their retreat, usually in concentric form, reduces the extent of the territory to be defended, with a larger proportion of heavy weapons available to defend each of the remaining sectors. During the encirclement of Budapest the length of the front line decreased by 90 percent and the territory held by the defense shrank to 3 percent of its original size within seven weeks. At the same time the rate of the decrease slowed: on 24 December the front line measured 87 kilometers in length, on 15 January, 21 kilometers, and on 11 February, 5 kilometers. The number of defenders declined even more slowly. On 24 December 1944 their ration strength (excluding the wounded) was 79,000 and their combat strength approximately 35,000; on 24 January 1945 about 40,000 and 15,000, respectively; and on 11 February 1945 about 32,000 and 11,000.

8

Soviet Marshal Vasili I. Chuikov on the Battle of Berlin[1]

1945

Imagine a crowd of youths, four hundred strong. Not one of them older than fifteen, all wearing their black school-uniform tunics. They are marching along the street towards the fighting area. They are heading towards our assault groups. On their shoulders are white 'Faustpatronen', set upon yard-long poles, and looking rather like water carafes. Hitler has sent these children to fight tanks.

'What are we to do—let them come on, or open fire?' radioed our officers.

'Refrain from firing: find some way of disarming them.'

Yellow flares sent up to show where our front line was failed to stop the boys. Now they are close to our positions, and on seeing guns and vehicles, they rush forward madly. The 'Faustpatronen' flew, blowing men and horses to ribbons. We had to open fire in answer. Seeing those in front falling, the rest turned back.

This happened in broad daylight, on 26 April, after the capture of Tempelhof aerodrome. The crowd of boys came out of the Tiergarten, and moved down the Kolonnenstrasse towards the positions of the 28th Guard Corps.

Who could thus have sent young boys to a certain death? Only a madman, a raving maniac.

---

1 Chuikov describes an encounter with elements of the Hitler Youth. A *Faustpatronen* was a smaller version of the *Panzerfaust*, a German anti-tank weapon roughly equivalent to a bazooka.

CHAPTER 12

ASIA AND THE PACIFIC

Introduction

Described by historian John Dower as a "war without mercy," the fighting in the Pacific featured fierce combat and heavy casualties. Japanese soldiers often fought to death, refusing to surrender. Tales of Japanese atrocities spread quickly among American soldiers and marines who, in turn, made little effort to take prisoners until late in the war.

Japan invaded the Philippines, a U.S. territory, on December 8, 1941. The campaign featured fierce fighting as Japanese soldiers steadily pushed back the islands' American and Filipino defenders who fought desperately despite severe supply shortages. After they surrendered on May 6, 1942, Japanese soldiers marched them across the island of Bataan. Several thousand of them died during this "Death March." Among the survivors was William E. Dyess, who escaped from captivity and wrote about his experiences. The excerpt in this chapter describes the murder of American prisoner (Document 1). Accounts such as this one further inflamed passions and further inflamed passions and encouraged combatants to fight without mercy for thier enemies.

Early in the war, American leaders adopted a strategy of "island hopping." Rather than attacking and capturing every Japanese-held island, they attacked only those needed to support the advance of U.S. forces across, particularly islands that offered good anchorages for the fleet or sites for air bases. As a result, fighting in the Pacific featured regular peaks and troughs as U.S. and

Allied amphibious forces invaded and conquered Japanese-held islands and then paused to recover and prepare for the next invasion.

Following success at the Battles of Coral Sea and Midway, the United States began its counteroffensive on the Solomon Islands with invasions of Guadalcanal and the much smaller nearby island of Tulagi (August 7, 1942). U.S. marines quickly captured Tulagi, but fighting for Guadalcanal, an island of 2,000 square miles, lasted six months. Japan fiercely contested the invasion and repeatedly sent additional troops in transports and small warships to reinforce its garrison and engage the marines. Nicknamed the "Tokyo Express" by Americans, cruisers and battleships sometimes escorted the transports and shelled American positions at night, particularly the Henderson Field airstrip, before sailing for home. Surprised by the initial American invasion, Japan reinforced its forces on the island and the nights of September 12–14 launched a succession of heavy attacks on thinly held marine positions. The fiercest fighting took place along Edson's Ridge, called "Bloody Ridge" by the marines, and the excerpt from Kerry Lane's *Guadalcanal Marine* (2004) captures its intensity (Document 2).

After the war, many American veterans wrote their memoirs, among them Eugene Sledge, whose book *With the Old Breed* (1981) captured his first-hand experiences fighting on the islands of Peleliu and Okinawa. Then a young marine, Sledge attended college after the war and had a successful career as a biology professor. The passage "Assault into Hell" (Document 3) describes the amphibious invasion of Peleliu. Although Americans had learned much from their prior invasions, so, too, had the Japanese, and both sides applied these lessons at Peleliu.

During war, military units record their own accounts of important events and military operations. This chapter includes an extract from the Report of the 4th Division, U.S. Marine Corps (Document 8), which participated in the June 15, 1944, amphibious invasion of Saipan. Three weeks of heavy fighting culminated with the mass suicide of several thousand Japanese soldiers and civilians, many of whom jumped off cliffs to their deaths despite American encouragement to surrender. The enclosed extract describes the mopping up operations on Saipan, which continued for another week.

U.S. marines faced even heavier fighting when they invaded Iwo Jima eight months later. On February 19, 1945, three marine divisions (3rd, 4th, and 5th) landed on Iwo Jima, a small, volcanic island expertly and fiercely defended by 21,000 Japanese soldiers, only about 200 of whom surrendered. The rest fought to the death, inflicting the highest losses the marines had ever suffered: 6,821 dead and almost 20,000 wounded. More than one in three marines who landed on Iwo Jima was killed or wounded. Rabbi Roland B. Gittelsohn, the Marine Corps' first Jewish chaplain, landed with the 5th Marine Division, and after the conclusion of the heaviest fighting delivered a moving eulogy for the many fallen. The division chaplain asked Gittelsohn to deliver the eulogy to the entire division, but religious prejudice prevented this, and separate Catholic, Jewish, and Protestant eulogies were delivered. Roughly 1,500 Jews served in the invading marine divisions, and Gittelsohn delivered his moving eulogy to them (Document 4).

Americans stationed in India joked that SEAC (Southeast Asia Command) actually stood for "Save England's Asian Colonies." This joke highlighted tensions between the otherwise close allies over colonialism and the post-war world. General Archibald Wavell, the British Viceroy of India, wrote to Prime Minister Winston Churchill to explain India's politics, India's large and well-organized independence movement, and Indians' growing demand for independence (Document 5). Although U.S. military leaders ordered their troops to avoid involvement in Indian politics (Document 6), independence leader Mahatma Gandhi wrote the U.S. Congress to seek American support for independence (Document 7).

Following the Soviet Union's entry into the Pacific War and the American dropping of atomic bombs on Hiroshima and Nagasaki, Japanese Emperor Hirohito, who had remained silent for most of the war, asserted his authority and insisted Japan surrender. Following an unsuccessful coup by senior military officers who wanted to continue the war, the emperor's recorded surrender message was broadcast to the Japanese people (Document 9). It was the first time most of them heard his voice.

1

BATAAN DEATH MARCH

DESCRIBING THE FIRST MURDER ON THE MARCH

The victim, an air force captain, was being searched by a private. Standing by was a Jap commissioned officer, hand on sword hilt. These men were nothing like the toothy, bespectacled runts whose photographs are familiar to most newspaper readers. They were cruel of face, stalwart, and tall. ... He didn't seem to be paying much attention. There was no expression in his eyes, only a sort of unseeing glare.

The private, a little squirt, was going through the captain's pockets. All at once he stopped and sucked in his breath with a hissing sound. He had found some Jap yen.

He held these out, ducking his head and sucking in his breath to attract notice. The big Jap looked at the money. Without a word he grabbed the captain by the shoulder and shoved him down to his knees. He pulled the sword out of the scabbard and raised it high over his head, holding it with both hands. The private skipped to one side.

Before we could grasp what was happening, the black-faced giant had swung his sword. I remember how the sun flashed on it. There was a swish and a kind of chopping thud, like a cleaver going through beef.

William E. Dyess "Bataan Death March," *The Dyess Story: Eye-Witness Account of the Death March From Bataan,* ed. Charles Leavelle, pp. 7-8, 93-94. 1944.

The captain's head seemed to jump off his shoulders. It hit the ground in front of him and went rolling crazily from side to side between the lines of prisoners.

The body fell forward. I have seen wounds, but never such a gush of blood as this. The heart continued to pump for a few seconds and at each beat there was another great spurt of blood. The white dust around our feet was turned into crimson mud. I saw that the hands were opening and closing spasmodically. Then I looked away.

When I looked again the big Jap had put up his sword and was strolling off. The runt who had found the yen was putting them into his pocket. He helped himself to the captain's possessions."

This was the first murder. In the year to come there would be enough killing of American and Filipino soldier prisoners to rear a mountain of dead.

Our Jap guards now threw off all restraint. They beat and slugged prisoners, robbing them of watches, fountain pens, money, and toilet articles. Now, as never before, I wanted to kill Japs for the pleasure of it.

The thing that almost drove me crazy was the certainty that the officer who had just been murdered couldn't have taken those yen from a dead Jap, He had been in charge of an observation post far behind the lines. I doubt that he ever had seen a dead Jap.

Gradually I got control of myself. By going berserk now I would only lose my own life without hope of ever helping to even the score.

Describing a Stop on the March

Just ahead of me, in the afternoon heat, were two American enlisted men, stumbling along near the point of collapse. I wasn't in much better shape. At this moment we came abreast of a calasa [covered cart] which had stopped beside the road.

An American colonel who also had been watching the two enlisted men, observed that no Jap guard was near us. He drew the two soldiers out of line and helped them into the cart, then got in also. The Filipino driver tapped his pony. The cart had moved only a few feet when the trick was discovered.

Yammering Jap guards pulled the three Americans from the cart and dragged the Filipino from the driver's seat. A stocky Jap noncommissioned officer seized the heavy horsewhip. The enlisted men were flogged first. The crackling lash slashed their faces and tore their clothing. The searing pain revived them for a moment. Then they fell to the ground. The blows thudded upon their bodies. They lost consciousness.

The colonel was next. He stood his punishment a long time. His fortitude enraged the Jap, who put all his strength behind the lash. When the American officer finally dropped to his knees his face was so crisscrossed with bloody welts it was unrecognizable.

The trembling Filipino driver fell at the first cut of the whip. He writhed on the ground. The lash tore his shirt and the flesh beneath it. His face was lacerated and one eye swollen shut. When the whipper grew weary, he ordered the driver on his way. The colonel, bleeding and staggering, was kicked back into the line of American prisoners.

I don't know what became of the enlisted men. I never saw them again. During the remaining two miles we marched to San Fernando I listened for shots, but heard none. The soldiers probably were bayoneted.

The sun still was high in the sky when we straggled into San Fernando, a city of 36,000 population, and were put in a barbed wire compound. ... We were seated in rows for a continuation of the sun treatment. Conditions here were the worst yet.

The prison pen was jammed with sick, dying, and dead American and Filipino soldiers. They were sprawled amid the filth and maggots that covered the ground. Practically all had dysentery. Malaria and dengue fever appeared to be running unchecked. There were symptoms of other tropical diseases I didn't even recognize.

Jap guards had shoved the worst cases beneath the rotted flooring of some dilapidated building. Many of these prisoners already had died. The others looked as though they couldn't survive until morning.

2

SECOND ASSAULT ON BLOODY RIDGE

Like all Marines, the pioneers were first and foremost riflemen. They were rushed up to the line during skirmishes when every man and every rifle was needed. They responded to trouble calls. The second assault on Bloody Ridge was one of those times.

In late October, our company was rushed into the lines with the 1st Battalion, 7th Marines. Once again the B Company Pioneers moved up to fill a gap that had been breached in a few places on the ridge. It was a debacle, but I think we held our own. The infantry was delighted to have the pioneers go into the lines with them because we had such firepower. We had machine guns galore. We also had the semiautomatic weapon of choice, the M-1 Garand rifle, recently obtained through moonlight requisition from the Army's 3rd Battalion, 164th Infantry Regiment.

On October 25, the men of B Company Pioneers awoke to the sounds of a fierce battle being waged south of Henderson Field. Little did we know at the time that our company would be joining the fray before the end of the day. A desperate battle was once again underway on Bloody Ridge. The Marine unit defending the ridge perimeter overlooking the airfield was Lt. Col. "Chesty" Puller's 1st Battalion. Puller had to cover the whole sector of 2500 yards with his understrength battalion, which required spreading his men thin and putting in the line all except those in the mortar section.

When the Sendai Division set out toward Edson's Ridge, Lt. Gen. Masao Maruyama appraised his officers and men of the stakes: "This is the decisive battle between Japan and the United States in which the rise and fall of the Japanese Empire will be decided. If we do not succeed in the occupation of these islands, no one should expect to return alive to Japan. We must over-come the hardships caused by the lack of material and push on unendingly by displaying invincible teamwork. Hit the proud enemy with an iron fist so he will not be able to rise again."[1]

On the night of October 24, in a blinding rainstorm, Lt. Gen. Maruyama's forces had launched their attack against Col. Puller's 1st Battalion. The attack began about 2130 hours, when a Marine listing post opened fire on the advance elements of the Japanese 29th Infantry Regiment, and pulled back to our lines. The Japanese had finally hacked their way through the jungle to the south of the Marines and were launching their attack. They had crossed the upper reaches of the Lunga River and were now just south of Bloody Ridge.

To support their attacks, they had nothing more than machine guns. All of their artillery and mortars had been abandoned along the Maruyama Trail. Gen. Maruyama had hoped for bright moonlight to orientate his troops, but the clouds and rain made the night black. The clash with the outpost was unavoidable and tipped off the Marines. The front lines were quiet for about two hours, until suddenly they attacked Puller's battalion east of Bloody Ridge.

Six battalions of the Sendai Division charged out of the jungle, attacking in Puller's area near the ridge and the flat ground to the east. The Marines replied with everything they had, calling in artillery, firing mortars, and relying heavily on crossing fields of machine-gun fire to cut down the enemy infantrymen. A wedge was driven into the Marine lines, but that was eventually straightened out with repeated counterattacks. Puller soon realized a strong Japanese force capable of repeated attacks was hitting his battalion. He called for reinforcements, and the Army's 3rd Battalion, 164th Infantry, commanded by Lt. Col. Robert K. Hall, was ordered forward. Also ordered forward was B Company Pioneers.

By 0330 on the morning of October 25, the Army battalion was completely integrated into the 1st Battalion, 7th Marines lines and the enemy attacks were getting weaker and weaker. The return fire laid down by Puller's reinforced battalion, including a smothering artillery barrage, was just too much to take. Gen. Maruyama pulled his men back to regroup and prepare to attack again.

Meanwhile, in our bivouac area, B Company made final preparations to go forward. The men busily cleaned and checked their weapons to insure that they were operating properly. Ammunition was distributed for the extra bandoleers and machine-gun belts they carried. Canisters of grenades and packages of C-rations were also passed out. Those items were carried in their combat packs.

Late in the afternoon, word was passed: "Stand by to move out." B Company Pioneers formed up in a column of platoons formation. A forward hand signal by Capt. Stephens started us on a force march that would take us from Kukum Beach to the ridge, where we would fill in a gap between two front-line units in Puller's extended line.

Light was fading fast as we crossed the mouth of the Lunga River. The skipper had us pick up the pace almost to a dogtrot. Night drops on you quickly in the jungle, and he didn't want us caught out in the dark before we reached the ridge. It was imperative that we occupy our unfamiliar defensive positions during daylight hours.

Once we reached the communication trail that led to the Puller zone, there was a guide from one of those units waiting to lead us in. When we reached the crest of the ridge, additional guides were waiting to drop off squad-sized units in fighting positions already prepared along the ridgeline. It was evident by the odor and the marks of battle that these fighting positions had been manned the previous night. The Marine pioneers were quite surprised to find machine guns, ammunition cans, and boxes of grenades in many of the fighting holes they were to occupy.

After we established radio communications with Col. Puller's battalion command post, my attention was focused primarily on making sure security was adequate in and around the company command bunker. After being briefed by a member of Puller's staff on the field telephone, Capt. Stephens requested that I accompany him on a quick tour of our lines. We really had to move out fast because darkness was setting in. We stopped briefly at some of the fighting positions along the ridgeline we were to defend. The men appeared to be in good spirits and eager to take on the enemy. Capt. Stephens had a brief conversation with his platoon commanders before we returned to the command bunker.

By the time we arrived back at the command center, the top of the ridgeline was already blanketed in a damp, heavy fog. Marines from the headquarters platoon assigned to man fighting positions in the sector around the center had already donned their ponchos to ward off the dampness of the night. Inside the command bunker, the radio was crackling with fast and furious reports of enemy activity in the area. There was no light in the bunker except for a flashlight occasionally used by the radioman. One of the men attached from the battalion communications section was manning an open field phone to Col. Puller's command post. Field phones were also opened down the line so that all platoon commanders could hear every message.

One message heard over the open phone resonated with every Marine on the ridge: "Colonel," Capt. Regan Fuller said to Puller, "I'm just about out of ammo. I've used up almost three and a half units of fire." Col. Puller said, "You've got bayonets, haven't you?" Fuller replied, "Sure. Yes, Sir." Puller said, "Alright, then. Hang on." B Company, 1st Pioneers was ready for its night of trial. Rain began to fall. It would be a long night.

After dark on the night of the 25th, the Japanese repeated the pattern of attack used the previous night. With only machine guns to augment their hand-carried weapons, groups of 20 to 200 Japanese soldiers charged out of the darkness to assault the entire length of the Puller-Hall line. The machine-gun companies with supporting riflemen against the junction of the Marine and Army battalions, where a trail led north to the airfield. The heavy concentration of artillery, mortars, small arms, and the four canister-firing 37s cut down the repeated Japanese assaults. A Company from the 1st Marine Division reserve (B Company Pioneers) came forward to reinforce, and the line held.

The Japanese took staggering losses, but continued hammering against the Marine lines throughout the night. But both of the assaults on the night of October 25–26 were thrown back. At dawn on the 26th it looked as though some enemy men might break through in the south. Col. Twining, the D-3, sent a precautionary message to the air command: "Jap's are driving hard toward Fighter Strip One. We'll probably stop them but take security measures around planes." He sent the engineers to act as security guards at the strip.

The Sendai Division hit Puller again about 1915 hours that night—the third successive night of trying to work along the east slope of Bloody Ridge. But the Marines were no longer the tenuous, hastily improvised group it had been before the arrival of the reinforcements. A lack of reserves had plagued the Marine command throughout the campaign. During the first battle at Bloody Ridge, it consisted of one understrength battalion. But Army and Marines lines south of the airfield, breached in a few places, were restored and held. The Sendai Division's back had been broken. It was clear that with the aid of the 11th Artillery and the final support of Army and Marine reinforcements, Puller's forces had been able to fend off the enemy. At daybreak the Marine positions were secure and the enemy had retreated. They would not come back. The grand Japanese offensive of the Sendai Division was over.

One of the mainstays of the Marine defense of Henderson Field was artillery in well-placed positions. Both the 37-mm antitank gun, in a sandbagged bunker, and the 75-mm howitzer were used with devastating effect against enemy formations. Often, Marine artillery fire would fall upon the Japanese before they had an opportunity to adequately prepare for an attack.

By the time the night was over, the 29th Japanese Infantry had lost 553 killed or missing and 479 wounded. The 16th Japanese Regiment's losses are uncounted, but the 164th burial parties handled 975 bodies. The Americans estimated that about 3500 enemy troops had died during the attacks. Once again, the "automatic artillery," so labeled by the Japanese in the Edson's Ridge and the Matanikau battles, helped to turn the tide. What was left of Gen. Maruyama force now straggled back over the Maruyama Trail, losing most of its seriously wounded men, as had the Kawaguchi force in the same situation during the first battle of Bloody Ridge.

That fighting in late October was probably as important as any combat on Guadalcanal. Once again, the Marines showed the Japanese that even with their bushido beliefs, they couldn't break the Marines. In the long run, that battle was the key to our victory on Guadalcanal.

Amid all the heroics of the three nights of fighting, many men were singled out for recognition, and there was an equally large number who performed great deeds that were never recognized. One Marine who distinguished himself throughout this action was Sgt. "Manila John" Basilone, who, operating in imminent danger and constantly exposing himself to hostile fire, kept the machine guns in his section of the front lines operating under almost impossible conditions. For his constant feats of heroism in this action he was awarded the Congressional Medal of Honor.

A platoon sergeant by the name of Mitchell Paige won the Congressional Medal of Honor for holding the Japanese at bay as they overran the eastern portion of the ridge. By holding his position against seemingly insurmountable odds, Paige was able to disrupt the Japanese and prevent them from outflanking the Marine positions. In a further heroic action, Paige led a group of Marines in an attack that broke the back of the final Japanese assault. In that attack, Paige cradled a .30-caliber water-cooled machine gun in his arms as he ran forward firing into the Japanese.

For his courageous leadership and successful defense against heavy odds, Lt. Col. Puller was awarded his third Navy Cross. The action that brought him the medal occurred on the night of October 24–25. For a desperate three hours his battalion stretched over a mile-long front. It was the only defense between vital Henderson Field and a regiment of seasoned Japanese troops. In pouring jungle rain the Japanese smashed repeatedly at his thin line, as Chesty moved up and down its length encouraging his men and direct the defense. After reinforcements arrived, he commanded the augmented unit until late the next afternoon. The defending Marines suffered fewer than

70 casualties in the engagement, while 1400 of the enemy were killed. The Marines recovered several truckloads of abandoned Japanese equipment.

A few days after his men had fought off an assault on the ridge, Puller led his battalion in a new engagement to block off any Japanese attempt to escape inland. He was one of the casualties of the eight-day engagement. Chesty's wounds were significant, but not immediately life threatening. He was wounded by mortar fire, collecting, as he put it, "a fanny full of shrapnel." When the battalion medical officer pinned a casualty tag on him and ordered him evacuated, the colonel shouted: "Evacuate me hell! Take that tag and stick it you know where. I will remain in command." But the next day he was ordered to leave and yield command to Maj. John E. Weber, his battalion executive officer.

3

"ASSAULT INTO HELL" ON THE FIGHTING FOR PELELIU

Hhour, 0800. Long jets of red flame mixed with thick black smoke rushed out of the muzzles of the huge battleships' 16-inch guns with a noise like a thunderclap. The giant shells tore through the air toward the island, roaring like locomotives.

* * *

We waited a seeming eternity for the signal to start toward the beach. The suspense was almost more than I could bear. Waiting is a major part of war, but I never experienced any more supremely agonizing suspense that the excruciating torture of those moments before we received the signal to begin the assault on Peleliu. I broke out in a cold sweat as the tension mounted with the intensity of the bombardment. My stomach was tied in knots. I had a lump in my throat and swallowed only with great difficulty. My knees nearly buckled, so I clung weakly to the side of the [amphibious] tractor [amtrac]. I felt nauseated and feared that my bladder would surely empty itself and reveal me to be the coward I was. But the men around me looked just about the way I felt. Finally, with a sense of fatalistic relief mixed with a flash of anger at the navy officer who was our wave commander, I saw him wave a flag toward the beach. Our driver revved the engine. The treads churned up the water, and we started in—the second wave ashore.

Eugene Sledge, "Assault Into Hell," *With the Old Breed*, pp. 55-57. Copyright © 2007 by Random House LLC. Reprinted with permission.

351

We moved ahead, watching the frightful spectacle. Huge geysers of water rose around the amtracs ahead of us as they approached the reef. The beach was now marked along its length by a continuous sheet of flame backed by a thick wall of smoke. It seemed as though a huge volcano had erupted from the sea, and rather than heading for an island, we were being drawn into the vortex of a flaming abyss. For many it was to be oblivion.

* * *

The Lieutenant braced himself and pulled out a half-pint whisky bottle.

"This is it, boys," he yelled.

He held out the bottle to me, but I refused. Just sniffing the cork under those conditions might have made me pass out. He took a long pull on the bottle, and couple of men did the same. Suddenly a large shell exploded with a terrific concussion, and a huge geyser rose up just to our right front. It barely missed us. The engine stalled. The front of the tractor lurched to the left and bumped hard against the rear of another amtrac that was either stalled or hit. I never knew which.

We sat stalled, floating in the water for some terrifying moments. We were sitting ducks for the enemy gunners. I looked forward through the hatch behind the driver. He was wrestling frantically with the control levers. Japanese shells were screaming into the area and exploding all around us. Sgt. Johnny Marmet leaned toward the driver and yelled something. Whatever it was, it seemed to calm the driver, because he got the engine started. We moved forward again amid the geysers of exploding shells.

Our bombardment began to lift off the beach and move inland. Our dive-bombers also moved inland with their strafing and bombing. The Japanese increased the volume of their fire against the wave of amtracs. Above the din I could hear the ominous sound of shell fragments humming and growling through the air.

"Stand by" someone yelled.

I picked up my mortar ammo bag and slung it over my left shoulder, buckled by helmet chin strap, adjusted my carbine sling over my right shoulder, and tried to keep my balance. My heart pounded Our amtrac came out of the water and moved a few yards up the gently sloping sand.

"Hit the beach!" yelled an NCO moments before the machine lurched to a stop.

The men piled over the sides as fast as they could. I followed Snafu, climbed up, and planted both feet firmly on the left side so as to leap as far away from it as possible. At that instant a burst of machine-gun fire with white hot tracers snapped through the air at eye level, almost grazing my face. I pulled back my head like a turtle, lost my balance, and fell awkwardly forward down into the sand in a tangle of ammo bag, pack, helmet, carbine, gas mask, cartridge belt, and flopping canteens. "Get off the beach! Get off the beach!" raced through my mind.

* * *

Shells crashed all around. Fragments tore and whirred, slapping on the sand and splashing into the water a few yards behind us. The Japanese were recovering from the shock of our prelanding bombardment. Their machine-gun and rifle fire got thicker, snapping viciously overhead in increasing volume.

Our amtrac spun around and headed back out as I reached the edge of the beach and flattened on the deck. The world was a nightmare of flashes, violent explosions, and snapping bullets. Most of what I saw blurred. My mind was benumbed by the shock of it.

I glanced back across the beach and saw a DUKW (rubber-tired amphibious truck) roll up on the sand at a point near where we had just landed. The instant the DUKW stopped, it was engulfed in thick, dirty black smoke as a shell scored a direct hit on it. Bits of debris flew into the air. I watched with the odd, detached fascination peculiar to men under fire, as a flat metal panel about two feet square spun high into the air then splashed into shallow water like a big pancake. I didn't see any men get out of the DUKW.

Eulogy for the Dedication of the 5th Marine Division Cemetery on Iwo Jima

March 1945

This is perhaps the grimmest, and surely the holiest task we have faced since D-Day. Here before us lie the bodies of comrades and friends. Men who until yesterday or last week laughed with us, joked with us, trained with us. Men who were on the same ships with us, and went over the sides with us as we prepared to hit the beaches of this island. Men who fought with us and feared with us. Somewhere in this plot of ground there may lie the man who could have discovered the cure for cancer. Under one of these Christian crosses, or beneath a Jewish Star of David, there may now rest a man who was destined to be a great prophet–to find the way, perhaps, for all to live in plenty, with poverty and hardship for none. Now they lie here silently in this sacred soil, and we gather to consecrate this earth in their memory.

It is not easy to do so. Some of us have buried our closest friends here. We saw these men killed before our very eyes. Any one of us might have died in their places. Indeed, some of us are alive and breathing at this very moment only because men who lie here beneath us had the courage and strength to give their lives for ours. To speak in memory of such men as these is not easy. Of them too can it be said with utter truth: "The world will little note, nor long remember what we say here. It can never forget what they did here."

No, our poor power of speech can add nothing to what these men and the other dead of our Division who are not here have already done. All that we

Roland B. Gittelsohn, "Eulogy for the Dedication of the 5th Marine Division Cemetery on Iwo Jima," pp. 1-3. 1945.

even hope to do is follow their example. To show the same selfless courage in peace that they did in war. To swear that by the grace of God and the stubborn strength and power of human will, their sons and ours shall never suffer these pains again. These men have done their jobs well. They have paid the ghastly price of freedom. If that freedom be once again lost, as it was after the last war, the unforgivable blame will be ours, not theirs. So it is we the living who are here to be dedicated and consecrated.

We dedicate ourselves, first, to live together in peace the way they fought and are buried in this war. Here lie men who loved America because their ancestors generations ago helped in her founding, and other men who loved her with equal passion because they themselves or their own fathers escaped from oppression to her blessed shores. Here lie officers and men, negroes and whites, rich men and poor–together. Here no man prefers another because of his faith or despises him because of his color. Here there are no quotas of how many from each group are admitted or allowed. Among these men there is no discrimination. No prejudices. No hatred. Theirs is the highest and purest democracy.

Any man among us the living who fails to understand that will thereby betray those who lie here dead. Whoever of us lifts up his hand in hate against a brother, or thinks himself superior to those who happen to be in the minority, makes of this ceremony and of the bloody sacrifice it commemorates, an empty, hollow mockery. To this, then, as our solemn, sacred duty, do we the living now dedicate ourselves: to the rights of Protestants, Catholics and Jews, of white men and negroes alike, to enjoy the democracy for which all of them here have paid the price.

To one thing more do we consecrate ourselves in memory of those who sleep beneath these crosses and stars. We shall not foolishly suppose, as did the last generation of America's fighting men, that victory on the battlefield will automatically guarantee the triumph of democracy at home. This war, with all its frightful heartache and suffering, is but the beginning our generation's struggle for democracy. When the last battle has been won, there will be those at home, as there were the last time, who will want us to turn our backs in selfish isolation on the rest of organized humanity, and thus to sabotage the very peace for which we fight. We promise you who lie here: we will not do that! We will join hands with Britain, China, Russia in peace, even as we have in war, to build the kind of world for which you died.

When the last shot has been fired, there will still be those whose eyes are turned backward, not forward, who will be satisfied with those wide extremes of poverty and wealth in which the seeds of another war can breed. We promise you, our departed comrades: this too we will not permit. This war has been fought by the common man; its fruits of peace must be enjoyed by the common man! We promise, by all that is sacred and holy, that your sons, the sons of miners and millers, the sons of farmers and workers, the right to a living that is decent and secure.

When the final cross has been placed in the last cemetery, once again there will be those to whom profit is more important than peace, who will insist with the voice of sweet reasonableness and appeasement that it is better to trade with the enemies of mankind, than by crushing them, to lose their profit. To you who sleep here silently, we give our promise: we will not listen! We will not forget that some of you were burnt with oil that came from American wells, that many of you were killed with shells fashioned from American steel. We promise that when once again men profit at your expense, we shall remember how you looked when we placed you reverently, lovingly, in the ground.

Thus do we memorialize those who, having ceased living with us, now live within us. Thus do we consecrate ourselves the living to carry on the struggle they began. Too much blood has gone into this soil for us to let it lie barren. Too much pain and heartache have fertilized the earth on which we stand. We here solemnly swear: this shall not be in vain! Out of this, and from the suffering and sorrow of those who mourn this, will come—we promise—the birth of a new freedom for the sons of men everywhere.

Amen.

5

GENERAL WAVELL REPORTS TO CHURCHILL ON SITUATION IN INDIA

OCTOBER 24, 1944

My Dear Prime Minister

I will begin by saying that my primary reason for writing is that I feel very strongly that the future of India is the problem on which the British Commonwealth and the British reputation will stand or fall in the post-war period. To my mind, our strategic security, our name in the world for statesmanship and fair dealing and much of our economic well-being will depend on the settlement we make in India. ...

... I agree in the main with what I think if your conviction, that in a mistaken view of Indian conditions and in an entirely misplaced sentimental liberalism we took the wrong turn 25 or 30 years ago; but we cannot put back the clock and must deal with existing conditions and pledges ...

* * *

When we started, 20 or 30 years [ago], on the political reform of India, we laid down a course from which we cannot now withdraw. It may have been a mistaken course, and it would probably have been better to have prescribed economic development first; but I am afraid it is too late to reverse the policy now And the general policy, of giving India self-government at an early date, was confirmed not long ago in the Cripps offer.

Source: http://www.bl.uk/reshelp/findhelpregion/asia/india/indianindependence/ww2/ww28/index.html

Nor do I think that in any case we can hold India down by force. Indians are a docile people, and a comparatively small amount of force ruthlessly used might be sufficient; but it seems to me clear that the British people will not consent to be associated with a policy of repression, nor will world opinion approve it, not will British soldiers wish to stay here in large numbers after the war to hold the country down. There must be acquiescence in the British connection if we are to continue to keep India within the Commonwealth.

India will never, with any time that we can foresee, be an efficient country, organised and governed on western lines. In her development to self-government we have got to be prepared to accept a degree of inefficiency comparable to that in China, Iraq, or Egypt. We must do our best to maintain the standards of efficiency we have tried to inculcate, but we cannot continue to resist reform because it will make the administration less efficient.

The present Government of India cannot continue indefinitely, or even for long. Though ultimate responsibility still rests with His Majesty's Government, His Majesty's Government has no longer the power to take effective action. We shall drift increasingly into situations—financial, economic, or political—for which India herself will be responsible but for which His Majesty's Government will get the discredit. ...

If our aim is to retain India as a willing member of the British Commonwealth, we must make some imaginative and constructive move without delay. We have every reason to mistrust Gandhi and Jinnah, and their followers. But the Congress and the League are the dominant parties in Hindu and Muslim India, and will remain so. They control the Press, the electoral machine, and money bags; and have the prestige of established parties. Even if Gandhi and Jinnah disappeared tomorrow ... I can see no prospect of our having more reasonable people to deal with ...

When we should make our fresh move is a difficult problem. I am quite clear that it should be made some considerable time before the end of the Japanese war. When the Japanese war ends, we shall have to release our political prisoners. They will find India unsettled and discontented. ... They will find fertile field for agitation, unless we have previously diverted their energies into some more profitable channel, i.e., into dealing with the administrative problems of India and into trying to solve the constitutional problem [of India]. We cannot move without taking serious risks, but the most serious risk of all is that India after the war will become a running sore which will sap the strength of the British Empire. I think it is still possible to keep India within the Commonwealth, though I do not think it will be easy to do so. If we fail to make any effort now we may hold India down uneasily for some years, but in the end she will pass into chaos and probably into other hands.

To be effective any move we make must be such as to capture the Indian imagination. If India is not to be ruled by force, it must be ruled by the heart rather than by the head. Our move must be sincere and friendly, and our outlook toward India must change accordingly. ...

It will not be easy to do, there is very deep-rooted feeling of suspicion to overcome, but certain steps could be taken which would help to reduce the mistrust and enmity now generally felt. In fact, if we want India as a Dominion after the war, we must begin treating her much more like a Dominion now.

6

Orders to American Military Forces in India

August 12, 1942

1. The sole purpose of the American forces in India is to prosecute the war of the United Nations against the Axis powers. In the prosecution of the war in that area the primary aim of the Government of the United States is to aid China.

2. American forces are not to indulge to the slightest degree in activities of any other nature unless India should be attacked by the Axis powers, in which event American troops would aid in defending India.

3. American forces in India will exercise scrupulous care to avoid the slightest participation in India's internal political problems, or even the appearance of so doing.

4. In event of internal disturbances American forces will resort to defensive measures only should their own personal safety or that of other American citizens be endangered or for the necessary protection of American military supplies and equipment.

"Orders to American Military Forces in India," Ibiblio, 1942.

7

GANDHI, MESSAGE TO AMERICA

OCTOBER 31, 1942

As I am supposed to be the spirit behind the much discussed and equally well abused resolution of the Working Committee of the Indian National Congress on independence, it has become necessary for me to explain my position, for I am not unknown to you.

I have in America perhaps the largest number of friends in the West—not even excepting Great Britain. British friends knowing me personally are more discerning than the American. In America I suffer from the well-known malady called hero worship. Good Dr. Holmes, until recently of the Unity Church of New York, without knowing me personally became my advertising agent. Some of the nice things he said about me I never knew myself. So I receive often embarrassing letters from America expecting me to perform miracles. Dr. Holmes was followed much later by Bishop Fisher who knew me personally in India. He very nearly dragged me to America but fates had ordained otherwise and I could not visit your vast and great country with its wonderful people.

Moreover, you have given me a teacher in Thoreau, who furnished me through his essay on the "Duty of Civil Disobedience" scientific confirmation of what I was doing in South Africa. Great Britain gave me Ruskin, whose "Unto This Last" transformed me overnight from a lawyer and a city-dweller into a rustic living away from Durban on a farm, three miles from the nearest railway station, and Russia gave me in Tolstoi, a teacher who furnished a reasoned basis for my non-violence. He blessed my movement in South

Gandhi, "Message to America," Ibiblio, 1942.

Africa when it was still in its infancy and of whose wonderful possibilities I had yet to learn. It was he who had prophesied in his letter to me that I was leading a movement which was destined to bring a message of hope to the down-trodden people of the earth. So you will see that I have not approached the present task in any spirit of enmity to Great Britain and the West. After having imbibed and assimilated the message of "Unto This Last" I could not be guilty of approving of Fascism or Nazism, whose cult is suppression of the individual and his liberty.

I invite you to read my formula of withdrawal or as it has been popularly called "Quit India" with this background. You may not read into it more than the context warranted.

I claim to be a votary of truth from my childhood. It was the most natural thing to me. My prayerful search gave me the revealing maxim "Truth is God" instead of the usual one "God is Truth." That maxim enables me to see God face to face as it were. I feel him pervade every fibre of my being. With this Truth as witness between you and me, I assert that I would not have asked my country to invite Great Britain to withdraw her rule over India irrespective of any demand to the contrary, if I had not seen at once that for the sake of Great Britain and the Allied cause it was necessary for Britain boldly to perform the duty of freeing India from bondage.

By that supreme act of justice Britain would have taken away all cause for the seething discontent of India. She will turn the growing ill will into active good will. I submit that it is worth all the battleships and airships that your wonder working engineers and financial resources can produce.

I know that interested propaganda has filled your ears and eyes with distorted visions of the Congress position. I have been painted as a hypocrite and enemy of Britain under disguise. My demonstrable spirit of accommodation has been described as my inconsistency, proving me to be an utterly unreliable man. I am not going to burden this letter with proof in support of my assertions. If the credit which I have enjoyed in America will not stand me in good stead, nothing I may argue in self defense will carry conviction.

You have made common cause with Great Britain. You cannot therefore disown responsibility for anything that her representatives do in India. You will do a grievous wrong to the Allied cause, if you do not sift the Truth from the chaff whilst there is yet time. Just think of it. Is there anything wrong in the Congress demanding unconditional recognition of India's independence? It is being said: "But this is not the time." We say: This is the psychological moment for that recognition. For then and then only can there be irresistible opposition to Japanese aggression. It is of immense value to the Allied cause if it is also of equal value to India.

I want you to look upon the immediate recognition of India's independence as a war measure of first class magnitude.

8

REPORT OF 4TH U.S. 4TH MARINE DIVISION ON THE FIGHTING ON SAIPAN

JULY 31, 1944

NARRATIVE OF THE ASSAULT

Tractor Battalion was utilized by RCT 23 to reduce enemy resistance remaining in caves along the west coast. Considerable difficulty was experienced in forcing civilians to come out of caves accessible only from the water.

Operations during the day resulted in an advance of 2500 yards and the capture of 0–9. All organized resistance had ceased and the Island of SAIPAN was officially declared secured at 1615, 9 July 1944.

SUBSEQUENT OPERATIONS (10 JULY TO 15 JULY)

During this period the Division was given the mission of completing the mopping up of that portion of SAIPAY Island north of grid line 26, with the exception of a western sector assigned to the 2d Marine Division. Thereafter, reorganization was to be initiated in preparation for further amphibious operations.

RCT 24 and RCT 25 were ordered to retrace their forward advance with the task of thoroughly combing the area southward to grid line 25. Isolated groups located mainly in caves and ravines, were destroyed as the two RCTs proceeded south on the mission assigned.

"Report of 4th U.S. 4th Marine Division on the Fighting on Saipan," 1944, pp. 44-45.

RCT 23 remained in the area north of grid line 26, conducted anti-sniper patrols, provided outposts for the coastline, and progressively assumed responsibility for RCT 24 and RCT 25 zones of action as these units withdrew.

Intermingling of civilians with fanatical Japanese soldiers, who used them for shields and prohibited them from surrendering, complicated the problem of completely clearing the area of enemy troops. The fact that both civilians and soldiers sought refuge in common beach caves which were inaccessible, except from the sea, further hindered the rapid accomplishment of the mission. Casualties among our own troops, suffered in attempts to entice civilians and soldiers to surrender, prompted the issuance of the following directive in Division Operation Order No. 32–44 relative to the policy to be followed: "Destroy enemy elements encountered in assigned zones. Mopping up operations to be conducted consistent with least loss of life own troops. Lives of non-combatants to be preserved consistent with accomplishment of this mission."

Persistent and zealous efforts to induce surrender of civilians, including extensive use of public address systems by interpreters, were made throughout the period, but the process was slow and arduous duo to the stubbornness and fanatical attitude of Japanese.

RCT 24 and RCT 25 completed assigned missions on D-plus-28 (13 July) and both RCTs proceeded to designated assembly areas where rehabilitation; reorganization) maintenance and repair of equipment and staff planning for further operations were initiated.

On D-plus-30 (15 July), the 14th Marines passed the control of its three 105mm Howitzer Battalions to XXIV Corps Artillery in preparation for intensification of the bombardment of TINIAN.

On D-plus-31 (15 July), the Division command post moved to a new position on the eastern coast of MAGICIENNE BAY.

RCT 23 continued mopping up operations in the assigned zone of responsibility until relieved by SAIPAN Garrison Forces on D-plus-31 (16 July) when it moved to its assigned assembly area.

9

Emperor of Japan Orders the Surrender of All Japanese Troops

To the Officers and Men of the Imperial Forces

Three years and eight months have elapsed since we declared war on the United States and Britain. During this time our beloved men of the army and navy, sacrificing their lives, have fought valiantly on disease-stricken and barren lands and on tempestuous waters in the blazing sun, and of this we are deeply grateful.

Now that the Soviet Union has entered the war against us, to continue the war under the present internal and external conditions would be only to increase needlessly the ravages of war finally to the point of endangering the very foundation of the Empire's existence

With that in mind and although the fighting spirit of the Imperial Army and Navy is as high as ever, with a view to maintaining and protecting our noble national policy we are about to make peace with the United States, Britain, the Soviet Union and Chungking.

To a large number of loyal and brave officers and men of the Imperial forces who have died in battle and from sicknesses goes our deepest grief. At the same time we believe the loyalty and achievements of you officers and men of the Imperial forces will for all time be the quintessence of our nation.

Source: http://www.taiwandocuments.org/surrender07.htm.

We trust that you officers and men of the Imperial forces will comply with our intention and will maintain a solid unity and strict discipline in your movements and that you will bear the hardest of all difficulties, bear the unbearable and leave an everlasting foundation of the nation.

CHAPTER 13

D-DAY AND WESTERN EUROPE, 1944–1945

Introduction

British, Canadian, and U.S. troops landed in Normandy, France, on June 6, 1944, beginning the liberation of Western Europe from Nazi rule. The next seven months, lasting through the Battle of the Bulge (December 16, 1944—January 25, 1945), Germany's failed winter counteroffensive, were a period of intense, almost continuous combat that exhausted soldiers. Casualties were such that personnel shortages forced Britain to consolidate many regiments. American divisions were chronically short of combat infantrymen. Chapter 13 covers the advance of Allied armies from the Normandy Invasion through Germany's May 1945 surrender and the end of the war in Europe.

General Dwight D. Eisenhower, a protégé of U.S. Army Chief of Staff George Marshall, commanded the Anglo-American invasion of North Africa. He proved an able diplomat as well as military commander, worked well with both British and American leaders, and was assigned to prepare for the invasion of Normandy (Document 1). Later, Eisenhower was appointed to command the Allied invasion, a massive undertaking and the largest amphibious invasion in history. Eisenhower's order of the day for June 6, 1944 (Document 2) encourages Allied troops on the day of invasion. Among the soldiers who landed on Normandy was Forest Pogue, a combat historian who had a distinguished scholarly career after the war. For many years, he was in charge of editing General Eisenhower's papers. In an excerpt from his memoirs (Document 3),

Pogue recounts reactions to Eisenhower's order and describes the first days of the invasion.

Although fooled by an elaborate Allied deception campaign to expect the invasion further to the east at the Pas de Calais, the Germans, commanded by Field Marshall Erwin Rommel, the famed "Desert Fox," had fortified the Normandy beaches and defended them fiercely. The German response to the invasion was hindered by disagreements between Rommel and Field Marshall Gerd von Rundstedt, his nominal superior, overwhelming Allied air superiority, and the lack of reinforcements to replace their growing casualties. Rommel outlined the deteriorating situation to Hitler on July 15 (Document 4). Two days later, Rommel was seriously injured in an Allied air attack. Three days after that, a group of senior German officers attempted to assassinate Hitler, but failed.

French resistance groups supplied the invading Allied armies with important information on German defenses. The night before the invasion, they sabotaged bridges and railroads across France, delaying the arrival of German reinforcements in Normandy. The Allies poured reinforcements into Normandy and steadily expanded their beachhead in June. At the end of July, they broke through German defenses and surrounded and destroyed most of the German army in France opposing them. By mid-August, they neared Paris. Inside the city, the French resistance rose against their German occupiers and seized control of large parts of the city. This "Day of the Barricades" is described by historian Michael Neiberg in an excerpt from his book *The Blood of Free Men: The Liberation of Paris, 1944* (Document 5). Thanks to its rapid liberation, Paris emerged from the war relatively undamaged.

Allied armies liberated most of France, but their advance then stalled due to lack of supplies. Antwerp, a major port in Belgium that Allied planners hoped to reopen quickly instead required heavy and prolonged fighting by Canadian troops to secure. As increasing Allied supplies finally flowed through the port, Germans targeted it with rocket attacks and built up forces for a major offensive to capture it. Launched through the dense forests of the Ardennes, the mid-December German offensive caught Allied commanders and soldiers by surprise, and in the first days of the Battle of the Bulge, German armies made rapid progress despite fierce American defense of St. Vith and Bastogne, towns that occupied key crossroads. Eduardo A. Peniche, a member of the U.S. 101st Airborne Division, describes a firefight near Bastogne in the "Mad Minute at Longchamps" in which American paratroopers fought off a massed German tank attack (Document 6).

In contrast to its practice in later wars, U.S. soldiers served for the duration of the war, rather than fixed one-year tours of duty. Despite this, American divisions were chronically short combat infantrymen. Great Britain suffered even worse shortages of personnel in the last 18 months of war. The result, not surprisingly, was high rates of combat exhaustion, particularly among infantrymen who often faced prolonged combat with little chance for rest. In an excerpt from his book *Browned Off and Bloody-Minded: The British Soldier Goes to War 1939–1945* (2015), Alan Allport describes how British soldiers coped with the rigors of combat and managed to both hate their enemies and display compassion toward them (Document 7).

Although U.S. casualties in World War II were lower than many of its Allies, particularly the Soviet Union, they were still large, and increased dramatically in the last 18 months of war. In his final report on the war, U.S. Army Chief of Staff General George Marshall tallied "The Price of Victory" (Document 8), noting the high casualty rates of U.S. infantry regiments, the medical advancements that saved lives and dramatically reduced deaths from disease, the many awards for bravery, and the continuing problem of treating combat fatigue.

1

General Eisenhower Ordered to Prepare Invasion of Normandy (D-Day)

Directive to Supreme Commander, Allied Expeditionary Force

1. You are hereby designated as Supreme Allied Commander of the forces placed under your orders for operations for liberation of Europe from Germans. Your title will be Supreme Commander Allied Expeditionary Force.

2. Task. You will enter the continent of Europe and, in conjunction with the other United Nations, undertake operations aimed at the heart of Germany and the destruction of her armed forces. The date for entering the Continent is the month of May, 1944. After adequate channel ports have been secured, exploitation will be directed towards securing an area that will facilitate both ground and air operations against the enemy.

3. Notwithstanding the target date above you will be prepared at any time to take immediate advantage of favorable circumstances, such as withdrawal by the enemy on your front, to effect a reentry into the Continent with such forces as you have available at the time; a general plan for this operation when approved will be furnished for your assistance.

4. Command. You are responsible to the Combined Chiefs of Staff and will exercise command generally in accordance with the diagram at Appendix. Direct communication with the United States and British Chiefs of Staff is authorized in the interest of facilitating your operations and for arranging necessary logistical support.

5. Logistics. In the United Kingdom the responsibility for logistics organization, concentration, movement and supply of forces to meet the requirements of your plan will rest with British Service Ministries so far as British Forces are concerned. So far as United States Forces are concerned, this responsibility will rest with the United States War and Navy Departments. You will also be responsible for coordinating the requirements of British and United States Forces under your command.

6. Coordination of operations of other Forces and Agencies. In preparation for your assault on enemy occupied Europe, Sea and Air Forces agencies of sabotage, subversion and propaganda, acting under a variety of authorities are now in action. You may recommend any variation in these activities which may seem to you desirable.

7. Relationship with United Nations Forces in other areas. Responsibility will rest with the Combined Chiefs of Staff for supplying information relating to operations of the Forces of the U.S.S.R. for your guidance in timing your operations. It is understood that the Soviet Forces will launch an offensive at about the same time as OVERLORD with the object of preventing the German forces from transferring from the Eastern to the Western Front. The Allied Commander in Chief, Mediterranean Theater, will conduct operations designed to assist your operation, including the launching of an attack against the south of France at about the same time as OVERLORD. The scope and timing of his operations will be decided by the Combined Chiefs of Staff. You will establish contact with him and submit to the Combined Chiefs of Staff you views and recommendations regarding operations from the Mediterranean in support of your attack from the United Kingdom. The Combined Chiefs of Staff will place under your command the forces operating in Southern France as soon as you are in a position to assume such command. You will submit timely recommendations compatible with this regard.

8. Relationship with Allied Governments—the re-establishment of Civil Governments and Liberated Allied Territories and the administration of enemy territories. Further instructions will be issued to you on these subjects at a later date.

2

GENERAL EISENHOWER'S ORDER OF THE DAY

JUNE 6, 1944

SUPREME HEADQUARTERS
ALLIED EXPEDITIONARY FORCE

Soldiers, Sailors, and Airmen of the Allied Expeditionary Force!
You are about to embark upon the Great Crusade, toward which we have striven these many months. The eyes of the world are upon you. The hope and prayers of liberty-loving people everywhere march with you. In company with our brave Allies and brothers-in-arms on other Fronts, you will bring about the destruction of the German war machine, the elimination of Nazi tyranny over the oppressed peoples of Europe, and security for ourselves in a free world.

Your task will not be an easy one. Your enemy is will trained, well equipped and battle-hardened. He will fight savagely.

But this is the year 1944! Much has happened since the Nazi triumphs of 1940–41. The United Nations have inflicted upon the Germans great defeats, in open battle, man-to-man. Our air offensive has seriously reduced their strength in the air and their capacity to wage war on the ground. Our Home Fronts have given us an overwhelming superiority in weapons and munitions of war, and placed at our disposal great reserves of trained fighting men. The tide has turned! The free men of the world are marching together to Victory!

"Eisenhower's June 6, 1944 Order of the Day," *The Papers of Dwight David Eisenhower: The War Years*, ed. Alfred D. Chadler, pp. 1913-1914. Johns Hopkins University Press, 1970.

I have full confidence in your courage, devotion to duty and skill in battle. We will accept nothing less than full Victory!

Good luck! And let us beseech the blessing of Almighty God upon this great and noble undertaking.

3

Forest Pogue Describes D-Day Invasion

June 1944

At noon [June 5] we received General Eisenhower's order of the day together with our cookies. Those who read it said little. The only comment I got down in my diary was that several said "Bull." Fox and I compared notes and we agreed that the men were somewhat cynical and uninspired about their task, but determined. They spent their time no longer at cards now that the money was in the hands of a few, but swapped yarns and exchanged items of clothing with the sailors. This pastime, which threatened to change the colors of the services, was eventually forbidden. The evening was cool and windy, and we made little speed. We went to bed early since we supposed we would be awakened by firing.

Tuesday, 6 June (D-Day)

> Awakened at 10 to hear that it had been announced that after heavy bombing and bombardment U.S. and British troops had landed on the French coast. No great enthusiasm evinced by troop, although they were pleased.
>
> Started turning southward from English coast at 7 p.m. There are now 60–70 craft in sight (the radio says 4000 took part). Water relatively calm (although we rocked a bit at noon and I felt a little sick). Became cool near evening. At 7 as we turned towards

France a message was read from General Eisenhower urging proper treatment of peoples of France. Another message—from General Montgomery—wished the men good hunting. Neither message got any response from the men. It has been difficult to get any atmosphere of—or preparation. The Captain found it necessary to urge watchfulness and care in the Navy personnel since they were imitating the Army's lack of care. In the midst of so many boats, the idea of despair seems to them remote and absurd. There is absolutely nothing to indicate that the men are stirred in the least.

We have been told that we will stand off the coast of France between 6–7 and that we will go off on Rhino ferries and LCI's. We were told to expect air attack.

The clouds lifted in afternoon and except for cool breeze the weather is fine. Planes were in evidence throughout the day.

Land barely in sight astern at 7:30. At 9:30 were told we were 54 miles from French coast. Bed at 11. Slept poorly because 5 of us were sleeping on top of 5 cases of K rations in truck.

During the next six weeks, it was to be the task of some five combat historians to collect as much as we could of the D-Day story from officers and men of the 1st and 29th Divisions, the Rangers, the 4th Division, and the 82d and 101st Airborne Divisions. My share was the interviewing of assault troops from the 116th and 115th Regimental Combat Teams and a few from the 16th Infantry Regiment. ...

My own picture of D-Day was gleaned from dozens of interviews with officers and men who went in during the morning of 6 June. Some I talked to shortly after they were wounded, others I interviewed as they rested near the front lines, and some gave their stories weeks later. A short outline of that morning is given below.

The ships that took the assault elements to Normandy had been loaded, much like ours, in many coves and inlets in Wales, southern England, and the eastern counties. On the evening of 5 June they had proceeded from the rendezvous area near the Isle of Wight southward toward France. Shortly after midnight, minesweepers of the Allied fleet began to clear channels through the minefields for the ships. British and American airborne units took off from English fields and flew overhead to drop over their objectives—the British east of the Orne and the Americans in the Cotentin Peninsula. The British reached their bridgehead early and secured it, while the American forces, scattered to a considerable degree, had a tough job of assembling for concerted action.

Toward daylight the planes and ships took up their task of softening up the enemy, the chief change in plan being that mentioned earlier in which the air force struck a few miles inland instead of at the beaches. On the western limit of Omaha Beach, the Rangers scrambled ashore to find that the six guns they were to knock out were pulled back out of their way.

By daylight, ship channels had been cleared to the beaches and the small landing craft had been filled with men from the LSTs and larger transports and were on their way in from rendezvous points some ten miles out. The floating tanks were started in, as were guns in small craft. Only five out of thirty-two DDs survived of those that attempted to float in under their own power, while most of those in the other tank battalion, sent in at the last minute by boat, got in safely. In one field artillery battalion all but one gun was lost when the craft carrying them capsized.

The accounts of the early landings tend to follow the same pattern. Heavy seas threatened to swamp the smaller craft and made many of the soldiers seasick. Enemy fire struck numerous craft or forced navy crews to unload in deep water. Poor visibility, obstacles, and inexperience led other navy crews to land on the wrong beaches. Many of the soldiers in the first waves had to wade ashore carrying heavy equipment, which they often disposed of in deep water. At the extreme ends of the beaches, the cliffs interfered to some extent with the enemy fire and gave our troops some protection. In front of Vierville, the men hid behind the seawall that ran along the beach, and near Saint-Laurent-sur-Mer they found mounds of shingles to use as cover. Accounts of the first hours on the beaches speak of efforts of officers and non-coms to organize their units and get them off the beaches, but often those who tried to direct the attack fell as soon as they exposed themselves to the enemy. In some cases, platoons stuck together, but in others sections landed some distance apart—and there were instances where dispersed elements attached themselves to entirely different regiments and divisions and did not return to their parent organization for two or three days.

* * *

On the 16th Infantry's beaches, Colonel George Taylor, the RCT commander, gained lasting fame by saying to his officers and men: "The only people on the beach are the dead and those who are going to die—now let's get the hell out of here." In a short time he had the men in his sector moving. He and Colonel Canham were promoted to the rank of brigadier general for their work on D-Day.

The manner of the advance up the bluffs differed somewhat among the various units. Some stayed behind the seawall until units in the second and third waves came in through them and went up the cliffs. Others, after being reorganized, pressed forward and by noon were on top of the bluffs.

By midnight on 6 June all of the regiments in the 1st Division (the 16th, 18th, and 26th) and two from the 29th (the 116th and 115th) had been landed on Omaha Beach. The 2d and 5th Ranger Battalions were in position to their right. Heavy seas, landings on the wrong beaches, intense fire from well-entrenched positions, the foundering of DD tanks and artillery pieces, abnormally high casualties among officers, failure to open all the beach exits, beach congestion, the slowness of some of the assault waves to move forward from the seawall, the difficulty of using the full force of naval gunfire because of the fear of inflicting losses on the infantrymen, the lack of sufficient gaps in underwater obstacles and beach obstacles, and the failure, for various reasons, of air bombardment to take out beach fortifications all placed V Corps a considerable distance from its D-Day objectives, and, as a result of the presence of the German 352d Division in the area, in danger of a counterattack before the time estimated. In the face of this situation, the regiments were reorganized, defenses were set up for the night, and preparations made for a vigorous offensive to attain the D-Day objectives as quickly as possible.

4

FIELD MARSHAL ERWIN ROMMEL REPORTS TO HITLER ON D-DAY LANDINGS

JULY 15, 1944

The situation on the Normandy Front is growing worse every day and is now approaching a grave crisis.

Due to the severity of the fighting, the enemy's enormous use of material—above all, artillery and tanks—and the effect of his unrestricted command of the air over the battle area, our casualties are so high that the fighting power of our divisions is rapidly diminishing. Replacements from home are few in number and, with the difficult transport situation, take weeks to get to the front. As against 97,000 casualties (including 2,360 officers)—i.e. an average of 2,500 to 3,000 a day—replacements to date number 10,000, of whom about 6,000 have actually arrived at the front.

Material losses are also huge and have so far been replaced on a very small scale; in tanks, for example, only 17 replacements have arrived to date as compared with 225 losses.

The newly arrived infantry divisions are raw and, with their small establishment of artillery, anti-tank guns and close combat anti-tank weapons, are in no state to make a lengthy stand against major enemy attacks coming after hours of drum-fire and heavy bombing. The fighting has shown that with this use of material by then enemy, even the bravest army will be smashed piece by piece, lose men, arms and territory in the process.

Due to the destruction of the railway system and the threat of the enemy air force to roads and tracks up to 90 miles behind the front, supply conditions are so bad that only the barest essentials can be brought to the front. It is consequently now necessary to exercise the greatest economy in all fields, and especially in artillery and mortar ammunition. These conditions are unlikely to improve, as enemy action is steadily reducing the transport capacity available. Moreover, this activity in the air is likely to become even more effective as the numerous air-strips in the bridgehead are taken into use.

No new forces of any consequence can be brought up to the Normandy front except by weakening Fifteenth Army's front on the Channel, or the Mediterranean front in southern France. Yet the Seventh Army's front, taken over all, urgently requires two fresh divisions, as the troops in Normandy are exhausted.

On the enemy's side, fresh forces are great quantities of war material are flowing into his front every day. His supplies are undisturbed by our air force. Enemy pressure is growing steadily stronger.

In these circumstances we must expect that in the foreseeable future the enemy will succeed in breaking through out thin front, above all Seventh Army's, and thrusting deep into France. Apart from the Panzer Group's sector reserves, which are at present tied down by the fighting on their own front and—due to the enemy's command of the air—can only move by night, we dispose of no mobile reserve for defense against such a breakthrough. Action by our air force will, as in the past, have little effect.

The troops are everywhere fighting heroically, but the unequal struggle is approaching its end. It is urgently necessary for the proper conclusion to be drawn from this situation. As C.-in-C. of the Army Group I feel myself duty bound to speak plainly in this point.

5

THE DAYS OF THE BARRICADES

AUGUST 21–22

Parisians had responded with enthusiasm to the call, erecting four hundred barricades in two days. By the end of the battle for Paris, the city had more than six hundred barricades in place. Most were built in the traditional Parisian style, using paving stones hacked out of the roads by the sweat and muscle of the neighborhood's young men. Anything that might help support a barricade was soon added, including disabled vehicles, felled trees, and broken pieces of furniture. Some barricades were just a few large branches stretched across a road. Others were as deep as six feet and as high as four feet. In many cases, Parisians added portraits of Hitler or other symbols of the German occupation to the front, thus requiring any German troops to open fire on photographs of the führer or Nazi flags if they attacked. It may have been a small token of resistance, but it was symbolic nonetheless. Other barricades flew French tricolors or improvised Soviet, British, or American flags.

The barricades served both symbolic and strategic purposes. From a symbolic standpoint, they showed that the city belonged to the FFI and to the people of Paris. The formation of barricades recalled heroic periods in French history and connected the events of 1944 to those of the historic days of 1789, 1830, and 1848. They showed that a battle was well and truly underway, and they served as a rallying point for neighborhood action. The construction of the barricades involved thousands of people, young and old, rich and poor, male and female. Even children participated, bringing supplies to the barricades' defenders and, like Victor Hugo's young hero Gavroche, often exposing themselves to danger in the process.

Sylvia Beach, an American expatriate who owned the Shakespeare and Company bookstore, marveled at the sights of the barricades in her neighborhood, writing: "The children engaged in our defense piled up furniture, stoves, dustbins, and so on at the foot of the Rue de l'Odéon, and behind these barricades youths with FFI armbands and a strange assortment of old-fashioned weapons aimed at the Ger-mans stationed on the steps of the theater at the top of the street." The uprising that had begun as a movement of select, clandestine groups had now expanded to include a wide array of Parisians, all of whom fought for a common cause. The password of the St. Michel neighborhood's barricades was "Vengeance."

The sight of entire communities openly working to defend themselves underscored the communal nature of the new struggle. Another famous Parisienne, Simone de Beauvoir, recalled children behind the barricades singing, "Nous ne les reverrons plus / C'est fini, ils sont foutus" (We will not see them again / It's all over, they are screwed). The barricades thus had an important symbolic purpose in a city desperate to recover some of its own self-respect. FFI member Jean Reybaz watched in wonder as children in his working-class neighborhood piled paving stones into the baskets of their bicycles and took them to barricades that needed reinforcement. Philippe Barat, an FFI commander who was in charge of the barricades in the critical St. Michel area, recalled that the neighborhood "was suddenly filled with a motley and strange crowd that formed a vast, marvelous fraternity. The rich and the poor, the aristocrat and the worker, came together so that the Germans would take from their capital the memory of a city that had a true soul." Even allowing for some exaggeration in the heat of the moment, Barat had a point. For the first time in four years (at least), the people of Paris were standing together. As Gilles Perrault, a teenager at the time, thoughtfully noted, many of the barricades were not as much an action aimed at the Germans as "a matter between us and our long humiliation."

From a tactical perspective, the barricades were unlikely to present much of an obstacle to a determined German attack; nevertheless, they served an important military purpose. Barat noted that they provided Parisians, many of whom had never held a gun in their lives, a modicum of protection that was crucially important to sustaining their morale. The men in his FFI cell were desperately anxious to fight—on hearing of the truce they had screamed, "No truce! War to the Death! Now more than ever!" But they had no real experience of fighting and no idea how to combat the materially superior Germans. The barricades gave them a place to assemble and site their few weapons. One barricade in the St. Michel area, for example, had thirty-seven men defending it, but just two rifles and a revolver. Fighting together as a community gave Parisians a strength they would not have had as individuals or pairs. As a result, the barricades took on an importance far out of proportion to their tactical value. Barat wrote that "words cannot express the fever of combat, the intoxication, the enthusiasm" that people felt as they took up an active role in their own liberation.

When properly located and reinforced, moreover, the barricades could still play a strategic role. FFI leaders knew that the Germans were unlikely to risk losing a precious tank to demolish a barricade that was inexpensive to construct and simple to rebuild. FFI section chiefs carefully determined where to construct the barricades and instructed people how best to defend them in order to achieve the maximum effect. Barat's area in St. Michel sat along the route between the German tank park in the Jardin du Luxembourg and the Préfecture de Police. It therefore dominated one of the most important streets in the city on these days, the Boulevard St. Michel. Barat was determined to make his neighborhood a bastion of the FFI and a death trap for any Germans who dared to cross.

Barat oversaw the establishment of nine major barricades in St. Michel. The most important, made up of overturned trucks, paving stones, and sandbags, went up just west of the Boulevard St. Michel on the Quai des Grands Augustins. It was more than ten feet high and almost six feet deep, making it undoubtedly one of the strongest barricades in the city. It successfully prevented the movement of German tanks along the Left Bank of the Seine, thus protecting the southern approaches to the Île de la Cité. Other barricades blocked off the Boulevard St. Michel and the Rue St. Jacques at both the river and along the Boulevard St. Germain. Two barricades near the prominent fountain of St. Michel (the protector of Paris) stretched halfway across the boulevard to keep the interior lines of communication around the Rue St. Severin open for the FFI. In this neighborhood, at least, the barricades were not constructed randomly, but according to a plan that made maximum use of their strength.

Barricades located in less important areas or that were less sturdily constructed still had their own roles to play. The barricades canalized German movements, forcing them to move around the obstacles or engage them directly. When they chose the former, they moved into alleys and side streets, where FFI teams were waiting for them with Molotov cocktails and whatever other weapons they could amass. When they chose the latter, they had to stop, which left them open to attack. In either case, Resistance fighters ambushed them, seized prisoners of war, and, more crucially, captured badly needed German weapons and ammunition. The barricades also presented a new and unwelcome problem for the Germans, who had grown accustomed to open lines of communication.

The Germans, and for that matter the French, often had no idea which streets were open and which were barricaded. The result was a communications headache for the Germans that sowed confusion and fear, placing them in the uncomfortable role of being on the defensive amid a hostile population. The barricades isolated the Ger-man strongpoints from one another. German units saw their supplies and reinforcements choked off as the roads literally closed in around them. When the Germans came out of their strongpoints to clear barricades, they found themselves engaged in disorienting street fighting for which they had no training. German attacks rarely succeeded, because the Germans could not survive outside their strongpoints for long before being surrounded. Even when the Germans damaged the barricades, teams of neighborhood volunteers quickly repaired them.

The mass confusion in the streets impacted the Germans much more than it did the FFI. Rol's fighters could easily move in pairs or small groups through the streets without fear of being intercepted by either the Germans or the police, who were protecting the prefecture and the commissariats. They could also use the corridors of the Métro and the sewer system to move under-ground, where the Germans could not see them and the barricades did not inhibit them. From his headquarters underneath the Denfert-Rochereau Métro station, Rol could keep in contact with the neighborhoods and even direct reinforcements to threatened areas where necessary. Rol's staff marked each barricade on a giant map, giving the FFI an enormous intelligence advantage over the Germans. The prefecture, too, acted as a command post. Its fully functioning telephone system helped the FFI to direct reinforcements and supplies to crisis areas.

The heady atmosphere in Paris transformed it into a new city as residents felt freedom for the first time in years. Rol's courageous wife, Cécile, recalled these days as the first time she could walk through the streets of Paris without having to look behind to see who was following her. Parisians finally felt safe enough to use the telephones and say in public what had been on their minds throughout the occupation. "One could say out loud that Hitler was a bastard and Pétain an old traitor," recalled one Parisian with joy. Others were inspired by the sight of the French police patrolling the area around the prefecture in a captured German armored car with the word "POLICE" painted hastily on its sides. "People stared at us stupefied," the driver of the vehicle later noted. "They couldn't believe their eyes. Everywhere we went they cheered us and applauded us." The FFI flew a large tricolor flag over the recently liberated

Cherche-Midi prison and stretched another across an adjacent road. A German armored vehicle passing by shot it down, but thirty minutes later a new one took its place. That flag flew throughout the rest of the liberation.

The Resistance leaders attempted to channel these newfound energies into the ongoing battle raging within the city. One communist proclamation urged Parisians to join the fight, saying that "the hour has come to chase out the invader, the hour has come to once again proclaim the Republic at the Hôtel de Ville, by Parisians themselves. TO ARMS CITIZENS!" The Communist Party also posted notices urging Parisians to disregard the false truce. "Paris wants to fight!" they read. And fight Paris did. All but three of the city's arrondissements saw action on August 21 and 22.

6

"Mad Minute at Longchamps," Battle of the Bulge

The new year of 1945 was welcomed with a big bang in our sector; it seemed that our Division's artillery and mortars had joined every gun on the 3d Army front in a midnight barrage, all of them pouring high explosives toward the German lines. By this date, the entire Bastogne area was deep in snow that had been coming down at intervals during the seven days of the siege.

... Our main mission was to protect the road block on that road [leading into Bastogne].

* * *

On Jan. 3, 1945, the 502d Parachute Infantry Regiment was attacked in force and its MLR was overrun by enemy armor. The action began around 1330 hours. The enemy armor came down the road which runs southward from Compogne to Longchamps. In a well-planned maneuver, the German tanks, about 15 or 17 of them, fanned out for the attack. They were followed by infantrymen and panzer-grenadiers. It was a fierce and determined attack against our front. As the German tanks and infantry began to advance against our position and towards the road block, our Squad Leader, Sgt. Joe O'Toole (Vincennes, IN) gave us orders to engage the enemy—enemy fire as effectively raking our positions. The entire Longchamps-Monaville front was under attack!

Eduardo A. Peniche, "Mad Minute at Longchamps," *Veterans of the Battle of the Bulge*, ed. Robert Van Houten, pp. 44-45. Copyright © 1991 by Turner Publishing Company. Reprinted with permission.

I am sure that at that moment everyone else was as scared as I was ... Pfc. Alfred Steen (The Bronx, NY) was ready to load the piece again as Pfc. Darrell Garner (Florence, SC) our gunner was finding the range.

I quickly moved two more AT shells to the gun position making sure that they had AP fuse, a new type of high velocity shell.

Several airbursts exploded between us and the roadblock; our machine gunners to our right were keeping the grenadiers from reaching the road block. As a Tiger tank approached the point in the road, we hit it twice; the second shot took its turret off and as the crew was leaving the burning tank, they were riddled with machine-gun fire—our AP ammunition was proving to be very effective AT ordnance. Behind our position one or two armored vehicles ... sporadically came up the ridge to lob a shell or two against the attacking force. German 88's were proving to be accurate and devastating—shells and bullets were spraying our emplacement. In reality, once an AT gun is committed to battle, its position is easily spotted and the situation becomes do-or-die. There are no avenues of retreat nor room for maneuver.

I crawled back to our ammo dump to bring more AT shells and assisted in loading the gun.

As we destroyed a second tank, all hell broke loose around us. We were determined to offer a heavy resistance, but the German gunners zeroed in on our emplacement; we were being hit with everything the enemy could fire. It was the hour of the mad minute. It was that terrifying moment when all the weapons on the line seemed to explode violently all at once. The incoming shells were so numerous that the ground felt tremoring. Our gun took a direct hit and was destroyed. All three of us, O'Toole, Garner and myself were hit by shrapnel. The battle raged all around us, the TDs [tank destroyers] and our mortars were hitting the advancing German infantry. The German tanks were not advancing but were continuing in their murderous fire. The mad minute indeed was upon us at Longchamps and yet, our other AT squads were joining the firefight.

By this time, I crawled to assist O'Toole who had been severely wounded. He had been hit in the hip and the leg; he was bleeding profusely and looked as if he were going into shock. To mitigate the pain he had given himself a shot of morphine. Darrell was hit in the face and shoulder; my left leg was numb above the knee, but my knee was hurting a lot. I looked down and saw the blood on my muddy trousers. Voices and moans of some other men could be heard. I remember praying both in English and Spanish. As I crawled on the snow toward the ridge, I heard the bullets and the shrapnel cutting the air above me, but I needed to reach our CP just behind the knoll. We needed medical attention.

The entire mad episode could not have lasted more than 15 or 20 minutes.

While the medic was tending my wound (foreign body, left knee), I heard our rounds heading toward the advancing Germans. It was then that I realized how close I had been to being killed in action. ... Casualties on both sides proved numerous.

* * *

The crisis at Longchamps was over for the moment. Our wounded were being evacuated to field hospitals. My ambulance was on its way to Arlon. The troops on the stretcher below me mumbled something and I agreed; for us the Battle of the Bulge was over.

7

CATEGORIES OF COURAGE

One reason why soldiers could endure the horrors of the front line does not sit well with the liberal values of twenty-first century Britain: because some of them enjoyed it. Battle freed life from all its petty complexities. Spit-and-polish bullshit ended when the bullets began to fly. The nearer you were to the enemy, the fewer base-wallahs and other detested rear-echelon types you had to concern yourself with. "What a clarity and a simplicity it really had!" as one soldier put it. Plus there was the sheer thrill of the hunt and the kill. Some men thrived on the adrenalin rush of danger. ... a platoon sergeant called Whitemark underwent a transformation after D-Day ... a man who had previously been an unruly and persistent defaulter, was revealed, to everyone's surprise, to be a natural leader. He seemingly had no sense of fear, and was able to communicate his own cool serenity to the other soldiers around him, even under the worst of fire. He volunteered for patrols, carried them out without fuss, and was soon known for killing the enemy with calm efficiency. He expressed no interest in life after the war, or any particular desire to see it come to an end. The battlefield was his element. When asked why he enjoyed life on the front line so much, Whitemark could only grin and reply enigmatically, *"Ah, sir, I'm the nomadic type."*

Raleigh Trevelyan's first experience of killing in cold blood was one of unalloyed pleasure. As the German he had shot through the head collapsed from sight, Trevelyan felt a swell of ecstasy inside himself, the same raw

Alan Allport, "Categories of Courage," *Browned Off and Bloody-Minded: The British Soldier Goes to War*, 1939-1945, pp. 262-265. Copyright © 2015 by IB Taurus. Reprinted with permission.

thrill he had experienced as a boy when he stalked roosting pigeons and wild rabbits on expeditions in the woods. "I was triumphant ... before long I was pouring out the story to an audience, flatteringly impress." ... The first man Corporal Harry "Smudger" Smith of the Royal Engineers killed in Normandy was a German sniper he stabbed in the back with a bayonet. "He gave a little grunt, and then he was down, dead at once," he recalled later. "I saw he was SS. So it seemed a great thing to me, something I'd never done before. It was interesting, I'd enjoyed doing it, and although it was murder, I'd no regrets."

The idea that the conflict between the British Army and *Wehrmacht* was (As Rommel put it) a *Krieg ohne Hass*—a war without hate—needs to be carefully qualified. Unarmed prisoners were sometimes cut down in cold blood by both sides. Tank crews trapped in their knock-out vehicles were killed by vengeful infantrymen. ... There was little sentimentality on either side. ... The dismembering of enemy corpses is something we associate more with the Pacific island campaigns fought between the Americans and the Japanese more than the western European theater, but it happened there too. One of Stanley Whitehouse's comrades briskly hacked the fingers of any dead Germans he found in order to remove their rings. Dudley Anderson saw British troops extracting gold teeth from the mouths of dead *Landsers*. ...

Yet hatred of the other side tended to be the product of raw, nerve-rattled emotions rather than cold calculation. Where it existed, it was usually direct at particular enemy formations out of a sense of moral outrage—usually from a belief, real or imagined, that they had "broken the rules" first, and so had forfeited the right to sympathy. The Waffen SS were regarded (with good reason) as troops who gave no quarter, and therefore could expect non in return. Soldiers of the Black Watch in Normandy were disinclined to accept German surrenders because of allegations that Scottish medics had been fired upon while attending to the wounded in battle. Particular enemy tactics were regarded as contemptible, even if one's own side used them too. Snipers were loathed by regular infantrymen and rarely had their surrenders accepted. ...

Complicating this moral outrage, however, was a countercurrent of compassion for enemy troops—the recognition that they, too, were front-line soldiers going through hardships and indignities no less than the British themselves. "The did what they had to do just as we did," thought John Kenneally. "They stuck their faces into the same ground as we did; they were covered in the same filth and rubble as we were." ... "We received them as comrades," wrote Rex Wingfield of one group of Germans his platoon captured.

The first German Anthony Babington killed was a young officer, "slender, fair-haired, and boyish," and not at all like the image of the Beastly Hun that had been conjured up by his training sergeant back in Britain. Babington fired a bullet into the man's chest and the *Wehrmacht* officer died instantly, falling back with a look of "pain and surprise" on his face. It was all done "compulsively, without forethought" or hesitation. Yet afterward, Babington had a powerful urge to go back to the site and pray over the dead man's body. He consoled himself with the thought that the bullet might have been fired by one of his comrades, even though he knew this wasn't really plausible.

8

"THE PRICE OF VICTORY"

A rmy casualties in all theaters from 7 December 1941 until the end of the period of this report total 943,222, including 201,367 killed, 570,783 wounded, 114,205 prisoners, 56,867 missing; of the total wounded, prisoners, or missing more than 633,200 have returned to duty, or have been evacuated to the United States.

The great strategic bombardment strikes on Germany and the inauguration of the Mediterranean campaign pushed our total casualty rate above 5,000 a month in 1943. In the first five months of 1944 the increasing tempo of the air attack and the fighting in Italy drove our losses, killed, wounded, missing, and prisoners, to 13,700 men a month. Once ashore in Western Europe, the casualty rate leaped to 48,000 a month and increased to 81,000 by December. The average for the last seven months of the year was 59,000.

Out in the Pacific the advance on Japan cost 3,200 men a month throughout 1944. In the first seven months of this year the rate increased to 12,750 as we closed on the Japanese Islands.

The heaviest losses have been on the ground where the fighting never ceases night or day. Disregarding their heavy losses to disease and exposure, the combat divisions have taken more than 81 percent of all our casualties. However, though the percentage of the total is small, the casualties among the combat aircrews have been very severe. By the end of July the Army Air Forces had taken nearly 120,000 casualties. Of this total 36,698 had died. The

George Marshall, "The Price of Victory" *General Marshall's Report: The Winning of the War in Europe and the Pacific: Biennial Report of the Chief of Staff of the United States Army July 1, 1943 to June 30, 1945, to the Secretary of War*, pp. 201-204. 1945.

air raids over enemy territory gave Air Force casualties the heaviest weighting of permanency. The wounded of the Ground Forces drove their total casualties high, but with the exceptional medical care the Army has had in this war, the wounded had good chances to recover.

* * *

In the Army at large, the infantry comprises only 20.5 percent of total strength overseas, yet it has taken 70 percent of the total casualties. Enemy fire is no respecter of rank in this war; 10.2 percent of the casualties have been officers, a rate slightly higher than that for enlisted men.

The improvement of battle surgery and medical care, on the other hand, reduced the rate of death from wounds to less man one-half the rate in World War I, and permitted more than 58.8 percent of men wounded in this war to return to duty in the theaters of operations.

As staggering as our casualties have been, the enemy forces opposing us suffered many times more heavily; 1,592,600 Germans, Italians, and Japanese troops were killed for the 201,367 American soldiers who died. It is estimated that permanently disabled enemy total 303,700. We captured and disarmed 8,150,447 enemy troops.

* * *

The remarkable reduction in the percentage of deaths from battle wounds is one of the most direct and startling evidences of the great work of the Army medical service. In the last two years Army hospitals treated 9,000,000 patients; another 2,000,000 were treated in quarters and more than 80,000,000 cases passed through the dispensaries and received outpatient treatment. This tremendous task was accomplished by 45,000 Army doctors assisted by a like number of nurses and by more than one-half million enlisted men, including battalion-aid men, whose courage and devotion to duty under fire has been as great as that of the fighting men they assisted.

One of the great achievements of the Medical Department was the development of penicillin therapy which has already saved the lives of thousands. Two years ago penicillin, because of an extraordinarily complicated manufacturing process, was so scarce the small amounts available were priceless. Since then mass production techniques have been developed and the Army is now using 2,000,000 ampoules a month.

Despite the fact that United States troops lived and fought in some of the most disease-infested areas of the world, the death rate from non-battle causes in the Army in the last two years was approximately that of the corresponding age group in civil life—about 3 per 1,000 per year. The greater exposure of troops was counterbalanced by the general immunization from such diseases as typhoid, typhus, cholera, tetanus, smallpox, and yellow fever, and, obviously, by the fact that men in the Army were selected for their physical fitness.

The comparison of the non-battle death rate in this and other wars is impressive. During the Mexican War, 10 percent of officers and enlisted men died each year of disease; the rate was reduced to 7.2 percent of Union troops in the Civil War; to 1.6 percent in the Spanish War and the Philippine Insurrection; to 1.3 percent in World War I; and to 0.6 percent of the troops in this war.

Insect-borne diseases had a great influence on the course of operations throughout military history. Our campaigns on the remote Pacific Islands would have been far more difficult than they were except for the most rigid sanitary discipline and the development of highly effective insecticides and repellents. The most powerful weapon against disease-bearing lice, mosquitoes, flies, fleas, and other insects was a new chemical compound commonly known as DDT. In December 1943 and early 1944, a serious typhus epidemic developed in Naples. The incidence had reached 50 cases a day. DDT dusting stations were set up and by March more than a million and a quarter persons had been processed through them. These measures and an extensive vaccination program brought the epidemic under control within a month. Shortly after the invasion of Saipan an epidemic of dengue fever developed among the troops. After extensive aerial spraying of DDT in mosquito-breeding areas, the number of new cases a day few more than 80 percent in two weeks. The danger of scrub typhus in the Pacific Islands and in Burma and China was reduced measurably by the impregnation of clothing with dimethyl phthalate.

The treatment of battle neurosis progressed steadily so that between 40 and 60 percent of men who broke down in battle returned to combat and another 20 to 30 percent returned to limited duties. In the early stages of the War less than 10 percent of these men were reclaimed for any duty.

The development of methods of handling whole blood on the battlefield was a great contribution to battle surgery. Though very useful, plasma is not nearly as effective in combating shock and preparing wounded for surgery as whole blood. Blood banks were established in every theater and additional quantities were shipped by air from the United States, as a result of the contribution of thousands of patriotic Americans. An expendable refrigerator was developed to preserve blood in the advanced surgical stations for a period of usefulness of 21 days.

So that no casualty is discharged from the Army until he has received full benefit of the finest hospital care this Nation can provide, the Medical Service has established a reconditioning program. Its purpose is to restore to fullest possible physical and mental health any soldier who has been wounded or fallen ill in the service of his country.

* * *

It is impossible for the Nation to compensate for the services of a fighting man. There is no pay scale that is high enough to buy the services of a single soldier during even a few minutes of the agony of combat, the physical miseries of the campaign, or of the extreme personal inconvenience of leaving his home to go out to the most unpleasant and dangerous spots on earth to serve his Nation. But so that our troops might know that the Nation realizes this simple truth, the Army made it a determined policy to decorate men promptly for arduous service and for acts of gallantry while they were fighting.

Exclusive of the Purple Heart, which a man receives when he is wounded, often right at the forward dressing station, the Army awarded 1,400,409 decorations for gallantry and meritorious service since we entered the war. The Nation's highest award, the Congressional Medal of Honor, was made to 239 men, more than 40 percent of whom died in their heroic service; 3,178 Distinguished Service Crosses have been awarded; 630 Distinguished Service Medals; 7,192 awards of the Legion of Merit; 52,831 Silver Stars; 103,762 Distinguished Flying Crosses; 8,592 Soldiers Medals; 189,309 Bronze Stars; and 1,034,676 Air Medals. ...

CHAPTER 14

THE AFTERMATH OF WAR

Introduction

This final chapter addresses the end of the war and visions for the postwar order. Cities around the world were in ruins. Tens of millions of people were displaced and homeless, including survivors of the Holocaust and forced labor programs. More than 50 million people died as a result of the war. The Second World War reshaped both the global balance of power and the domestic affairs of many nations. It set in motion the process of decolonization, and Europe's major powers—willingly or not—ceded control of most of their overseas colonies over the next generation. European nations similarly found themselves displaced as the world's dominant economic and military powers by the United States and the Soviet Union whose Cold War struggle originated in the postwar aftermath. As the Soviet Union solidified its hold on Eastern Europe and imposed communism and centrally planned economies, the United States encouraged capitalism and free trade through a host of new international organizations and agreements including the General Agreement on Trade and Tariffs (GATT), International Monetary Fund (IMF), and World Bank. It provided financial and other aid through the Marshall Plan, which helped Western European nations rebuild from the war, but also tied them to the U.S. economy.

In the last year of war, the major Allied leaders met in two conferences, Yalta (February 4–11, 1945) and Potsdam (July 17–August 2, 1945) at which they sought to coordinate their final military operations, reconcile their competing visions for the postwar order, and establish institutions and agreements that would prevent future war. Both became subjects of fierce and prolonged debate in succeeding decades as scholars questioned the motives of the leaders involved, their diplomatic successes and failures, and their role in creating the postwar international environment and Cold War. The Yalta agreement (Document 1), included provisions creating the United Nations, the establishment of governments in liberated European nations, reparations, and trials of war criminals. Most importantly, from the perspective of the United States, the Soviet Union agreed to join the war against Japan following Germany's defeat. With the war in Europe over, the Potsdam agreement (Document 2) sought to more clearly define Allied expectations and deal with urgent matters ranging from refugees to German disarmament. The Allies also issued a warning to Japan, the Potsdam Declaration (see Chapter 8) urging its immediate surrender.

The Allied governments brought to trial leading German officials for war crimes. The best known of these are the series of 13 trials held in Nuremberg (1945–1949), particularly the first one, whose 20 defendants included Herman Goering and other senior Nazi military and political leaders. Numerous trials followed these, as evidence emerged and escaped Nazis were located and captured, among them Adolf Eichmann, one of the architects of the Final Solution, who was captured in Argentina in 1960 and then tried in Israel. Before the Second World War, war crimes trials were rare and they lacked significant precedent in international law. In his opening address at the first Nuremberg trial (Document 5), U.S. chief prosecutor Robert H. Jackson, a former U.S. Attorney General and Supreme Court Justice, sought to establish the importance and legitimacy of the trials, as well as documenting the sheer magnitude of Nazi crimes.

Wartime mobilization transformed domestic society, particularly among the Western democracies. Civil rights organizations pressed for reform, and governments built on the foundation provided by Depression Era and wartime activism to enact sweeping social welfare programs. In the United States, President Franklin D. Roosevelt pushed the "G.I Bill of Rights" through Congress, which offered veterans a host of benefits including job training, college education, unemployment payments, and home and business loans (Document 3). The U.S. Army and Navy issued a host of pamphlets explaining these benefits and encouraged service members to take advantage of them (Document 4).

Susan B. Anthony II, daughter of the famous suffragist, hoped that the opportunities created for women during the war would set the pattern for the postwar years with women increasing their participation in the work force and entering careers previously closed to them in ever growing numbers. In *Out of the Kitchen—Into the War* (1943), she encouraged women to join the military, work in war industries, and support the war effort (Document 6). In turn, she argued, American society had an obligation to preserve and expand opportunities for women who should have equal opportunities to participate in government and the workplace. To do otherwise, she suggests, would be to imitate the fascist governments against which the United States fought.

During the war, President Roosevelt assured Americans that they were fighting against a great evil and for four freedoms: freedom of speech, freedom of worship, freedom from fear, and freedom from want. As the war entered its final stages in 1944, Roosevelt focused on the last of these, freedom from want. Like many of his contemporaries, he saw the origins of the Great Depression and World War II in the messy aftermath of the First World War and American isolationism. In proposing an "Economic Bill of Rights" (Document 7), he sought to extend a package of benefits similar to that of the G.I. Bill to all Americans, guaranteeing their economic security. Although often overlooked, he also emphasized that U.S. security required engagement with the world, not isolation from it.

Thirteen months before President Roosevelt, British economist William Beveridge encouraged his nation to embrace similar reforms to eliminate squalor, ignorance, want, idleness, and disease. His report (Document 8) helped launch a series of reform programs in Britain, which laid the foundation for large, postwar welfare programs. Although the U.S. Congress failed to pass a similarly sweeping package of reforms, rejecting in particular a system of national health care, welfare programs in the United States also expanded over the next generation.

A host of new international agreements similarly sought to avoid problems of the past and harmonize international relations. The Bretton Woods Agreement (Document 9), for example, established an international currency exchange system based on the U.S. dollar, the world's strongest currency, which facilitated postwar trade. It also created the International Monetary Fund (IMF) and the International Bank for Reconstruction and Development, which played critical roles in postwar recovery and the reestablishment of international commerce among European and American nations. Although Soviet representatives attended the talks, the Soviet Union declined to participate in any of the institutions created at Bretton Woods.

Most policy makers came to believe that American isolationism following the First World War fatally weakened the interwar international system, helping lead to both the Great Depression and Second World War. Most American leaders were determined to avoid this mistake, among them both new President Harry Truman and General George Marshall, who became his secretary of state after the war. On June 4, 1947, Marshall delivered a speech (Document 10) at Harvard University that called not only for American engagement in the world, but active and substantial U.S. assistance for European nations then struggling to recover and rebuild from the war. In the resulting Marshall Plan (officially called the European Recovery Plan), the United States provided $13 billion of aid to European nations, including Germany, which contributed substantially to their economic recovery.

Hundreds of thousands of military personnel were captured by the enemy during the war, and spent months or even years in prisoner of war (POW) camps. An excerpt from Antonio Thompson, *Men in German Uniform: POWs in America during World War II* (2010), "Leaving a Place Called Amerika" (Document 11), describes the experiences of the 370,000 German POWs held in the United States, many of whom picked crops or did other work.

1

YALTA CONFERENCE PUBLIC STATEMENT

PROTOCOL OF PROCEEDINGS OF CRIMEA CONFERENCE

FEBRUARY 4–11, 1945

The Crimea Conference of the heads of the Governments of the United States of America, the United Kingdom, and the Union of Soviet Socialist Republics, which took place from Feb. 4 to 11 [1945], came to the following conclusions:

I. WORLD ORGANIZATION

It was decided:

1. That a United Nations conference on the proposed world organization should be summoned for Wednesday, 25 April, 1945, and should be held in the United States of America.
2. The nations to be invited to this conference should be:
   a. the United Nations as they existed on 8 Feb. 1945; and
   b. Such of the Associated Nations as have declared war on the common enemy by 1 March 1945. ...

"Yalta Conference Public Statement: Protocol of Proceedings of Crimea Conference," Avalon Project, pp. 1-7. 1945.

Territorial trusteeship:

It was agreed that the five nations which will have permanent seats on the Security Council should consult each other prior to the United Nations conference on the question of territorial trusteeship.

The acceptance of this recommendation is subject to its being made clear that territorial trusteeship will only apply to

a. existing mandates of the League of Nations;

b. territories detached from the enemy as a result of the present war;

c. any other territory which might voluntarily be placed under trusteeship; and

d. no discussion of actual territories is contemplated at the forthcoming United Nations conference or in the preliminary consultations, and it will be a matter for subsequent agreement which territories within the above categories will be place under trusteeship.

II. Declaration of Liberated Europe

The following declaration has been approved:

The Premier of the Union of Soviet Socialist Republics, the Prime Minister of the United Kingdom and the President of the United States of America have consulted with each other in the common interests of the people of their countries and those of liberated Europe. They jointly declare their mutual agreement to concert during the temporary period of instability in liberated Europe the policies of their three Governments in assisting the peoples liberated from the domination of Nazi Germany and the peoples of the former Axis satellite states of Europe to solve by democratic means their pressing political and economic problems.

The establishment of order in Europe and the rebuilding of national economic life must be achieved by processes which will enable the liberated peoples to destroy the last vestiges of Nazism and fascism and to create democratic institutions of their own choice. This is a principle of the Atlantic Charter—the right of all people to choose the form of government under which they will live—the restoration of sovereign rights and self-government to those peoples who have been forcibly deprived to them by the aggressor nations.

To foster the conditions in which the liberated people may exercise these rights, the three governments will jointly assist the people in any European liberated state or former Axis state in Europe where, in their judgment conditions require,

a. to establish conditions of internal peace;
b. to carry out emergency relief measures for the relief of distressed peoples;
c. to form interim governmental authorities broadly representative of all democratic elements in the population and pledged to the earliest possible establishment through free elections of Governments responsive to the will of the people; and
d. to facilitate where necessary the holding of such elections. ...

By this declaration we reaffirm our faith in the principles of the Atlantic Charter, our pledge in the Declaration by the United Nations and our determination to build in cooperation with other peace-loving nations world order, under law, dedicated to peace, security, freedom and general well-being of all mankind.

* * *

V. Reparation

* * *

1. Germany must pay in kind for the losses caused by her to the Allied nations in the course of the war. Reparations are to be received in the first instance by those countries which have borne the main burden of the war, have suffered the heaviest losses and have organized victory over the enemy.
2. Reparation in kind is to be exacted from Germany in three following forms:
    a. Removals within two years from the surrender of Germany or the cessation of organized resistance from the national wealth of Germany located on the territory of Germany herself as well as outside her territory ... these removals to be carried out chiefly for the purpose of destroying the war potential of Germany.

b. Annual deliveries of goods from current production for a period to be fixed.

c. Use of German labor.

* * *

VI. Major War Criminals

The conference agreed that the question of the major war criminals should be the subject of inquiry by the three Foreign Secretaries for report in due course after the close of the conference.

VII. Poland

The following declaration on Poland was agreed by the conference:

"A new situation has been created in Poland as a result of her complete liberation by the Red Army. This calls for the establishment of a Polish Provisional Government which can be more broadly based than was possible before the recent liberation of the western part of Poland. The Provisional Government which is now functioning in Poland should therefore be reorganized on a broader democratic basis with the inclusion of democratic leaders from Poland itself and from Poles abroad.

* * *

Agreement Regarding Japan

The leaders of the three great powers—the Soviet Union, the United States of America and Great Britain—have agreed that in two or three months after Germany has surrendered and the war in Europe is terminated, the Soviet Union shall enter into war against Japan on the side of the Allies on condition that:

1. The status quo in Outer Mongolia (the Mongolian People's Republic) shall be preserved.

2. The former rights of Russia violated by the treacherous attack of Japan in 1904 [the Russo-Japanese War] shall be restored ...

For its part, the Soviet Union expresses it readiness to conclude with the National Government of China a pact of friendship and alliance between the U.S.S.R. and China in order to render assistance to China with its armed forces for the purpose of liberating China from the Japanese yoke.

2

THE BERLIN (POTSDAM) CONFERENCE DECLARATION

JULY 17–AUGUST 2, 1945

II. THE PRINCIPLES TO GOVERN THE TREATMENT OF GERMANY IN THE INITIAL CONTROL PERIOD

A. POLITICAL PRINCIPLES

1. In accordance with the Agreement on Control Machinery in Germany, supreme authority in Germany is exercised, on instructions from their respective Governments, by the Commanders-in-Chief of the armed forces of the United States of America, the United Kingdom, the Union of Soviet Socialist Republics, and the French Republic, each in his own zone of occupation, and also jointly, in matters affecting Germany as a whole, in their capacity as members of the Control Council.

2. So far as is practicable, there shall be uniformity of treatment of the German population throughout Germany.

3. The purposes of the occupation of Germany by which the Control Council shall be guided are:

"Potsdam Conference Declaration," Avalon Project, pp. 1-17. 1945.

    i.   The complete disarmament and demilitarization of Germany and the elimination or control of all German industry that could be used for military production. To these ends:-

        a.   All German land, naval and air forces, the SS., SA., SD., and Gestapo, with all their organizations, staffs and institutions, including the General Staff, the Officers' Corps, Reserve Corps, military schools, war veterans' organizations and all other military and semi-military organizations, together with all clubs and associations which serve to keep alive the military tradition in Germany, shall be completely and finally abolished in such manner as permanently to prevent the revival or reorganization of German militarism and Nazism;

        b.   All arms, ammunition and implements of war and all specialized facilities for their production shall be held at the disposal of the Allies or destroyed. ...

    ii.   To convince the German people that they have suffered a total military defeat and that they cannot escape responsibility for what they have brought upon themselves ...

    iii.   To destroy the National Socialist Party and its affiliated and supervised organizations ... and to prevent all Nazi and militarist activity or propaganda.

    iv.   To prepare for the eventual reconstruction of German political life on a democratic basis and for eventual peaceful cooperation in international life by Germany.

4. All Nazi laws which provided the basis of the Hitler regime or established discriminations on grounds of race, creed, or political opinion shall be abolished. No such discriminations, whether legal, administrative or otherwise, shall be tolerated.

5. War criminals and those who have participated in planning or carrying out Nazi enterprises involving or resulting in atrocities or war crimes shall be arrested and brought to judgment. Nazi leaders, influential Nazi supporters and high officials of Nazi organizations and institutions and any other persons dangerous to the occupation or its objectives shall be arrested and interned.

* * *

B. ECONOMIC PRINCIPLES.

11. In order to eliminate Germany's war potential, the production of arms, ammunition and implements of war as well as all types of aircraft and sea-going ships shall be prohibited and prevented. ...

12. At the earliest practicable date, the German economy shall be decentralized for the purpose of eliminating the present excessive concentration of economic power as exemplified in particular by cartels, syndicates, trusts and other monopolistic arrangements.

13. In organizing the German Economy, primary emphasis shall be given to the development of agriculture and peaceful domestic industries.

* * *

III. REPARATIONS FROM GERMANY

1. Reparation claims of the U. S. S. R. shall be met by removals from the zone of Germany occupied by the U. S. S. R., and from appropriate German external assets.

2. The U. S. S. R. undertakes to settle the reparation claims of Poland from its own share of reparations.

3. The reparation claims of the United States, the United Kingdom and other countries entitled to reparations shall be met from the Western Zones and from appropriate German external assets.

* * *

VIII. POLAND

A. DECLARATION

We have taken note with pleasure of the agreement reached among representative Poles from Poland and abroad which has made possible the formation, in accordance with the decisions reached at the Crimea [Yalta] Conference, of a Polish Provisional Government of National Unity ...

The Three Powers are anxious to assist the Polish Provisional Government of National Unity in facilitating the return to Poland as soon as practicable of all Poles abroad who wish to go, including members of the Polish Armed Forces and the Merchant Marine. ...

The Three Powers note that the Polish Provisional Government of National Unity ... has agreed to the holding of free and unfettered elections as soon as possible on the basis of universal suffrage and secret ballot in which all democratic and anti-Nazi parties shall have the right to take part and to put forward candidates, and that representatives of the Allied press shall enjoy full freedom to report to the world upon developments in Poland before and during the elections.

B. Western Frontier of Poland

In conformity with the agreement on Poland reached at the Crimea Conference [Yalta] the three Heads of Government have sought the opinion of the Polish Provisional Government of National Unity in regard to the accession of territory in the north and west which Poland should receive. ... pending the final determination of Poland's western frontier, the former German territories east of a line running from the Baltic Sea immediately west of Swinamunde, and thence along the Oder River to the confluence of the western Neisse River and along the Western Neisse to the Czechoslovak frontier, including that portion of East Prussia not placed under the administration of the Union of Soviet Socialist ...

* * *

XII. Orderly Transfer of German Populations

The Three Governments, having considered the question in all its aspects, recognize that the transfer to Germany of German populations, or elements thereof, remaining in Poland, Czechoslovakia and Hungary, will have to be undertaken. They agree that any transfers that take place should be effected in an orderly and humane manner. ...

XIV. IRAN

It was agreed that Allied troops should be withdrawn immediately from Tehran, and that further stages of the withdrawal of troops from Iran should be considered at the meeting of the Council of Foreign Ministers to be held in London in September, 1945.

* * *

3

FRANKLIN ROOSEVELT SIGNS THE G.I. BILL

JUNE 22, 1944

This bill, which I have signed today, substantially carries out most of the recommendations made by me in a speech on July 28, 1943, and more specifically in messages to the Congress dated October 27, 1943, and November 23, 1943:

1. It gives servicemen and women the opportunity of resuming their education or technical training after discharge, or of taking a refresher or retrainer course, not only without tuition charge up to $500 per school year, but with the right to receive a monthly living allowance while pursuing their studies.

2. It makes provision for the guarantee by the Federal Government of not to exceed 50 percent of certain loans made to veterans for the purchase or construction of homes, farms, and business properties.

3. It provides for reasonable unemployment allowances payable each week up to a maximum period of one year, to those veterans who are unable to find a job.

4. It establishes improved machinery for effective job counseling for veterans and for finding jobs for returning soldiers and sailors.

5. It authorizes the construction of all necessary additional hospital facilities.

"FDR Statement on Signing the Servicemen's Readjustment Act (GI Bill)," 1945, pp. 1-2.

6. It strengthens the authority of the Veterans Administration to enable it to discharge its existing and added responsibilities with promptness and efficiency.

With the signing of this bill a well-rounded program of special veterans' benefits is nearly completed. It gives emphatic notice to the men and women in our armed forces that the American people do not intend to let them down.

By prior legislation, the Federal Government has already provided for the armed forces of this war: adequate dependency allowances; mustering-out pay; generous hospitalization, medical care, and vocational rehabilitation and training; liberal pensions in case of death or disability in military service; substantial war risk life insurance, and guaranty of premiums on commercial policies during service; protection of civil rights and suspension of enforcement of certain civil liabilities during service; emergency maternal care for wives of enlisted men; and reemployment rights for returning veterans.

This bill therefore and the former legislation provide the special benefits which are due to the members of our armed forces—for they "have been compelled to make greater economic sacrifice and every other kind of sacrifice than the rest of us, and are entitled to definite action to help take care of their special problems." While further study and experience may suggest some changes and improvements, the Congress is to be congratulated on the prompt action it has taken.

* * *

I trust that the Congress will also soon provide similar opportunities for postwar education and unemployment insurance to the members of the merchant marine, who have risked their lives time and again during this war for the welfare of their country.

But apart from these special benefits which fulfill the special needs of veterans, there is still much to be done.

As I stated in my message to the Congress of November 23, 1943, "What our servicemen and women want, more than anything else, is the assurance of satisfactory employment upon their return to civil life. The first task after the war is to provide employment for them and for our demobilized workers. ... The goal after the war should be the maximum utilization of our human and material resources."

As a related problem the Congress has had under consideration the serious problem of economic reconversion and readjustment after the war, so that private industry will be able to provide jobs for the largest possible number. This time we have wisely begun to make plans in advance of the day of peace, in full confidence that our war workers will remain at their essential war jobs as long as necessary until the fighting is over.

* * *

A sound postwar economy is a major present responsibility.

4

THE U.S. ARMY EXPLAINS GI BILL BENEFITS

1944

Education: Educational aid for veterans is available from the Veterans' Administration provided: (1) you were discharged under conditions other than dishonorable; (2) you were not over 25 at the time you entered service, or can demonstrate that your education or training was interrupted or interfered with by service; or you desire a refresher or retraining course; (3) you served 90 days or more (not counting the time in Army Specialized Training Program or Navy College Training Program, which course was a continuation of a civilian course and was pursued to completion, or as a Cadet or Midshipman in a Service Academy) or were discharged or released from actual service because of an actual service related injury or disability; and (4) you start such education not later than two years after discharge or end of war (whichever date is later).

Length of training. One year (or its equivalent in part-time study). If you complete these courses satisfactorily, you will be entitled to additional education or training not to exceed the length of time you spent in active service after 16 September 1940 and before the end of the present war ... No course of education or training shall exceed 4 years.

Expenses paid. The Veterans' Administration will pay to the educational or training institution the customary cost of tuition, and such laboratory, library, infirmary, and similar payments as are customarily charged, and may pay for books, supplies, equipment and such other necessary expenses (exclusive of

Additional Information for Soldiers Going Back to Civilian Life: a Supplement Explaining the Provisions of the "GI Bill of Rights," pp. 2-8. 1944.

board, lodging, other living expenses and travel) as are required. Such payments shall not exceed $500 for an ordinary school-year.

* * *

If Unemployed. To cover temporary periods of unemployment following discharge, financial help is available to you, either through State or Federal sources.

State Programs. State employment compensation programs provide weekly payments to unemployed workers based on their previous work in "covered" jobs—that is most jobs in private firms and industries ... Types of jobs not covered are farm work, household service, government and self-employment, and work for many small firms. ...

Federal Programs. Weekly allowances of unemployment compensation are available through a Federal program if you are not eligible under a State program. ... Under the Federal plan, you may receive four weeks of allowance for each calendar month of active service after 16 September 1940 and before the end of the present war, up to a total of 52 weeks. ...

Loans for Homes, Farms, Business. These three types of loans are available to veterans who served on or after 16 September 1940 and before the end of the present war, and who are discharged or released under conditions other than dishonorable, after active service of 90 days or more, or because of service-incurred disability. Applications must be made within two years after discharge or separation, or two years after the end of the war (whichever is later), but in no event more than five years after the end of the war.

The administrator of Veterans' Affairs will guarantee up to 50% of any such loan or loans, provided that the amount guaranteed shall not exceed a total of $2,000. The Administrator will pay the interest on the guaranteed amount for the first year. Loans guaranteed by the Administrator bear interest of not more than 4% per year and must be paid up within twenty years. ...

5

Justice Robert Jackson's Opening Statement at the Nuremberg Trial

The privilege of opening the first trial in history for crimes against the peace of the world imposes a grave responsibility. The wrongs which we seek to condemn and punish have been so calculated, so malignant, and so devastating, that civilization cannot tolerate their being ignored, because it cannot survive their being repeated. That four great nations, flushed with victory and stung with injury stay the hand of vengeance and voluntarily submit their captive enemies to the judgment of the law is one of the most significant tributes that Power has ever paid to Reason.

This ... inquest represents the practical effort of four of the most mighty of nations, with the support of 17 more, to utilize international law to meet the greatest menace of our times-aggressive war. The common sense of mankind demands that law shall not stop with the punishment of petty crimes by little people. It must also reach men who possess themselves of great power and make deliberate and concerted use of it to set in motion evils which leave no home in the world untouched. It is a cause of that magnitude that the United Nations will lay before Your Honors.

In the prisoners' dock sit twenty-odd broken men [who] represent sinister influences that will lurk in the world long after their bodies have returned to dust. We will show them to be living symbols of racial hatreds, of terrorism and violence, and of the arrogance and cruelty of power. They are symbols of fierce nationalisms and of militarism, of intrigue and war-making which

"Nuremberg Trial Opening Address," *Robert Jackson's Opening Address at Nuremberg Trials*, pp. 119-120, 134-135, 160-163, 170-173. 1945.

have embroiled Europe generation after generation ... Civilization can afford no compromise with the social forces which would gain renewed strength if we deal ambiguously or indecisively with the men in whom those forces now precariously survive.

... the catalog of crimes will omit nothing that could be conceived by a pathological pride, cruelty, and lust for power. ... They led their people on a mad gamble for domination. They diverted social energies and resources to the creation of what they thought to be an invincible war machine. They overran their neighbors. To sustain the "master race" in its war-making, they enslaved millions of human beings and brought them into Germany, where these hapless creatures now wander as "displaced persons". At length bestiality and bad faith reached such excess that they aroused the sleeping strength of imperiled Civilization. Its united efforts have ground the German war machine to fragments. But the struggle has left Europe a liberated yet prostrate land where a demoralized society struggles to survive. These are the fruits of the sinister forces that sit with these defendants in the prisoners' dock.

In justice to the nations and the men associated in this prosecution, I must remind you of certain difficulties which may leave their mark on this case. Never before in legal history has an effort been made to bring within the scope of a single litigation the developments of a decade, covering a whole continent, and involving a score of nations, countless individuals, and innumerable events. Despite the magnitude of the task, the world has demanded immediate action. ... I should be the last to deny that the case may well suffer from incomplete researches ... It is, however, a completely adequate case to the judgment we shall ask you to render and its full development we shall be obliged to leave to historians.

* * *

Unfortunately the nature of these crimes is such that both prosecution and judgment must be by victor nations over vanquished foes. The worldwide scope of the aggressions carried out by these men has left but few real neutrals. Either the victors must judge the vanquished or we must leave the defeated to judge themselves. After the First World War, we learned the futility of the latter course. ...

* * *

We will not ask you to convict these men on the testimony of their foes. There is no count in the Indictment that cannot be proved by books and records. The Germans were always meticulous record keepers, and these defendants ... arranged frequently to be photographed in action. We will show you their own films. You will see their own conduct and hear their own voices ...

  We would also make clear that we have no purpose to incriminate the whole German people. We know that the Party was not put in power by a majority of the German vote. ... If the German populace had willingly accepted the Nazi program, no Storm-troopers would have been needed in the early days of the Party and there would have been no need for concentration camps or the Gestapo, both of which institutions were inaugurated as soon as the Nazis gained control of the German State.

* * *

This war did not just happen it was planned and prepared for over a long period of time and with no small skill and cunning. The world has perhaps never seen such a concentration and stimulation of the energies of any people as that enabled Germany 20 years after it was defeated, disarmed, and dismembered to come so near carrying out its plan to dominate Europe. ... The Nazi Party from its inception ... contemplated war. ...

* * *

The most savage and numerous crimes planned and committed by the Nazis were those against the Jews. ... The avowed purpose was the destruction of the Jewish people as a whole ... [It] was so methodically and thoroughly pursued, that despite the German defeat and Nazi prostration this Nazi aim largely has succeeded. Only remnants of the European Jewish population remain ... Of the 9.6 million Jews who lived in Nazi-dominated Europe, 60% are authoritatively estimated to have perished. 5.7 million Jews are missing ... History does not record a crime ever perpetrated against so many victims or one ever carried out with such calculated cruelty. ...

* * *

How a government treats its own inhabitants generally is thought to be no concern of other governments ... But the German mistreatment of Germans is now known to pass in magnitude and savagery any limits of what is tolerable by modern civilization. ... Terrorism was the chief instrument for securing the cohesion of the German people in war purposes. Moreover, the cruelties in Germany served as atrocity practice to discipline the membership of the criminal organization to follow the pattern later in occupied countries.

... I am one who received during this war most atrocity tales with suspicion and skepticism. But the proof here will be so overwhelming that I venture to predict not one word I have spoken will be denied. These defendants will only deny personal responsibility or knowledge.

* * *

Even the most warlike of peoples have recognized in the name of humanity some limitations on the savagery of warfare. Rules to that end have been embodied in international conventions to which Germany became a party. ... We will show by German documents that these rights were denied, that prisoners of war were given brutal treatment and often murdered. ...

* * *

The real complaining party at your bar is Civilization. ... It does not expect that you can make war impossible. It does expect that your juridical action will put the forces of international law, its precepts, its prohibitions and, most of all, its sanctions, on the side of peace, so that men and women of good will, in all countries, may have "leave to live by no man's leave, underneath the law."

6

OUT OF THE KITCHEN

Susan B. Anthony II

Riveting the wing of a plane in the great roar of the Michigan bomber plant, standing watch on the long voyage to Murmansk, or running a tractor over the broad fields of Kansas, the minds of American women and men meet on the two major conditions of their lives.

They are thinking, first, that they must keep them flying, keep them sailing, and keep producing to crush the fascists in overwhelming and decisive defeat.

They are thinking, second, of what is going to happen to *them,* to their families, and to their lives, when war ends.

* * *

The woman who remembers or whose mother tells her of the mass expulsion of women from industry that followed World War I is apt to say, "Why should I leave home today, take training for a job, when they'll just kick me out tomorrow when the war is over?"

This lowered morale and lowered energy output for winning the war is the reason why I am talking now about postwar America.

The kind of war we wage now will directly determine the kind of peace we will enjoy for generations to come. The only possible excuse for thinking now of postwar problems is to release the maximum energy, build the

Susan B. Anthony II, "Out of the Kitchen," *Out of the Kitchen—Into the War: Woman's Winning Role in the Nation's Drama*, pp. 240-246. 1943.

highest morale for the one and only task that confronts us—that of defeating the fascists.

* * *

... What assurance have the women of America that maximum exertion of their energies now will give them not only a place in the war today but a place in the world tomorrow?

The premedical student, the young college science major, the women who require training for their careers are anxious to know whether the long and expensive years of preparation will be wasted in long expensive years of unemployment. The housewife who has wrenched herself out of her accustomed home grooves, the girl who left a good job to join the WAVES as an apprentice seaman, the woman who pulled stakes from teaching and went to the bomber plant—all these deserve an answer to their question. ...

If we are to win the war it is clear that nursery schools, public cafeterias, housing projects, medical services, recreation facilities, and special services for maternity cases are vital necessities. But they are more than that—they are the key to the postwar position of women and a promise to men and women of a standard of living that will enable three-fifths of a nation to be well housed, well fed, and well cared for.

* * *

Victory can no longer be regarded as separate from the assurance to our people of a future that will hold a place for them. To arouse the spirit of victory the people must be given a demonstration of what democracy means, what full employment means, what public service means.

We are in a death struggle against fascism—a system whose ideology and practice reduces men and women to slaves, living on starvation levels. What better proof could we offer the American people of our absolute irreconcilability with Hitler's methods than to start now to provide employment and security for all?

The war today is giving employment to a part of the largest body of unemployed persons in the nation—women. The peace tomorrow must also give them employment. ...

* * *

[Women] need the assurance that never again will they be deprived of the right to work, and the right to hold top positions. Temporary orders permitting equal pay for equal work, transitory demands of employers for their services, are not enough. ...

... The right to vote has been relied upon as the complete answer to our demands for a voice in the highest councils of the Government. In almost doubling the number of women workers this was doubles the justice of our demands for an equal place in the legislatures, on the court benches, and in law enforcement.

No longer can women be satisfied with a backseat in Congress, with one seat in the President's circle of advisers and administrators, with no seat on the Supreme Court bench. ... We would be but a poor pretender to democracy if, after having worked our women to the utmost to win the war, we barred them from a meaningful role in the peace. How can we claim to be purified of fascist tendencies in our own nation if we permit a fascist concept of women to prevail?

* * *

Fascism is determined to make women servants of the house. Democracy must encourage women to be servants of the world. The conditions of war pulling women out of the house. The peace must not push them back into the house, unless they wish to go there.

We must recognize that women's place is in the world as much as man's is. Woman's place is in the factory, in the office, in the professions, in the fields, and at the council table—wherever human labor, human effort, is needed to produce and create. In the postwar world there must be an abolition of the false distinctions between men and women—between "men's jobs" and "women's jobs." Personal ability and choice, not sex, must determine the jobholder. Present discriminations must be done away with, for they work against men as well as women.

7

PRESIDENT ROOSEVELT PROPOSES ECONOMIC BILL OF RIGHTS

This Nation in the past two years has become an active partner in the world's greatest war against human slavery.

* * *

But I do not think that any of us Americans can be content with mere survival. Sacrifices that we and our allies are making impose upon us all a sacred obligation to see to it that out of this war we and our children will gain something better than mere survival.

We are united in determination that this war shall not be followed by another interim which leads to new disaster—that we shall not repeat the tragic errors of ostrich isolationism—that we shall not repeat the excesses of the wild twenties when this Nation went for a joy ride on a roller coaster which ended in a tragic crash.

When Mr. Hull went to Moscow in October, and when I went to Cairo and Teheran in November, we knew that we were in agreement with our allies in our common determination to fight and win this war. But there were many vital questions concerning the future peace, and they were discussed in an atmosphere of complete candor and harmony.

In the last war such discussions, such meetings, did not even begin until the shooting had stopped and the delegates began to assemble at the peace table.

"President Roosevelt Proposes Economic Bill of Rights," pp. 1-9. 1944.

There had been no previous opportunities for man-to-man discussions which lead to meetings of minds. The result was a peace which was not a peace.

That was a mistake which we are not repeating in this war.

* * *

The one supreme objective for the future, which we discussed for each Nation individually, and for all the United Nations, can be summed up in one word: Security.

And that means not only physical security which provides safety from attacks by aggressors. It means also economic security, social security, moral security—in a family of Nations.

* * *

In this war, we have been compelled to learn how interdependent upon each other are all groups and sections of the population of America.

* * *

It is our duty now to begin to lay the plans and determine the strategy for the winning of a lasting peace and the establishment of an American standard of living higher than ever before known. We cannot be content, no matter how high that general standard of living may be, if some fraction of our people—whether it be one-third or one-fifth or one-tenth—is ill-fed, ill-clothed, ill housed, and insecure.

This Republic had its beginning, and grew to its present strength, under the protection of certain inalienable political rights—among them the right of free speech, free press, free worship, trial by jury, freedom from unreasonable searches and seizures. They were our rights to life and liberty.

As our Nation has grown in size and stature, however—as our industrial economy expanded—these political rights proved inadequate to assure us equality in the pursuit of happiness.

We have come to a clear realization of the fact that true individual freedom cannot exist without economic security and independence. "Necessitous men are not free men." People who are hungry and out of a job are the stuff of which dictatorships are made.

In our day these economic truths have become accepted as self-evident. We have accepted, so to speak, a second Bill of Rights under which a new basis of security and prosperity can be established for all regardless of station, race, or creed.

Among these are:

The right to a useful and remunerative job in the industries or shops or farms or mines of the Nation;

The right to earn enough to provide adequate food and clothing and recreation;

The right of every farmer to raise and sell his products at a return which will give him and his family a decent living;

The right of every businessman, large and small, to trade in an atmosphere of freedom from unfair competition and domination by monopolies at home or abroad;

The right of every family to a decent home; The right to adequate medical care and the opportunity to achieve and enjoy good health;

The right to adequate protection from the economic fears of old age, sickness, accident, and unemployment;

The right to a good education.

All of these rights spell security. And after this war is won we must be prepared to move forward, in the implementation of these rights, to new goals of human happiness and well-being.

America's own rightful place in the world depends in large part upon how fully these and similar rights have been carried into practice for our citizens. For unless there is security here at home there cannot be lasting peace in the world.

* * *

Our fighting men abroad—and their families at home—expect such a program and have the right to insist upon it. It is to their demands that this Government should pay heed rather than to the whining demands of selfish pressure groups who seek to feather their nests while young Americans are dying.

* * *

I have often said that there are no two fronts for America in this war. There is only one front. There is one line of unity which extends from the hearts of the people at home to the men of our attacking forces in our farthest outposts. When we speak of our total effort, we speak of the factory and the field, and the mine as well as of the battleground—we speak of the soldier and the civilian, the citizen and his Government.

Each and every one of us has a solemn obligation under God to serve this Nation in its most critical hour—to keep this Nation great—to make this Nation greater in a better world.

8

BEVERIDGE REPORT ON SOCIAL INSURANCE AND ALLIED SERVICES

1942

Statement of a reconstruction policy by a nation at war is statement of the uses to which that nation means to put victory, when victory is achieved. In a war which many nations must wage together as whole-hearted allies, if they are to win victory, such a statement of the uses of victory may be vital. This was recognised by the leaders of the democracies east and west of the Atlantic in putting their hands to a charter which, in general terms, set out the nature of the world which they desired to establish after the war.

The Atlantic Charter has since then been signed on behalf of all the United Nations. The fifth clause of the charter declares the desire of the American and the British leaders "to bring about the fullest collaboration between all nations in the economic field, with the object of securing for all improved labour standards, economic advancement, and social security." The proposals of this Report are designed as a practical contribution towards the achievement of the social security which is named in the closing words. The proposals [in this report] cover ground which must be covered, in one way or another, in translating the words of the Atlantic Charter into deeds.

They represent, not an attempt by one nation to gain for its citizens advantages at the cost of their fellow fighters in a common cause, but a contribution to that common cause. They are concerned not with increasing the wealth of the British people, but with so distributing whatever wealth is available to them in total, as to deal first with first things, with essential physical needs.

"Beveridge Report," Report on Social Insurance and Allied Services, pp. 1-3. 1942.

They are a sign of the belief that the object of government in peace and in war is not the glory of rulers or of races, but the happiness of the common man. That is a belief which, through all differences in forms of government, unites not only the democracies whose leaders first put their hands to the Atlantic Charter, but those democracies and all their Allies. It unites the United Nations and divides them from their enemies.

At the request of His Majesty's Government, the Inter-departmental Committee have pursued the task of surveying the social services of Britain and examining plans for their reconstruction during the most savage, most universal and most critical war in which Britain has ever been engaged. It would be wrong to conclude this Report without expressing gratitude to all those who in such a crisis have, nevertheless, found time and energy to assist the Committee in this task, who, triumphing over difficulties of dispersal, of loss of staff, of absorption in urgent tasks of war, have prepared memoranda, attended to give evidence, and have discussed their problems with so much frankness and public spirit. ... There are difficulties in planning reconstruction of the social services during the height of war, but there are also advantages in doing so. The prevention of want and the diminution and relief of disease—the special aim of the social services—are in fact a common interest of all citizens. It may be possible to secure a keener realisation of that fact in war than it is in peace, because war breeds national unity. It may be possible, through sense of national unity and readiness to sacrifice personal interests to the common cause, to bring about changes which, when they are made, will be accepted on all hands as advances, but which it might be difficult to make at other times. There appears at any rate to be no doubt of the determination of the British people, however hard pressed in war, not to live wholly for war, not to abandon care of what may come after. That, after all, is in accord with the nature of democracies, of the spirit in which they fight and of the purpose for which they fight. They make war, today more consciously than ever, not for the sake of war, not for dominion or revenge, but war for peace. If the united democracies today can show strength and courage and imagination equal to their manifest desire, can plan for a better peace even while waging total war, they will win together two victories which in truth are indivisible.

Freedom from want cannot be forced on a democracy or given to a democracy. It must be won by them. Winning it needs courage and faith and a sense of national unity: courage to face facts and difficulties and overcome them; faith in our future and in the ideals of fair-play and freedom for which century after century our forefathers were prepared to die; a sense of national unity overriding the interests of any class or section. The Plan for Social

Security in this Report is submitted by one who believes that in this supreme crisis the British people will not be found wanting, of courage and faith and national unity, of material and spiritual power to play their part in achieving both social security and the victory of justice among nations upon which security depends.

9

BRETTON WOODS AGREEMENT SUMMARY

This Conference at Bretton Woods, representing nearly all the peoples of the world, has considered matters of international money and finance which are important for peace and prosperity. The Conference has agreed on the problems needing attention, the measures which should be taken, and the forms of international cooperation or organization which are required. The agreements reached on these large and complex matters are without precedent in the history of international economic relations.

I. THE INTERNATIONAL MONETARY FUND

Since foreign trade affects the standard of life of every people, all countries have a vital interest in the system of exchange of national currencies and the regulations and conditions which govern its working. Because these monetary transactions are international exchanges, the nations must agree on the basic rules which govern the exchanges if the system is to work smoothly. When they do not agree, and when single nations and small groups of nations attempt by special and different regulations of the foreign exchanges to gain trade advantages, the result is instability, a reduced volume of foreign trade, and damage to national economies. This course of action is likely to lead to economic warfare and to endanger the world's peace.

"Bretton Woods Agreement: Summary," 1945, pp. 1-2.

429

The Conference has therefore agreed that broad international action is necessary to maintain an international monetary system which will promote foreign trade. The nations should consult and agree on international monetary changes which affect each other. They should outlaw practices which are agreed to be harmful to world prosperity, and they should assist each other to overcome short-term exchange difficulties.

The Conference has agreed that the nations here represented should establish for these purposes a permanent international body, *The International Monetary Fund*, with powers and resources adequate to perform the tasks assigned to it. ...

II. The International Bank for Reconstruction and Development

It is in the interest of all nations that post-war reconstruction should be rapid. Likewise, the development of the resources of particular regions is in the general economic interest. Programs of reconstruction and development will speed economic progress everywhere, will aid political stability and foster peace.

The Conference has agreed that expanded international investment is essential to provide a portion of the capital necessary for reconstruction and development.

The Conference has further agreed that the nations should cooperate to increase the volume of foreign investment for these purposes, made through normal business channels. It is especially important that the nations should cooperate to share the risks of such foreign investment, since the benefits are general.

The Conference has agreed that the nations should establish a permanent international body to perform these functions, to be called The International Bank for Reconstruction and Development.

It has been agreed that the Bank should assist in providing capital through normal channels at reasonable rates of interest and for long periods for projects which will raise the productivity of the borrowing country. ...

The Conference has recommended that in carrying out the policies of the institutions here proposed special consideration should be given to the needs of countries which have suffered from enemy occupation and hostilities.

The proposals formulated at the Conference for the establishment of the Fund and the Bank are now submitted, in accordance with the terms of the invitation, for consideration of the governments and people of the countries represented.

10

GEORGE MARSHALL PROPOSES "MARSHALL PLAN"

I need not tell you gentlemen that the world situation is very serious. That must be apparent to all intelligent people. I think one difficulty is that the problem is one of such enormous complexity that the very mass of facts presented to the public by press and radio make it exceedingly difficult for the man in the street to reach a clear appraisement of the situation. Furthermore, the people of this country are distant from the troubled areas of the earth and it is hard for them to comprehend the plight and consequent reactions of the long-suffering peoples, and the effect of those reactions on their governments in connection with our efforts to promote peace in the world.

In considering the requirements for the rehabilitation of Europe, the physical loss of life, the visible destruction of cities, factories, mines, and railroads was correctly estimated, but it has become obvious during recent months that this visible destruction was probably less serious than the dislocation of the entire fabric of European economy. For the past ten years conditions have been highly abnormal. The feverish preparation for war and the more feverish maintenance of the war effort engulfed all aspects of national economies. Machinery has fallen into disrepair or is entirely obsolete. Under the arbitrary and destructive Nazi rule, virtually every possible enterprise was geared into the German war machine. Long-standing commercial ties, private institutions, banks, insurance companies, and shipping companies disappeared through loss of capital, absorption through nationalization, or

George Marshall, "Marshall Plan Speech," pp. 1-3. 1947.

by simple destruction. In many countries, confidence in the local currency
has been severely shaken. The breakdown of the business structure of Europe
during the war was complete. Recovery has been seriously retarded by the fact
that two years after the close of hostilities a peace settlement with Germany
and Austria has not been agreed upon. But even given a more prompt solution of these difficult problems, the rehabilitation of the economic structure
of Europe quite evidently will require a much longer time and greater effort
than had been foreseen.

* * *

The truth of the matter is that Europe's requirements for the next three or
four years of foreign food and other essential products—principally from
America—are so much greater than her present ability to pay that she must
have substantial additional help, or face economic, social and political dete-
rioration of a very grave character.

The remedy lies in breaking the vicious circle and restoring the confidence
of the European people in the economic future of their own countries and of
Europe as a whole. The manufacturer and the farmer throughout wide areas
must be able and willing to exchange their products for currencies the continuing value of which is not open to question.

Aside from the demoralizing effect on the world at large and the possibilities
of disturbances arising as a result of the desperation of the people concerned,
the consequences to the economy of the United States should be apparent to
all. It is logical that the United States should do whatever it is able to do to
assist in the return of normal economic health in the world, without which
there can be no political stability and no assured peace. Our policy is directed
not against any country or doctrine but against hunger, poverty, desperation,
and chaos. Its purpose should be the revival of a working economy in the
world so as to permit the emergence of political and social conditions in
which free institutions can exist.

Such assistance, I am convinced, must not be on a piecemeal basis, as various crises develop. Any assistance that this Government may render in the
future should provide a cure rather than a mere palliative. Any government
that is willing to assist in the task of recovery will find full cooperation, I am
sure, on the part of the United States Government. Any government which
maneuvers to block the recovery of other countries cannot expect help from
us. Furthermore, governments, political parties, or groups which seek to

perpetuate human misery in order to profit there from politically or otherwise will encounter the opposition of the United States.

* * *

An essential part of any successful action on the part of the United States is an understanding on the part of the people of America of the character of the problem and the remedies to be applied. Political passion and prejudice should have no part. With foresight, and a willingness on the part of our people to face up to the vast responsibility which history has clearly placed upon our country, the difficulties I have outlined can and will be overcome.

11

LEAVING A PLACE CALLED AMERIKA

At one time, Camp Shanks and this lonely beach served the American invasion troops, which used this location as their springboard for their victorious push into Europe. Now we stand here, German prisoners of war with the same goal in our hearts, but instead intended on a peaceful return home. After they have pushed us around for years into all corners of the world, young Americans, our guards, stand with us also on the beach and shall return to the land of their fathers to keep the peace there. But the same joy is not to be seen in their faces as in ours.

—Former POW Helmut Hörner

With the surrender of Germany and the end of World War II, the United States began the repatriation process for the approximately 372,000 German POWs housed within its borders. The United States encountered and overcame a number of problems while housing these prisoners. Ultimately, it exceeded the guidelines set forth in the Geneva Convention. Although the Geneva Convention set some guidelines for establishing and operating the POW program, its vague articles left much room for interpretation. This required quite a bit of ingenuity, farsightedness, and compromise among the numerous agencies involved with the program. Government departments, civilian agencies, and labor unions all had a voice in the establishment of various aspects of the program, often causing much debate and delay in implementation of policy and procedure.

The POW program ended almost as quickly as it began. Branch camps closed and base camps consolidated beginning in 1945, often leaving no trace of their former inhabitants. The POWs realized that when the war ended they would go home and again they found themselves at their points of embarkation at Norfolk, Virginia; Camp Shanks, New York; and New Orleans, Louisiana. There they anxiously anticipated the arrival of U.S. transport ships, this time to return to Europe. While many may have respected the United States and others hated it, most desired to go home. Only the most intuitive among them and those privy to confidential information knew that they would be sent to France, Great Britain, Greece, Czechoslovakia, the Netherlands, and Norway, where they would remain POWs for up to three more years. The decision to transfer U.S.-held POWs to allied nations followed an agreement reached in November 1945 between the War Department and America's European allies to allow the POWs to aid in rebuilding these war-torn nations. Those POWs who participated in the reeducation program, however, returned directly to Germany in the hope that they would assume political offices and law enforcement positions.

The process of sending the POWs back to Europe took time. Practicality and a degree of stalling enabled American farmers to keep their workers for several months after Germany's surrender. The United States argued that with the war in Europe over, fewer transports existed for the Atlantic run. In fact, nearly all shipping now supported the war in the Pacific, which lasted until August 1945. Even with available shipping, the United States insisted that the administrative and security situation in Europe could not handle a large influx of POWs. One report from the *Washington Post* stated that "returning prisoners might soon band themselves into Freikorps, which could subsequently be united into a private army."

By the end of 1946, however, nearly all the POWs had left the United States, and the last men shipped out on June 30, 1947. The War Department issued an official statement in August 1947 that all 435,788 POWs held in the United States, with the exception of the seriously sick or injured and twenty-four escapees, had returned to Europe. This included not only the official number of 378,898 Germans but also 51,455 Italians and 5,435 Japanese. A spokesman for the War Department added that "considering the numbers we feel we got them out in a hurry." Nearly five hundred POWs died behind barbed wire in the United States, and they received burials in or near their camps.

The Western allies could weigh this against the situation in the Soviet Union, which released its last Axis POWs in 1956.

In some ways the extended stay in the United States was a benefit for the Germans, but they did not understand that until it was too late. They were held under the liberal U.S. interpretations of the Geneva Convention, but after returning to Europe, many went to France and other Allied countries, where they worked to rebuild these nations. Anger overcame many of the POWs as they learned that their next destination was not Germany but work in the ruins of one of its former enemies. Helmut Hörner, boarding the *Empress of York* on June 14, 1946, for what he thought would be the trip home, discovered the truth by accident. Above his bunk, someone had scrawled on the canvas: "10 March boarded in Camp Shanks. Goal Bremen—Hunger—Disembarked 22 March in Liverpool, England. Everything is only lies!" After a bout of anger and depression, Hörner accepted his fate. England was still closer to Germany. In January 1948, he returned to Germany, finally able to see his wife. Walter Schmid was transported aboard the *Aiken* to Belgium. The POWs found it confusing that they received new serial numbers. Schmid called it "silly for the few days we'd be here, since we were about to be released. We were allowed to write a postcard home, to let them know we were on our way." Schmid and his colleagues were again transferred, but this time to England, where they worked until sent back to Germany in May 1947.